The Greater & Lesser Keys of Solomon the King

by Samuel Liddell MacGregor Mathers & Aleister Crowley

Copyright © 2016 by Mockingbird Press

All rights reserved. The original works first published in 1904 &1888 are in the public domain and may be reproduced and copied at will. However, the compilation, construction, cover design, trademarks, derivations, etc., of this edition are copyrighted and may not be reproduced, distributed, or transmitted in any form or by any means, including photocopying, recording, or other electronic or mechanical methods, without the prior written permission of the publisher, except in the case of brief quotations embodied in critical reviews and certain other noncommercial uses permitted by copyright law. For permission requests, write to the publisher, addressed "Attention: Permissions Coordinator," at the email address below.

Mockingbird Press
www.mockingbirdpress.com
info@mockingbirdpress.com

Ordering Information:
Quantity sales. Special discounts are available on quantity purchases by corporations, associations, and others. For details, contact the publisher at the email address above.

Publisher's Cataloging-In-Publication Data
Mathers, Samuel
The Greater and Lesser Keys of Solomon the King / Samuel Liddell MacGregor Mathers; with Aleister Crowley.
Mathers, Samuel

ISBN-13:978-0-9981364-6-2
ISBN-10:0-9981364-6-8
1. Occult Sciences—Magic.. I. Mathers, S.L. MacGregor (Samuel Liddell MacGregor). II. Crowley, Aleister. III. The Greater and Lesser Keys of Solomon the King
BF1585-1623

CONTENTS

THE LESSER KEY OF SOLOMON

PART ONE: GOETIA 1

Preface 3

Preliminary Invocation 5

The Initiated Interpretation of Ceremonial Magic 7

Preliminary Definition of Magic 11

    Lemegeton Vel Clavicula Salomonis Regis 11

    The Whole Lemegeton or Clavicula 14

    The Book of Evil Spirits 16

Shemhamphorash 17

Observations 52

Classified List of the 72 Chief Spirits 53

The Magical Circle 55

The Magical Triangle of Solomon 57

The Hexagram of Solomon 59

The Pentagram of Solomon 60

The Magic Ring or Disc of Solomon 61

The Vessel of Brass 62

The Secret Seal of Solomon 64

The Other Magical Requisites 73

The Adoration at the Bath 74

    The Conjuration to Call Forth Any of the Aforesaid Spirits 75

    The Second Conjuration 77

    The Constraint 79

    The Invocation of the King 80

    The General Curse or Spirits' Chain 81

    The Conjuration of the Fire 82

    The Greater Curse 83

    The Address Unto the Spirit Upon His Coming 84

    The Welcome Unto the Spirit 86

PART TWO: EXPLANATION OF CERTAIN NAMES IN THE LEMEGETON 87

    Explanation of Names 88

    The Explanation of the Two Triangles in the Parchment 91

    An Explanation of Solomon's Triangle 92

PART THREE: CONJURATIONS 93

    Preamble 94

    Atte Ye Bathes of Art 95

    Atte Ye Induynge of Ye Holy Vestures 96

    Ye Fyrste Conjouratioun 97

    Ye Secounde Conjouratioun 98

    Ye Constraynte 99

    Ye Potent Invocatioun of Hys Kynge 100

    Ye Generall Curse 101

Yclept Ye Spirits' Chayne 101

Ye Conjouratioun of Ye Fyre 102

Ye Greter Curse 103

Ye Addresse Unto Ye Spirit On Hys Coming 104

*Ye Welcome Unto Y*ᴱ *Spirit Dygnytie* 105

Ye License to Ye Spirit YT He Maye Depart 106

THE GREATER KEY OF SOLOMON

BOOK ONE 108

    PREFACE 109

    PRELIMINARY DISCOURSE 112

    INTRODUCTION 113

        Table of the Planetary Hours 119

        Table of the Magical Names of the Hours and of the Angels who Rule them, Commencing at the First Hour After Midnight of Each Day, and Ending at the Ensuing Midnight 120

        Table of the Archangels, Angels, Metals, Days of the Week, and Colours attributed to each Planet. 121

        Note by Editor 121

    Concerning the Divine Love Which Ought to Precede the Acquisition of this Knowledge 123

    Of the Days, and Hours, and of the Virtues of the Planets 124

    Concerning the Arts 128

    The Confession to be Made by the Exorcist 135

Prayers and Conjurations 138

Stronger and More Potent Conjuration 142

An Extremely Powerful Conjuration 149

Concerning the Medals or Pentacles, and the Manner of Constructing Them 157

Of the Experiment Concerning Things Stolen, and How it Should be Preformed . 161

Of the Experiment of Invisibility and How it Should Be Preformed 164

To Hinder a Sportsman from Killing Any Game 166

How to Make the Magic Garters 167

How to Make the Magic Carpet Proper for Interrogating the Intelligences, So as to Obtain an Answer Regarding Whatsoever Matter One May Wish to Learn ... 168

How to Render Thyself Master of a Treasure Possessed by the Spirits 170

Of the Experiment of Seeking Favour and Love 172

How Operations of Mockery, Invisibility, and Deceit Should be Prepared 173

How Extraordinary Experiments and Operations Should be Prepared 174

Concerning the Holy Pentacles or Medals 175

THE PLATES 178

The Order of the Pentacles 179

BOOK TWO 207

At What Hour After the Preparation of All Things Necessary, We Should Bring the Exercise of the Art to Perfection 209

In What Manner the Master of the Art Should Keep, Rule, and Govern Himself 213

How the Companions of the Master of the Art Ought to Regulate and Govern Themselves 215

Concerning the Fasting, Care and Things to be Observed 217

Concerning the Baths and How They Are to Be Arranged 219

Of the Garments and Shoes of the Art 221

Of Places Wherein We May Conveniently Execute the Experiments and Operations of the Art 222

Of the Knife, Sword, Sickle, Poniard, Dagger, Lance, Wand, Staff, and Other Instruments of Magical Art 224

Of the Formation of the Circle 227

Concerning Incense, Suffumigations, Perfumes, Odors, and Similar Things Which Are Used in Magical Arts 229

Of Water, and Of the Hyssop 231

Of Light, and Of the Fire 232

Concerning the Precepts of the Art 233

Of the Pen, Ink, and Colours 235

Of the Pen, Of the Swallow, and Of the Crow 236

Of the Blood of the Bat, Pidgeon, and Other Animals 237

Of Virgin Parchment, Or Virgin Paper, and How it Should be Prepared 238

Of Wax and Virgin Earth 241

Concerning the Needle and Other Iron Instruments 242

Concerning the Silken Cloth 243

Concerning Characters, and the Consecration of the Magical Book 244

Concerning Sacrifices to the Spirits, and How They Should be Made 246

ANCIENT FRAGMENT OF THE KEY OF SOLOMON 248

THE QABALISTICAL INVOCATION OF SOLOMON..........................253

The Lesser Key of Solomon

by Samuel Liddell MacGregor Mathers &
Aleister Crowley

[1904]

PART ONE

GOETIA

Dedication

ΕΠΙΚΑΛΟΥΜΑΙ ΣΕ ΤΟΝ ΕΝ ΤΩ ΚΕΝΕΩ ΠΝΕΥΜΑΤΙ, ΔΕΙΝΟΝ, ΑΟΡΑΤΟΝ, ΠΑΝΟΤΡΑΤΟΡΑ, ΘΕΟΝ ΘΕΩΝ, ΦΘΕΡΟΠΟΙΟΝ, ΚΑΙ ΕΠΗΜΟΠΟΙΝ, Ο ΜΙΣΩΝ ΟΙΚΙΑΝ ΕΥΣΤΑΘΟΥΣΑΝ, ΩΣ ΕΞΕΒΡΑΣΘΗΣ ΕΚ ΤΗΣ ΑΙΓΥΠΤΙΟΥ ΚΑΙ ΕΞΩ ΧΩΡΑΣ.

ΕΠΟΝΟΜΑΣΘΗΣ Ο ΠΑΝΤΑ ΠΗΣΣΩΝ ΚΑΙ ΜΗ ΝΙΚΩΜΕΝΟΣ.

ΕΠΙΚΑΛΟΥΜΑΙ ΣΕ ΤΥΦΩΝ ΣΗΘ ΤΑΣ ΣΑΣ ΜΑΤΡΕΙΑΣ ΕΠΙΤΕΛΩ, ΟΤΙ ΕΠΙΚΑΛΟΥΜΑΙ ΣΕ ΤΟ ΣΟΝ ΑΥΘΕΝΤΙΚΟΝ ΣΟΥ ΟΝΟΜΑ ΕΝ ΟΙΣ ΟΥ ΔΥΝΗ ΠΑΡΑΚΟΥΣΑΙ ΙΩΕΡΒΗΘ, ΙΩΠΑΚΕΡΒΗΟ, ΙΩΒΟΛΧΩΣΗΘ, ΙΩΠΑΤΑΘΝΑΖ, ΙΩΣΩΡΩ, ΙΩΝΕΒΟΥΤΟΣΟΥΑΛΗΘ, ΑΚΤΙΩΦΙ, ΕΡΕΣΧΙΓΑΛ, ΝΕΒΟΠΟΩΑΛΗΘ, ΑΒΕΡΑΜΕΝΘΩΟΝ, ΛΕΡΘΕΞΑΝΑΞ, ΕΘΡΕΛΥΩΘ, ΝΕΜΑΡΕΒΑ, ΑΕΜΙΝΑ, ΟΛΟΝ ΗΚΕ ΜΟΙ ΚΑΙ ΒΑΔΙΣΟΝ ΚΑΙ ΚΑΤΕΒΑΛΕ ΤΟΝ ΔΕΙΝΟΝ ΜΑΘΕΡΣ. ΡΙΓΕΙ ΚΑΙ ΠΥΡΕΙΩ ΑΥΤΟΣ ΗΔΙΚΗΣΕΝ ΤΟΝ ΑΝΘΡΩΠΟΝ ΚΑΙ ΤΟ ΑΙΜΑ ΤΟΥ ΦΥΩΝΟΣ ΕΣΚΕΧΥΣΕΝ ΠΑΡ'ΕΑΥΤΩ.

ΔΙΑ ΤΟΥΤΟ ΤΑΥΤΑ ΠΟΙΕΩ ΚΟΙΝΑ.

Preface

This translation of the FIRST BOOK of the "Lemegeton" which is now for the first time made accessible to students of TALISMANIC MAGIC was done, after careful collation and edition, from numerous Ancient Manuscripts in Hebrew, Latin, and French, by G. H. Fra. D.D.C.F., by the order of the Secret Chief of the Rosicrucian Order.[1] The G. H. Fra., having succumbed unhappily to the assaults of the Four Great Princes (acting notably under Martial influences), it seemed expedient that the work should be brought to its conclusion by another hand. The investigation of a competent Skryer into the house of our unhappy Fra., confirmed this divination; neither our Fra. nor his Hermetic Mul. were there seen; but only the terrible shapes of the evil Adepts S.V.A.[2] and H., whose original bodies having been sequestered by Justice, were no longer of use to them. On this we stayed no longer Our Hand; but withdrawing Ourselves, and consulting the Rota, and the Books M. and Q. did decide to ask Mr. Aleister Crowley, a poet, and skilled student of Magical Lore, and an expert Kabbalist, to complete openly that which had been begun in secret.[3] This is that which is written: "His Bishoprick let another take." And again: "Oculi Tetragammaton." This is also that which is said: "Nomen Secundum refertur ad Gebhurah; qui est Rex Bittul atque Corruptio Achurajim Patris et Matris hoc indigitatur."

And so saying we wish you well.

---

[1] Mr. A. E. Waite writes ("Real History Of The Rosicrucians," p. 426): "I beg leave to warn my readers that all persons who proclaim themselves to be Rosicrucians are simply members of pseudo-fraternities, and that there is that difference between their assertion and the fact of the case in which the essence of a lie consists!" It is within the Editor's personal knowledge that Mr. Waite was (and still is probably) a member of a society claiming to be the R.C. fraternity As Mr. Waite constantly hints in his writing that he is in touch with initiated centres, I think the syllogism, whose premises are given above, is fair, if not quite formal.--ED.

[2] It was owing to our Fra. receiving this S.V.A. as his Superior, and giving up the Arcana of our Fraternity into so unhallowed a power, that We decided no longer to leave Our dignity and authority in the hands of one who could be thus easily imposed upon. (For by a childish and easy magical trick did S.V.A. persuade D.D.C.F. of that lie.)

[3] He that is appointed to complete in secret that which had been begun openly is R.R., and to be heard of at the care of the Editor.

Ex Deo Nascimur.
In Jesu Morimur.
Per S.S. Reviviscimus.

Given forth from our Mountain of A., this day of C.C. 1903 A. D.

Preliminary Invocation

Thee I invoke, the Bornless one.
Thee that didst create the Earth and the Heavens:
Thee that didst create the Night and the Day.
Thee that didst create the Darkness and the Light.
Thou art Osorronophris: Whom no man has seen at any time.
Thou art Jäbas
Thou art Jäpôs:
Thou hast distinguished between the Just and the Unjust.
Thou didst make the Female and the Male.
Thou didst produce the Seed and the Fruit.
Thou didst form Men to love one another, and to hate one another.

I am Mosheh Thy Prophet, unto Whom Thou didst commit Thy Mysteries, the Ceremonies of Ishrael:
Thou didst produce the moist and the, dry, and that which nourisheth all created Life.
Hear Thou Me, for I am the Angel of Paphrô Osorronophris: this is Thy True Name, handed down to the Prophets of Ishrael.

****

Hear Me:--
Ar: Thiao: Rheibet: Atheleberseth:
A: Blatha: Abeu: Ebeu: Phi:
Thitasoe: Ib: Thiao.

Hear Me, and make all Spirits subject unto Me: so that every Spirit of the Firmament and of the Ether; upon the Earth and under the Earth: on dry Land and in the Water: of Whirling Air, and of rushing Fire: and every Spell and Scourge of God may be obedient unto Me.

****

I invoke Thee, the Terrible and Invisible God: Who dwellest in the Void Place of the Spirit:--
Arogogorobraô: Sothou:
Modoriô: Phalarthaô: Döö: Apé, The Bornless One:

Hear Me: etc.

Hear me:--
Roubriaô: Mariôdam: Balbnabaoth: Assalonai: Aphniaô: I: Thoteth: Abrasar: Aëöôü: Ischure, Mighty and Bornless One!
Hear me: etc.

I invoke thee:--
   Ma: Barraiô: Jôêl: Kotha:
   Athorêbalô: Abraoth:
Hear Me: etc.

Hear me!
Aôth: Abaôth: Basum: Isak:
Sabaoth: Iao:

This is the Lord of the Gods:
This is the Lord of the Universe:
This is He Whom the Winds fear.

The Initiated Interpretation of Ceremonial Magic

It is loftily amusing to the student of Magical literature who is not quite a fool--and rare is such a combination!--to note the criticism directed by the Philistine against the citadel of his science. Truly, since our childhood has ingrained into us not only literal belief in the Bible, but also substantial belief in Alf Laylah wa Laylah, and only adolescence can cure us, we are only too liable, in the rush and energy of dawning manhood, to overturn roughly and rashly both these classics, to regard them both on the same level, as interesting documents from the standpoint of folk-lore and anthropology, and as nothing more.

Even when we learn that the Bible, by a profound and minute study of the text, may be forced to yield up Qabalistic arcana of cosmic scope and importance, we are too often slow to apply a similar restorative to the companion volume, even if we are the luck holders of Burton's veritable edition.

To me, then, it remains to raise the Alf Laylah wa Laylah into its proper place once more.

I am not concerned to deny the objective reality of all "magical" phenomena; if they are illusions, they are at least as real as many unquestioned facts of daily life; and, if we follow Herbert Spencer, they are at least evidence of some cause.[4]

Now, this fact is our base. What is the cause of my illusion of seeing a spirit in the triangle of Art?

Every smatterer, every expert in psychology, will answer: "That cause lies in your brain."

English children (pace the Education Act) are taught that the Universe lies in infinite Space; Hindu children, in the Akasa, which is the same thing.

Those Europeans who go a little deeper learn from Fichte, that the phenomenal Universe is the creation of the Ego; Hindus, or Europeans studying under Hindu Gurus, are told, that by Akasa is meant the Chitakasa. The Chitakasa is situated in the "Third Eye," i.e., in the brain. By assuming higher dimensions of space, we can assimilate this fact to Realism; but we have no need to take so much trouble.

This being true for the ordinary Universe, that all sense-impressions are

---

[4] This, incidentally, is perhaps the greatest argument we possess, pushed to its extreme, against the Advaitist theories.

dependent on changes in the brain,[5] we must include illusions, which are after all sense-impressions as much as "realities" are, in the class of "phenomena dependent on brain-changes."

Magical phenomena, however, come under a special sub-class, since they are willed, and their cause is the series of "real" phenomena, called the operations of ceremonial Magic.

These consist of

(1) Sight.
The circle, square, triangle, vessels, lamps, robes, implements, etc.

(2) Sound.
The invocations.

(3) Smell.
The perfumes.

(4) Taste.
The Sacraments.

(5) Touch.
As under (1).

(6) Mind.

The combination of all these and reflection on their significance.

These unusual impressions (1-5) produce unusual brain-changes; hence their summary (6) is of unusual kind. Its projection back into the apparently phenomenal world is therefore unusual.

Herein then consists the reality of the operations and effects of ceremonial magic,[6] and I conceive that the apology is ample, as far as the "effects" refer only to those phenomena which appear to the magician himself, the appearance of the spirit, his conversation, possible shocks from imprudence, and so on, even to ecstasy on the one hand, and death or madness on the other.

But can any of the effects described in this our book Goetia be obtained,

---

[5] Thought is a secretion of the brain (Weissmann). Consciousness is a function of the brain (Huxley).

[6] Apart from its value in obtaining one-pointedness.

and if so, can you give a rational explanation of the circumstances? Say you so?

I can, and will.

The spirits of the Goetia are portions of the human brain. Their seals therefore represent (Mr. Spencer's projected cube) methods of stimulating or regulating those particular spots (through the eye).

The names of God are vibrations calculated to establish:

(a) General control of the brain., (Establishment of functions relative to the subtle world.)

(b) Control over the brain in detail. (Rank or type of the Spirit.)

(c) Control of one special portion. (Name of the Spirit.)

The perfumes aid this through smell. Usually the perfume will only tend to control a large area; but there is an attribution of perfumes to letters of the alphabet enabling one, by a Qabalistic formula, to spell out the Spirit's name.

I need not enter into more particular discussion of these points; the intelligent reader can easily fill in what is lacking.

If, then, I say, with Solomon: "The Spirit Cimieries teaches logic," what I mean is: "Those portions of my brain which subserve the logical faculty may be stimulated and developed by following out the processes called 'The Invocation of Cimieries.'"

And this is a purely materialistic rational statement; it is independent of any objective hierarchy at all. Philosophy has nothing to say; and Science can only suspend judgment, pending a proper and methodical investigation of the facts alleged.

Unfortunately, we cannot stop there. Solomon promises us that we can (1) obtain information; (2) destroy our enemies; (3) understand the voices of nature; (4) obtain treasure; (5) heal diseases, etc. I have taken these five powers at random; considerations of space forbid me to explain all.

(1) Brings up facts from sub-consciousness.

(2) Here we come to an interesting fact. It is curious to note the contrast between the noble means and the apparently vile ends of magical rituals. The latter are disguises for sublime truths. "To destroy our enemies" is to realize the illusion of duality, to excite compassion. (Ah! Mr. Waite, the world of Magic is a mirror, wherein who sees muck is muck.)

(3) A careful naturalist will understand much from the voices of the animals he has studied long. Even a child knows the difference of a cat's miauling and purring. The faculty may be greatly developed.

(4) Business capacity may be stimulated.

(5) Abnormal states of the body may be corrected, and the involved tissues brought back to tone, in obedience to currents started from the brain.

So for all other phenomena. There is no effect which is truly and necessarily miraculous.

Our Ceremonial Magic fines down, then, to a series of minute, though of course empirical, physiological experiments, and whoso, will carry them through intelligently need not fear the result.

I have all the health, and treasure, and logic, I need; I have no time to waste. "There is a lion in the way." For me these practices are useless; but for the benefit of others less fortunate I give them to the world, together with this explanation of, and apology for, them.

I trust that the explanation will enable many students who have hitherto, by a puerile objectivity in their view of the question, obtained no results, to succeed; that the apology may impress upon our scornful men of science that the study of the bacillus should give place to that of the baculum, the little to the great--how great one only realizes when one identifies the wand with the Mahalingam, up which Brahma flew at the rate of 84,000 yojanas a second for 84,000 mahakalpas, down which Vishnu flew at the rate of 84,000 croces of yojanas a second for 84,000 crores of mahakalpas--yet neither reached an end.

But I reach an end.

    Boleskine House,
        Foyers, N.B.

Preliminary Definition of Magic

Lemegeton Vel Clavicula Salomonis Regis

MAGIC is the Highest, most Absolute, and most Divine Knowledge of Natural Philosophy,[7] advanced in its works and wonderful operations by a right understanding of the inward and occult virtue of things; so that true Agents[8] being applied to proper Patients,[9] strange and admirable effects will thereby be produced. Whence magicians are profound and diligent searchers into Nature; they, because of their skill, know how to anticipate an effort,[10] the which to the vulgar shall seem to be a miracle.

Origen saith that the Magical Art doth not contain anything subsisting, but although it should, yet that it must not be Evil, or subject to contempt or scorn; and doth distinguish the Natural Magic from that which is Diabolical.

Apollonius Tyannaeus only exercised the Natural Magic, by the which he did perform wonderful things.

Philo Hebraeus saith that true Magic, by which we do arrive at the understanding of the Secret Works of Nature, is so far from being contemptible that the greatest Monarchs and Kings have studied it. Nay! among the Persians none might reign unless he was skillful in this GREAT ART.

This Noble Science often degenerateth, from Natural becometh Diabolical, and from True Philosophy turneth unto Nigromancy.[11] The which is wholly to be charged upon its followers, who, abusing or not being capable of that High and Mystical Knowledge do immediately hearken unto the temptations of Sathan, and are misled by him into the Study of the Black Art. Hence it is that Magic lieth under disgrace, and they who seek after it are vulgarly esteemed Sorcerers.

The Fraternity of the Rosie Crusians thought it not fit to style themselves Magicians, but rather Philosophers. And they be not ignorant Empiricks,[12] but learned and experienced Physicians, whose remedies be not only Lawful but Divine.

---

[7] This Preliminary Definition of Magic is found in very few Codices, and is probably later than the body of the work.
[8] Or Actives.
[9] Or Passives.
[10] Or Effect.
[11] Or the Black Art, as distinct from mere Necromancy, or Divination by the Dead.
[12] Or Quacks and Pretenders.

The Brief Introductory Description

(N.B. This is taken from several MS. Codices, of which the four principal variations are here composed together in parallel columns as an example of the close agreement of the various texts of the Lemegeton.

For in the whole work the differences in the wording of the various Codices are not sufficient to require the constant giving of parallel readings; but except in the more ancient examples there is much deterioration in the Seals and Sigils, so that in this latter respect the more recent exemplars are not entirely reliable.

CLAVICULA SALOMONIS REGIS, which containeth all the Names, Offices, and Orders of all the Spirits that ever he had converse with, with the Seals and Characters to each Spirit and the manner of calling them forth to visible appearance:

In 5 parts, viz.:

(1) THE FIRST PART is a Book of Evil Spirits, called GOETIA, showing how he bound up those Spirits, and used them in general things, whereby he obtained great fame.

(2) THE SECOND PART is a Book of Spirits, partly Evil and partly Good, which is named THEURGIA-GOETIA, all Aërial Spirits, etc.

(3) THE THIRD PART is of Spirits governing the Planetary Hours, and what Spirits belong to every degree, of the Signs, and Planets in the Signs. Called the PAULINE ART, etc.

(4) THE FOURTH PART of this Book is called ALMADEL or SOLOMON, which containeth those Spirits which govern the Four Altitudes, or the 360 Degrees of the Zodiac.

These two last Orders of Spirits are Good, and to be sought for by Divine seeking, etc., and are called THEURGIA.

(5) THE FIFTH PART is a Book of Orations and Prayers that Wise Solomon used upon the Altar in the Temple. The which is called ARS NOVA, which was revealed unto Solomon by that Holy Angel of God called MICHAEL; and he also received many brief Notes written with the Finger of God, which were declared to him by the said Angel with Claps of Thunder; without which Notes King Solomon had never obtained his great knowledge, for by them in a short time he knew all Arts and Sciences both Good and

Bad; from these Notes it is called the NOTARY ART, etc.

The Whole Lemegeton or Clavicula

Now this Book containeth all the Names, Orders, and Offices of all the Spirits with which Solomon ever conversed, the Seals and Characters belonging to each Spirit, and the manner of calling them forth to visible appearance:

Divided into 5 special Books or parts, viz.:

(1) THE FIRST BOOK, or PART, which is a Book concerning Spirits of Evil, and which is termed THE GOETIA OF SOLOMON, sheweth forth his manner of binding these Spirits for use in things divers. And hereby did he acquire great renown.

(2) THE SECOND BOOK is one which treateth of Spirits mingled of Good and Evil Natures, the which is entitled THE THEURGIA-GOETIA, or the Magical Wisdom of the Spirits Aërial, whereof some do abide, but certain do wander and abide not.

(3) THE THIRD BOOK, called ARS PAULINA, or THE ART PAULINE, treateth of the Spirits allotted unto every degree of the 360 Degrees of the Zodiac; and also of the Signs, and of the Planets in the Signs, as well as of the Hours.

(4) THE FOURTH BOOK, called ARS ALMADEL SALOMONIS, or THE ART ALMADEL OF SOLOMON, concerneth those Spirits which be set over the Quaternary of the Altitudes.

These two last mentioned Books, the ART PAULINE and the ART ALMADEL, do relate unto Good Spirits alone, whose knowledge is to be obtained through seeking unto the Divine. These two Books be also classed together under the Name of the First and Second Parts of the Book THEURGIA OF SOLOMON.

(5) THE FIFTH BOOK of the Lemegeton is one of Prayers and Orations. The which Solomon the Wise did use upon the Altar in the Temple. And the titles hereof be ARS NOVA, the NEW ART, and ARS NOTARIA, the NOTARY ART. The which was revealed to him by MICHAEL, that Holy Angel of God, in thunder and in lightning, and he further did receive by the aforesaid Angel certain Notes written by the Hand of God, without the which that Great King had never attained unto his great Wisdom, for thus he knew all things and all Sciences and Arts whether Good or Evil.

CLAVICULA SALOMONIS REGIS, which containeth all the Names, Offices, and Orders of all the Spirits with. whom he ever held any converse; together with the Seals and Characters proper unto each Spirit, and the method of calling them forth to visible appearance:

In 5 parts, viz.:

(1) THE FIRST PART is a Book of Evil Spirits, called GOETIA, showing how he bound up those Spirits and used them in things general and several, whereby be obtained great fame.

(2) THE SECOND PART is a Book of Spirits, partly Evil and partly Good, which is called THEURGIA-GOETIA, all Aërial Spirits, etc.

(3) THE THIRD PART is of Spirits governing the Planetary Hours, and of what Spirits do belong to every Degree of the Signs, and of the Planets in the Signs. This is called the PAULINE ART, etc.

(4) THE FOURTH PART of this Book is called ALMADEL OF SOLOMON, the which containeth those Spirits which do govern the Four Altitudes, or the 360 Degrees of the Zodiac.

These two last Orders of Spirits are Good, and are called THEURGIA, and are to be sought for by Divine seeking, etc.

(5) THE FIFTH PART is a Book of Orations and Prayers which Wise Solomon did use upon the Altar in the Temple. The which is called ARS NOVA, the which was revealed to Solomon by that Holy Angel of God called Michael; and he also received many brief Notes written with the Finger of God, which were declared to him by the said Angel with Claps of Thunder; without which Notes King Solomon had never obtained his Great Wisdom, for by them in short time he gained Knowledge of all Arts and Sciences both Good and Bad; from these Notes it is called the NOTARY ART, etc.

The Book of Evil Spirits

THE KEY OF SOLOMON, which contains all the names, orders, and offices of all the Spirits that ever Solomon conversed with, together with the Seals and Characters belonging to each Spirit, and the manner of calling them forth to visible appearance:

In 4 parts:

(1) THE FIRST PART is a Book of Evil Spirits, called GOETIA, showing how he bound up those Spirits and used them in several things, whereby he obtained great fame.

(2) THE SECOND PART is a Book of Spirits, partly Good and partly Evil, which is named THEURGIA-GOETIA, all Aërial Spirits, etc.

(3) THE: THIRD PART is a Book governing the Planetary Houses, and what Spirits belong to every Degree of the Signs, and Planets in the Signs. Called the Pauline Art.

(4) THE FOURTH PART is a Book called the ALMADEL OF SOLOMON, which contains Twenty Chief Spirits who govern the Four Altitudes, or the 360 Degrees of the Zodiac.

These two last Orders of Spirits are Good, and called THEURGIA, and are to be sought after by Divine seeking.
These Most Sacred Mysteries were revealed unto Solomon.
Now in this Book LEMEGETON is contained the whole Art of King Solomon. And although there be many other Books that are said to be his, yet none is to be compared hereunto, for this containeth them all. Though there be titles with several other Names of the Book, as THE BOOK HELISOL, which is the very same with this last Book of Lemegeton called ARS NOVA or ARS NOTARIA, etc.
These Books were first found in the Chaldee and Hebrew Tongues at Jerusalem by a Jewish Rabbi; and by him put into the Greek language and thence into the Latin, as it is said.

SHEMHAMPHORASH

(1.) BAEL.--The First Principal Spirit is a King ruling in the East, called Bael. He maketh thee to go Invisible. He ruleth over 66 Legions of Infernal Spirits. He appeareth in divers shapes, sometimes like a Cat, sometimes like a Toad, and sometimes like a Man, and sometimes all these forms at once. He speaketh hoarsely. This is his character which is used to be worn as a Lamen before him who calleth him forth, or else he will not do thee homage.

(2.) AGARES.--The Second Spirit is a Duke called Agreas, or Agares. He is under the Power of the East, and cometh up in the form of an old fair Man, riding upon a Crocodile, carrying a Goshawk upon his fist, and yet mild in appearance. He maketh them to run that stand still, and bringeth back runaways. He teaches all Languages or Tongues presently. He hath power also to destroy Dignities both Spiritual and Temporal, and causeth Earthquakes. He was of the Order of Virtues. He hath under his government 31 Legions of Spirits. And this is his Seal or Character which thou shalt wear as a Lamen before thee.

(3.) VASSAGO.--The Third Spirit is a Mighty Prince, being of the same nature as Agares. He is called Vassago. This Spirit is of a Good Nature, and his office is to declare things Past and to Come, and to discover all things Hid or Lost. And he governeth 26 Legions of Spirits, and this is his Seal.

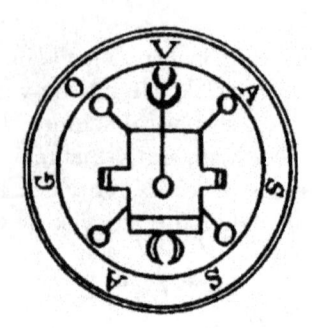

(4.) SAMIGINA, or GAMIGM.--The Fourth Spirit is Samigina, a Great Marquis. He appeareth in the form of a little Horse or Ass, and then into Human shape doth he change himself at the request of the Master. He speaketh with a hoarse voice. He ruleth over 30 Legions of Inferiors. He teaches all Liberal Sciences, and giveth account of Dead Souls that died in sin. And his Seal is this, which is to be worn before the Magician when he is Invocator, etc.

(5.) MARBAS.--The fifth Spirit is Marbas. He is a Great President, and appeareth at first in the form of a Great Lion, but afterwards, at the request of the Master, he putteth on Human Shape. He answereth truly of things Hidden or Secret. He causeth Diseases and cureth them. Again, he giveth great Wisdom and Knowledge in Mechanical Arts; and can change men into other shapes. He governeth 36 Legions of Spirits. And his Seal is this, which is to be worn as aforesaid.

(6.) VALEFOR.--The Sixth Spirit is Valefor. He is a mighty Duke, and appeareth in the shape of a Lion with an Ass's Head, bellowing. He is a good Familiar, but tempteth them he is a familiar of to steal. He governeth 10 Legions of Spirits. His Seal is this, which is to be worn, whether thou wilt have him for a Familiar, or not.

(7.) AMON.--The Seventh Spirit is Amon. He is a Marquis great in power, and most stern. He appeareth like a Wolf with a Serpents tail, vomiting out of his mouth flames of fire; but at the command of the Magician he putteth on the shape of a Man with Dog's teeth beset in a head like a Raven; or else like a Man with a Raven's head (simply). He telleth all things Past and to Come. He procureth feuds and reconcileth controversies between friends. He governeth 40 Legions of Spirits. His Seal is this which is to be worn as aforesaid, etc.

(8.)   BARBATOS.--The Eighth Spirit is Barbatos. He is a Great Duke, and appeareth when the Sun is in Sagittary, with four noble Kings and their companies of great troops. He giveth understanding of the singing of Birds, and of the Voices of other creatures, such as the barking of Dogs. He breaketh the Hidden Treasures open that have been laid by the Enchantments of Magicians. He is of the Order of Virtues, of which some part he retaineth still; and he knoweth all things Past, and to come, and conciliateth Friends and those that be in Power. He ruleth over 30 Legions of Spirits. His Seal of Obedience is this, the which wear before thee as aforesaid.

(9)   PAIMON.--The Ninth Spirit in this Order is Paimon, a Great King, and very obedient unto LUCIFER. He appeareth in the form of a Man sitting upon a Dromedary with a Crown most glorious upon his head. There goeth before him also an Host of Spirits, like Men with Trumpets and well sounding Cymbals, and all other sorts of Musical Instruments. He hath a great Voice, and roareth at his first coming, and his speech is such that the Magician cannot well understand unless he can compel him. This Spirit can teach all Arts and Sciences, and other secret things. He can discover unto thee what the Earth is, and what holdeth it up in the Waters; and what Mind is, and where it is; or any other thing thou mayest desire to know. He giveth Dignity, and confirmeth the same. He bindeth or maketh any man subject unto the Magician if he so desire it. He giveth good Familiars, and such as can teach all Arts. He is to be observed towards the West. He is of the Order of Dominations.[13] He hath under him 200 Legions of Spirits, and part of them are of the Order of Angels, and the other part of Potentates. Now if thou callest this Spirit Paimon alone, thou must make him some offering; and there will attend him two Kings called LABAL and ABALIM, and also other Spirits who be of the Order of Potentates in his Host, and 25 Legions. And those Spirits which be subject unto them are not always with them unless the Magician do compel them. His Character is this which must be worn as a

---

[13] Or Dominions, as they are usually termed.

Lamen before thee, etc.

(10.) BUER.--The Tenth Spirit is Buer, a Great President. He appeareth in Sagittary, and that is his shape when the Sun is there. He teaches Philosophy, both Moral and Natural, and the Logic Art, and also the Virtues of all Herbs and Plants. He healeth all distempers in man, and giveth good Familiars. He governeth 50 Legions of Spirits, and his Character of obedience is this, which thou must wear when thou callest him forth unto appearance.

(11.) GUSION.--The Eleventh Spirit in order is a great and strong Duke, called Gusion. He appeareth like a Xenopilus. He telleth all things, Past, Present, and to Come, and showeth the meaning and resolution of all questions thou mayest ask. He concileateth and reconcileth friendships, and giveth Honour and Dignity unto any. He ruleth over 40 Legions of Spirits. His Seal is this, the which wear thou as aforesaid.

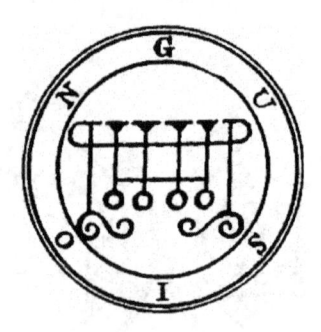

(12.) SITRI.--The Twelfth Spirit is Sitri. He is a Great Prince and appeareth at first with a Leopard's head and the Wings of a Gryphon, but after the command of the Master of the Exorcism he putteth on Human shape, and that very beautiful. He enflameth men with Women's love, and Women with Men's love; and causeth them also to show themselves naked if it be desired. He governeth 60 Legions of Spirits. His Seal is this, to be worn as a Lamen before thee, etc.

(13.) BELETH.--The Thirteenth Spirit is called Beleth (or Bileth, or Bilet). He is a mighty King and terrible. He rideth on a pale horse with trumpets and other kinds of musical instruments playing before him. He is very furious at his first appearance, that is, while the Exorcist layeth his courage; for to do this he must hold a Hazel Wand in his hand, striking it out towards the South and East Quarters, make a triangle, Δ, without the Circle, and then command him into it by the Bonds and Charges of Spirits as hereafter followeth. And if he doth not enter into the triangle, Δ, at your threats, rehearse the Bonds and Charms before him, and then he will yield Obedience and come into it, and do what he is commanded by the Exorcist. Yet he must receive him courteously because he is a Great King, and do homage unto him, as the Kings and Princes do that attend upon him. And thou must have always a Silver Ring on the middle finger of the left hand held against thy face,[14] as they do yet before AMAYMON. This Great King Beleth causeth all the love that may be, both of Men and of Women, until the Master Exorcist hath had his desire fulfilled. He is of the Order of Powers, and he governeth 85 Legions of Spirits. His Noble Seal is this, which is to be worn before thee at working.

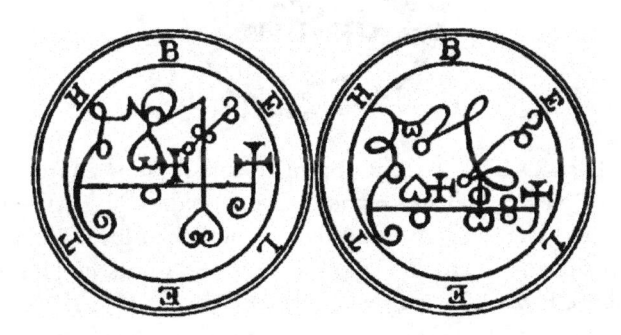

(14.) LERAJE, or LERAIKHA.--The Fourteenth Spirit is called Leraje (or Leraie). He is a Marquis Great in Power, showing himself in the likeness of an Archer clad in Green, and carrying a Bow and Quiver. He causeth all great Battles and Contests; and maketh wounds to putrefy that are made with Arrows by Archers. This belongeth unto Sagittary. He governeth 30 Legions of Spirits, and this is his Seal, etc.

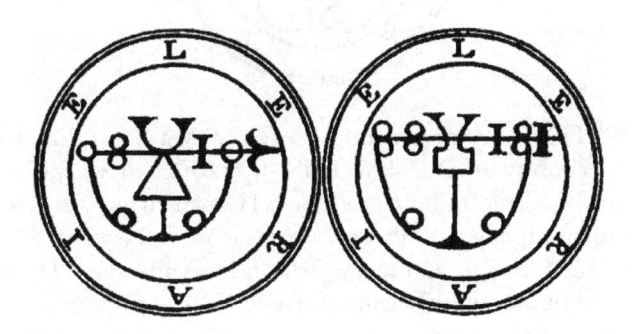

(15.) ELIGOS.--The Fifteenth Spirit in Order is Eligos, a Great Duke, and appeareth in the form of a goodly Knight, carrying a Lance, an Ensign, and a Serpent. He discovereth hidden things, and knoweth things to come; and of Wars, and how the Soldiers will or shall meet. He causeth the Love of Lords and Great Persons. He governeth 60 Legions of Spirits. His Seal is this, etc.

---

[14] To protect him from the flaming breath of the enraged Spirit; the design is given at the end of the instructions for the Magical Circle, etc., later on in the Goetia.

(16.) ZEPAR.--The Sixteenth Spirit is Zepar. He is a Great Duke, and appeareth in Red Apparel and Armour, like a Soldier. His office is to cause Women to love Men, and to bring them together in love. He also maketh them barren. He governeth 26 Legions of Inferior Spirits, and his Seal is this, which he obeyeth when he seeth it.

(17.) BOTIS.--The Seventeenth Spirit is Botis, a Great President, and an Earl. He appeareth at the first show in the form of an ugly Viper, then at the command of the Magician he putteth on a Human shape with Great Teeth, and two Horns, carrying a bright and sharp Sword in his hand. He telleth all things Past, and to Come, and reconcileth Friends and Foes. He ruleth over 60 Legions of Spirits, and this is his Seal, etc.

(18.) BATHIN.--The Eighteenth Spirit is Bathin. He is a Mighty and Strong Duke, and appeareth like a Strong Man with the tail of a Serpent, sitting upon a Pale-Coloured Horse. He knoweth the Virtues of Herbs and Precious Stones, and can transport men suddenly from one country to another. He ruleth over 30 Legions of Spirits. His Seal is this which is to be worn as aforesaid.

(19.) SALLOS.--The Nineteenth Spirit is Sallos (or Saleos). He is a Great and Mighty Duke, and appeareth in the form of a gallant Soldier riding on a Crocodile, with a Ducal Crown on his head, but peaceably. He causeth the Love of Women to Men, and of Men to Women; and governeth 30 Legions of Spirits. His Seal is this, etc.

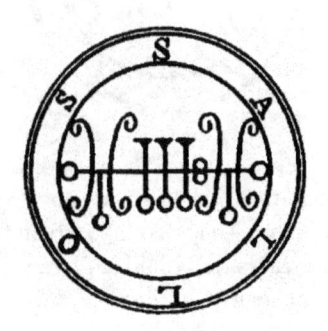

(20.) PURSON.--The Twentieth Spirit is Purson, a Great King. His appearance is comely, like a Man with a Lion's face, carrying a cruel Viper in his hand, and riding upon a Bear. Going before him are many Trumpets sounding. He knoweth all things hidden, and can discover Treasure, and tell all things Past, Present, and to Come. He can take a Body either Human or Aërial, and answereth truly of all Earthly things both Secret and Divine, and of the Creation of the World. He bringeth forth good Familiars, and under his Government there be 22 Legions of Spirits, partly of the Order of Virtues and partly of the Order of Thrones. His Mark, Seal, or Character is this, unto the which he oweth obedience, and which thou shalt wear in time of action, etc.

(21.) MARAX.--The Twenty-first Spirit is Marax.[15] He is a Great Earl and President. He appeareth like a great Bull with a Man's face. His office is to make Men very knowing in Astronomy, and all other Liberal Sciences; also he can give good Familiars, and wise, knowing the virtues of Herbs and Stones which be precious. He governeth 30 Legions of Spirits, and his Seal is this, which must be made and worn as aforesaid, etc.

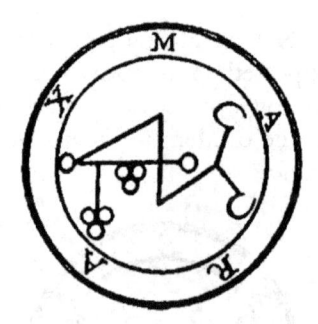

(22.) IPOS.--The Twenty-second Spirit is Ipos. He is an Earl, and a Mighty Prince, and appeareth in the form of an Angel with a Lion's Head, and a Goose's Foot, and Hare's Tail. He knoweth all things Past, Present, and to Come. He maketh men witty and bold. He governeth 36 Legions of Spirits. His Seal is this, which thou shalt wear, etc.

---

[15] In some Codices written Morax, but I consider the above the correct orthography.

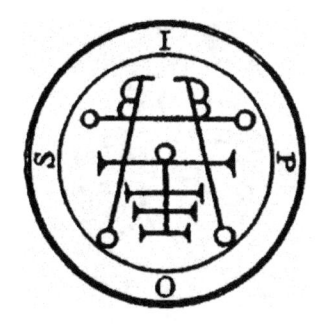

(23.) AIM.--The Twenty-third Spirit is Aim. He is a Great Strong Duke. He appeareth in the form of a very handsome Man in body, but with three Heads; the first, like a Serpent, the second like a Man having two Stars on his Forehead, the third like a Calf. He rideth on a Viper, carrying a Firebrand in his Hand, wherewith he setteth cities, castles, and great Places, on fire. He maketh thee witty in all manner of ways, and giveth true answers unto private matters. He governeth 26 Legions of Inferior Spirits; and his Seal is this, which wear thou as aforesaid, etc.

(24.) NABERIUS.--The Twenty-fourth Spirit is Naberius. He is a most valiant Marquis, and showeth in the form of a Black Crane, fluttering about the Circle, and when he speaketh it is with a hoarse voice. He maketh men cunning in all Arts and Sciences, but especially in the Art of Rhetoric. He restoreth lost Dignities and Honours. He governeth 19 Legions of Spirits. His Seal is this, which is to be worn, etc.

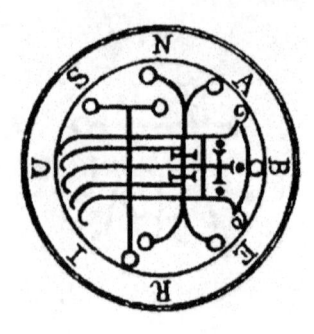

(25.) GLASYA-LABOLAS.--The Twenty-fifth Spirit is Glasya-Labolas. He is a Mighty President and Earl, and showeth himself in the form of a Dog with Wings like a Gryphon. He teacheth all Arts and Sciences in an instant, and is an Author of Bloodshed and Manslaughter. He teacheth all things Past, and to Come. If desired he causeth the love both of Friends and of Foes. He can make a Man to go Invisible. And he hath under his command 36 Legions of Spirits. His Seal is this, to be, etc.

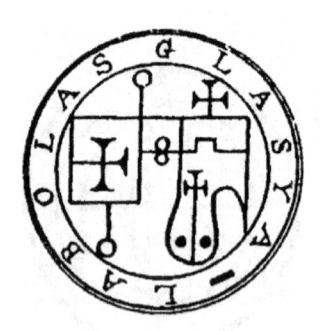

(26.) BUNE, or BIMÉ.--The Twenty-sixth Spirit is Buné (or Bim). He is a Strong, Great and Mighty Duke. He appeareth in the form of a Dragon with three heads, one like a Dog, one like a Gryphon, and one like a Man. He speaketh with a high and comely Voice. He changeth the Place of the Dead, and causeth the Spirits which be under him to gather together upon your Sepulchres. He giveth Riches unto a Man, and maketh him Wise and Eloquent. He giveth true Answers unto Demands. And he governeth 30 Legions of Spirits. His Seal is this, unto the which he oweth Obedience. He hath another Seal (which is the first of these, but the last is the best)

THE LESSER KEY OF SOLOMON

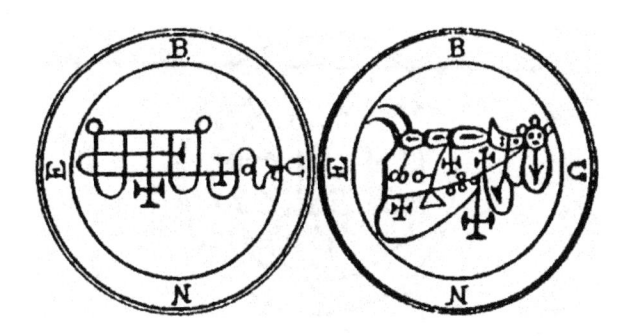

(27.) RONOVÉ.--The Twenty-seventh Spirit is Ronové. He appeareth in the Form of a Monster. He teacheth the Art of Rhetoric very well and giveth Good Servants, Knowledge of Tongues, and Favours with Friends or Foes. He is a Marquis and Great Earl; and there be under his command 19 Legions of Spirits. His Seal is this, etc.

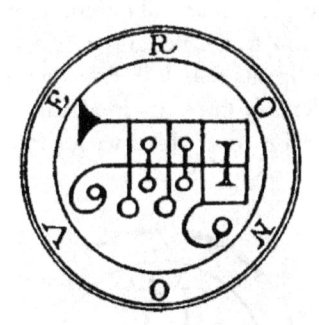

(28.) BERITH.--The Twenty-eighth Spirit in Order, as Solomon bound them, is named Berith. He is a Mighty, Great, and Terrible Duke. He hath two other Names given unto him by men of later times, viz.: BEALE, or BEAL, and BOFRY or BOLFRY. He appeareth in the Form of a Soldier with Red Clothing, riding upon a Red Horse, and having a Crown of Gold upon his head. He giveth true answers, Past, Present, and to Come. Thou must make use of a Ring in calling him forth, as is before spoken of regarding Beleth.[16] He can turn all metals into Gold. He can give Dignities, and can confirm them unto Man. He speaketh with a very clear and subtle Voice. He governeth 26 Legions of Spirits. His Seal is this, etc.

---

[16] See ante, Spirit No. 13.

(29.) ASTAROTH.--The Twenty.--ninth Spirit is Astaroth. He is a Mighty, Strong Duke, and appeareth in the Form of an hurtful Angel riding on an Infernal Beast like a Dragon, and carrying in his right hand a Viper. Thou must in no wise let him approach too near unto thee, lest he do thee damage by his Noisome Breath. Wherefore the Magician must hold the Magical Ring near his face, and that will defend him. He giveth true answers of things Past, Present, and to Come, and can discover all Secrets. He will declare wittingly how the Spirits fell, if desired, and the reason of his own fall. He can make men wonderfully knowing in all Liberal Sciences. He ruleth 40 Legions of Spirits. His Seal is this, which wear thou as a Lamen before thee, or else he will not appear nor yet obey thee, etc.

(30.) FORNEUS.--The Thirtieth Spirit is Forneus. He is a Mighty and Great Marquis, and appeareth in the Form of a Great Sea-Monster. He teacheth, and maketh men wonderfully knowing in the Art of Rhetoric. He causeth men to have a Good Name, and to have the knowledge and understanding of Tongues. He maketh one to be beloved of his Foes as well as of his Friends. He governeth 29 Legions of Spirits, partly of the Order of Thrones, and partly of that of Angels. His Seal is this, which wear thou, etc.

(31.) FORAS.--The Thirty-first Spirit is Foras. He is a Mighty President, and appeareth in the Form of a Strong Man in Human Shape. He can give the understanding to Men how they may know the Virtues of all Herbs and Precious Stones. He teacheth the Arts of Logic and Ethics in all their parts. If desired he maketh men invisible,[17] and to live long, and to be eloquent. He can discover Treasures and recover things Lost. He ruleth over 29 Legions of Spirits, and his Seal is this, which wear thou, etc.

(32.) ASMODAY.--The Thirty-second Spirit is Asmoday, or Asmodai. He is a Great King, Strong, and Powerful. He appeareth with Three Heads, whereof the first is like a Bull, the second like a Man, and the third like a Ram; he bath also the tail of a Serpent, and from his mouth issue Flames of Fire. His Feet are webbed like those of a Goose. He sitteth upon an Infernal Dragon, and beareth in his hand a Lance with a Banner. He is first and choicest under the Power of AMAYMON, he goeth before all other. When the Exorcist bath a mind to call him, let it be abroad, and let him stand on his feet all the time of action, with his Cap or Headdress off; for if it be on, AMAYMON will deceive him and call all his actions to be bewrayed. But as

---

[17] One or two Codices have "invincible," but "invisible" is given in the majority. Yet the form of appearance of Foras as a strong man might warrant the former, though from the nature of his offices the invincibility would probably be rather on the mental than on the physical plane.

soon as the Exorcist seeth Asmoday in the shape aforesaid, he shall call him by his Name, saying: "Art thou Asmoday?" and he will not deny it, and by-and-by he will bow down unto the ground. He giveth the Ring of Virtues; he teacheth the Arts of Arithmetic, Astronomy, Geometry, and all handicrafts absolutely. He giveth true and full answers unto thy demands. He maketh one Invincible. He showeth the place where Treasures lie, and guardeth it. He, amongst the Legions of AMAYMON governeth 72 Legions of Spirits Inferior. His Seal is this which thou must wear as a Lamen upon thy breast, etc.

(33.) GAAP.--The Thirty-third Spirit is Gaap. He is a Great President and a Mighty Prince. He appeareth when the Sun is in some of the Southern Signs, in a Human Shape, going before Four Great and Mighty Kings, as if he were a Guide to conduct them along on their way. His Office is to make men Insensible or Ignorant; as also in Philosophy to make them Knowing, and in all the Liberal Sciences. He can cause Love or Hatred, also he can teach thee to consecrate those things that belong to the Dominion of AMAYMON his King. He can deliver Familiars out of the Custody of other Magicians, and answereth truly and perfectly of things Past, Present, and to Come. He can carry and re-carry men very speedily from one Kingdom to another, at the Will and Pleasure of the Exorcist. He ruleth over 66 Legions of Spirits, and he was of the Order of Potentates. His Seal is this to be made and to be worn as aforesaid, etc.

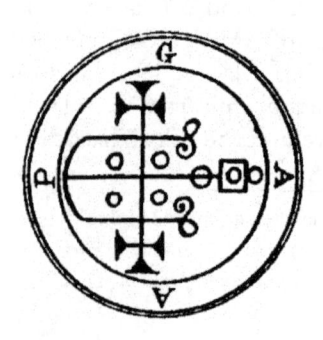

(34.) FURFUR.--The Thirty-fourth Spirit is Furfur. He is a Great and Mighty Earl, appearing in the Form of an Hart with a Fiery Tail. He never speaketh truth unless he be compelled, or brought up within a triangle, △. Being therein, he will take upon himself the Form of an Angel. Being bidden, he speaketh with a hoarse voice. Also he will wittingly urge Love between Man and Woman. He can raise Lightnings and Thunders, Blasts, and Great Tempestuous Storms. And he giveth True Answers both of Things Secret and Divine, if commanded. He ruleth over 26 Legions of Spirits. And his Seal is this, etc.

(35.) MARCHOSIAS.--The Thirty-fifth Spirit is Marchosias. He is a Great and Mighty Marquis, appearing at first in the Form of a Wolf[18] having Gryphon's Wings, and a Serpent's Tail, and Vomiting Fire out of his mouth. But after a time, at the command of the Exorcist he putteth on the Shape of a Man. And be is a strong fighter. He was of the Order of Dominations. He governeth 30 Legions of Spirits. He told his Chief, who was Solomon, that after 1,200 years he had hopes to return unto the Seventh Throne. And his Seal is this, to be made and worn as a Lamen, etc.

---

[18] On one Codex of the seventeenth century, very badly written, it might be read "Ox" instead of "Wolf."---TRANS. [For me he appeared always like an ox, and very dazed.--ED.]

(36.) STOLAS, OR STOLOS.--The Thirty-sixth Spirit is Stolas, or Stolos. He is a Great and Powerful Prince, appearing in the Shape of a Mighty Raven at first before the Exorcist; but after he taketh the image of a Man. He teacheth the Art of Astronomy, and the Virtues of Herbs and Precious Stones. He governeth 26 Legions of Spirits; and his Seal is this, which is, etc.

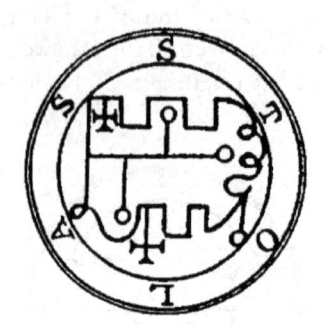

(37.) PHENEX.--The Thirty-Seventh Spirit is Phenex (or Pheynix). He is a great Marquis, and appeareth like the Bird Phoenix, having the Voice of a Child. He singeth many sweet notes before the Exorcist, which he must not regard, but by-and-by he must bid him put on Human Shape. Then he will speak marvellously of all wonderful Sciences if required. He is a Poet, good and excellent. And he will be willing to perform thy requests. He hath hopes also to return to the Seventh Throne after 1,200 years more, as he said unto Solomon. He governeth 20 Legions of Spirits. And his Seal is this, which wear thou, etc.

(38.) HALPHAS, or MALTHUS.--The Thirty-eighth Spirit is Halphas, or Malthous (or Malthas). He is a Great Earl, and appeareth in the Form of a Stock-Dove. He speaketh with a hoarse Voice. His Office is to build up Towers, and to furnish them with Ammunition and Weapons, and to send Men-of-War[19] to places appointed. He ruleth over 26 Legions of Spirits, and

---

[19] Or Warriors, or Men-at-Arms.

his Seal is this, etc.

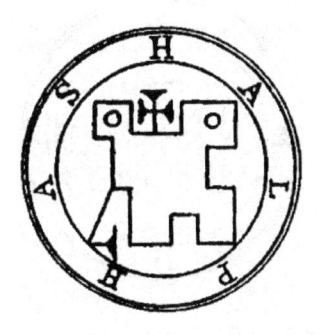

(39.) MALPHAS.--The Thirty-ninth Spirit is Malphas. He appeareth at first like a Crow, but after he will put on Human Shape at the request of the Exorcist, and speak with a hoarse Voice. He is a Mighty President and Powerful. He can build Houses and High Towers, and can bring to thy Knowledge Enemies' Desires and Thoughts, and that which they have done. He giveth Good Familiars. If thou makest a Sacrifice unto him he will receive it kindly and willingly, but he will deceive him that doth it. He governeth 40 Legions of Spirits, and his Seal is this, etc.

(40.) RAUM.--The Fortieth Spirit is Räum. He is a Great Earl; and appeareth at first in the Form of a Crow, but after the Command of the Exorcist he putteth on Human Shape. His office is to steal Treasures out King's Houses, and to carry it whither he is commanded, and to destroy Cities and Dignities of Men, and to tell all things, Past, and What Is, and what Will Be; and to cause Love between Friends and Foes. He was of the Order of Thrones. He governeth 30 Legions of Spirits; and his Seal is this, which wear thou as aforesaid.

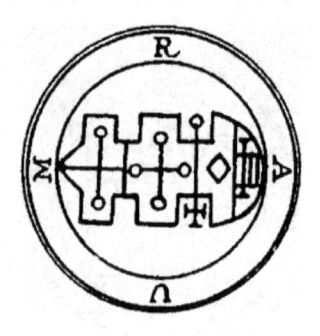

(41.) FOCALOR.--The Forty-first Spirit is Focalor, or Forcalor, or Furcalor. He is a Mighty Duke and Strong. He appeareth in the Form of a Man with Gryphon's Wings. His office is to slay Men, and to drown them in the Waters, and to overthrow Ships of War, for he hath Power over both Winds and Seas; but he will not hurt any man or thing if he be commanded to the contrary by the Exorcist. He also hath hopes to return to the Seventh Throne after 1,000 years. He governeth 30 Legions of Spirits, and his Seal is this, etc.

(42.) VEPAR.--The Forty-second Spirit is Vepar, or Vephar. He is a Duke Great and Strong and appeareth like a Mermaid. His office is to govern the Waters, and to guide Ships laden with Arms, Armour, and Ammunition, etc., thereon. And at the request of the Exorcist he can cause the seas to be right stormy and to appear full of ships. Also he maketh men to die in Three Days by Putrefying Wounds or Sores, and causing Worms to breed in them. He governeth 29 Legions of Spirits, and his Seal is this, etc.

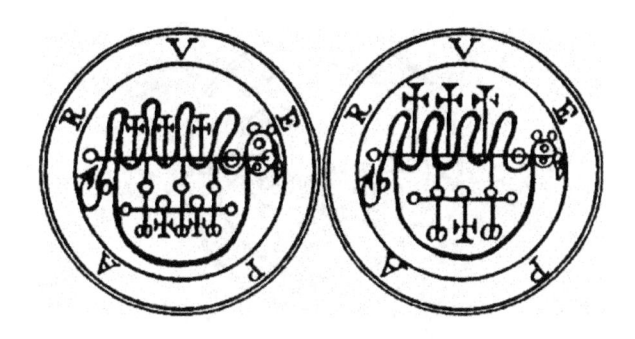

(43.) SABNOCK.--The Forty-third Spirit, as King Solomon commanded them into the Vessel of Brass, is called Sabnock, or Savnok. He is a Marquis, Mighty, Great and Strong, appearing in the Form of an Armed Soldier with a Lion's Head, riding on a pale-coloured horse. His office is to build high Towers, Castles and Cities, and to furnish them with Armour, etc. Also he can afflict Men for many days with Wounds and with Sores rotten and full of Worms. He giveth Good Familiars at the request of the Exorcist. He commandeth 50 Legions of Spirits; and his Seal is this, etc.

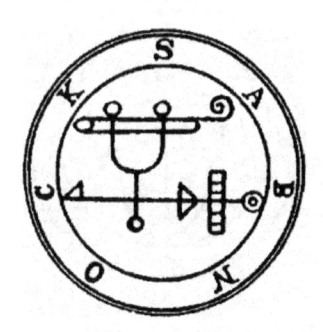

(44.) SHAN.--The Forty-fourth Spirit is Shax, or Shaz (or Shass). He is a Great Marquis and appeareth in the Form of a Stock-Dove, speaking with a voice hoarse, but yet subtle. His Office is to take away the Sight, Hearing, or Understanding of any Man or Woman at the command of the Exorcist; and to steal money out of the houses of Kings, and to carry it again in 1,200 years. If commanded he will fetch Horses at the request of the Exorcist, or any other thing. But he must first be commanded into a Triangle, ∆, or else he will deceive him, and tell him many Lies. He can discover all things that are Hidden, and not kept by Wicked Spirits. He giveth good Familiars, sometimes. He governeth 30 Legions of Spirits, and his Seal is this, etc.

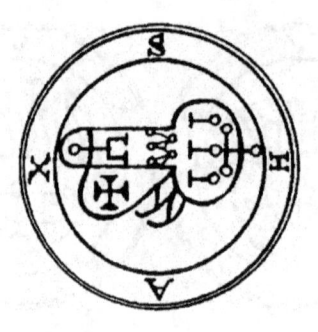

(45.) VINÉ.--The Forty-fifth Spirit is Viné, or Vinea. He is a Great King, and an Earl; and appeareth in the Form of a Lion,[20] riding upon a Black Horse, and bearing a Viper in his hand. His Office is to discover Things Hidden, Witches, Wizards, and Things Present, Past, and to Come. He, at the command of the Exorcist will build Towers, overthrow Great Stone Walls, and make the Waters rough with Storms. He governeth 36 Legions of Spirits. And his Seal is this, which wear thou, as aforesaid, etc.

(46.) BIFRONS.--The Forty-sixth Spirit is called Bifrons, or Bifröus, or Bifrovs. He is an Earl, and appeareth in the Form of a Monster; but after a while, at the Command of the Exorcist, he putteth on the shape of a Man. His Office is to make one knowing in Astrology, Geometry, and other Arts and Sciences. He teacheth the Virtues of Precious Stones and Woods. He changeth Dead Bodies, and putteth them in another place; also he lighteth seeming Candles upon the Graves of the Dead. He hath under his Command 6 Legions of Spirits. His Seal is this, which he will own and submit unto, etc.

---

[20] Or with the Head of a Lion, or having a Lion's Head, in some Codices.

The Lesser Key of Solomon

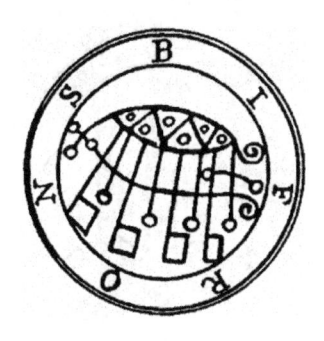

(47.) UVALL, VUAL, or VOVAL.--The Forty-seventh Spirit Uvall, or Vual, or Voval. He is a Duke, Great, Mighty, and Strong; and appeareth in the Form of a Mighty Dromedary at the first, but after a while at the Command of the Exorcist he putteth on Human Shape, and speaketh the Egyptian Tongue, but not perfectly.[21] His Office is to procure the Love of Woman, and to tell Things Past, Present, and to Come. He also procureth Friendship between Friends and Foes. He was of the Order of Potestates or Powers. He governeth 37 Legions of Spirits, and his Seal is this, to be made and worn before thee, etc.

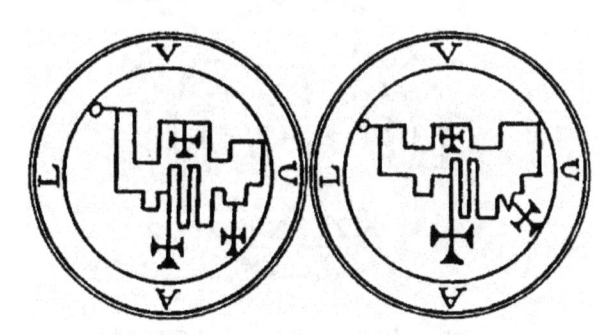

(48.) HAAGENTI.--The Forty-eighth Spirit is Haagenti. He is a President, appearing in the Form of a Mighty Bull with Gryphon's Wings. This is at first, but after, at the Command of the Exorcist he putteth on Human Shape. His Office is to make Men wise, and to instruct them in divers things; also to Transmute all Metals into Gold; and to change Wine into Water, and Water into Wine. He governeth 33 Legions of Spirits, and his Seal is this, etc.

---

[21] He can nowadays converse in sound though colloquial Coptic.--ED.

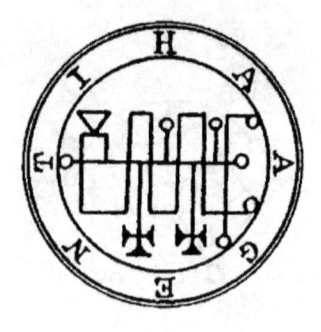

(49.) CROCELL.--The Forty-ninth Spirit is Crocell, or Krokel. He appeareth in the Form of an Angel. He is a Duke Great and Strong, speaking something Mystically of Hidden Things. He teacheth the Art of Geometry and the Liberal Sciences. He, at the Command of the Exorcist, will produce Great Noises like the Rushings of many Waters, although there be none. He warmeth Waters, and discovereth Baths. He was of the Order of Potestates, or Powers, before his fall, as he declared unto the King Solomon. He governeth 48 Legions of Spirits. His Seal is this, the which wear thou as aforesaid.

(50.) FURCAS.--The Fiftieth Spirit is Furcas. He is a Knight, and appeareth in the Form of a Cruel Old Man with a long Beard and a hoary Head, riding upon a pale-coloured Horse, with a Sharp Weapon in his hand. His Office is to teach the Arts of Philosophy, Astrology, Rhetoric, Logic, Cheiromancy, and Pyromancy, in all their parts, and perfectly. He hath under his Power 20 Legions of Spirits. His Seal, or Mark, is thus made, etc.

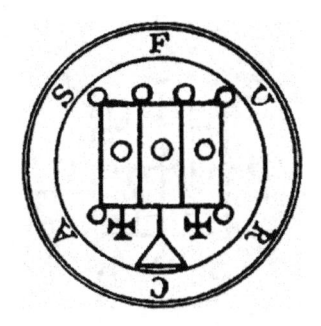

(51.) BALAM.--The Fifty-first Spirit is Balam or Balaam. He is a Terrible, Great, and Powerful King. He appeareth with three Heads: the first is like that of a Bull; the second is like that of a Man; the third is like that of a Ram. He hath the Tail of a Serpent, and Flaming Eyes. He rideth upon a furious Bear, and carrieth a Boshawk upon his Fist. He speaketh with a hoarse Voice, giving True Answers of Things Past, Present, and to Come. He maketh men to go Invisible, and also to be Witty. He governeth 40 Legions of Spirits. His Seal is this, etc.

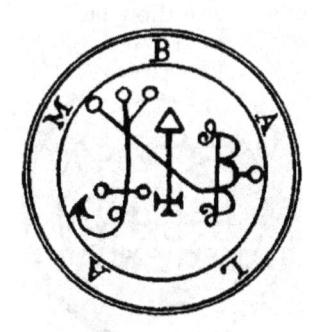

(52.) ALLOCES.--The Fifty-second Spirit is Alloces, or Alocas. He is a Duke, Great, Mighty, and Strong, appearing in the Form of a Soldier[22] riding upon a Great Horse. His Face is like that of a Lion, very Red, and having Flaming Eyes. His Speech is hoarse and very big.[23] His Office is to teach the Art of Astronomy, and all the Liberal Sciences. He bringeth unto thee Good Familiars; also he ruleth over 36 Legions of Spirits. His Seal is this, which, etc.

---

[22] Or Warrior.
[23] Thus expressed in the Codices.

(53.) CAMIO or CAIM.--The Fifty-third Spirit is Camio, or Caim. He is a Great President, and appeareth in the Form of the Bird called a Thrush at first, but afterwards he putteth on the Shape of a Man carrying in his Hand a Sharp Sword. He seemeth to answer in Burning Ashes, or in Coals of Fire. He is a Good Disputer. His Office is to give unto Men the Understanding of all Birds, Lowing of Bullocks, Barking of Dogs, and other Creatures; and also of the Voice of the Waters. He giveth True Answers of Things to Come. He was of the Order of Angels, but now ruleth over 30 Legions of Spirits Infernal. His Seal is this, which wear thou, etc.

(54.) MURMUR, or MURMUS.--The Fifty-fourth Spirit is called Murmur, or Murmus, or Murmux. He is a Great Duke, and an Earl; and appeareth in the Form of a Warrior riding upon a Gryphon, with a Ducal Crown upon his Head. There do go before him those his Ministers with great Trumpets sounding. His Office is to teach Philosophy perfectly, and to constrain Souls Deceased to come before the Exorcist to answer those questions which he may wish to put to them, if desired. He was partly of the Order of Thrones, and partly of that of Angels. He now ruleth 30 Legions of Spirits. And his Seal is this, etc.

(55.) OROBAS.--The Fifty-fifth Spirit is Orobas. He is a great and Mighty Prince, appearing at first like a Horse; but after the command of the Exorcist he putteth on the Image of a Man. His Office is to discover all things Past, Present, and to Come; also to give Dignities, and Prelacies, and the Favour of Friends and of Foes. He giveth True Answers of Divinity, and of the Creation of the World. He is very faithful unto the Exorcist, and will not suffer him to be tempted of any Spirit. He governeth 20 Legions of Spirits. His Seal is this, etc.

(56) GREMORY, or GAMORI.--The Fifty-sixth Spirit is Gremory, or Gamori. He is a Duke Strong and Powerful, and appeareth in the Form of a Beautiful Woman, with a Duchess's Crown tied about her waist, and riding on a Great Camel. His Office is to tell of all Things Past, Present, and to Come; and of Treasures Rid, and what they lie in; and to procure the Love of Women both Young and Old. He governeth 26 Legions of Spirits, and his Seal is this, etc.

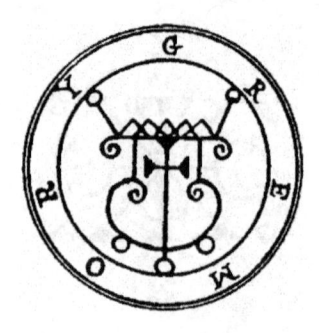

(57.) OSÉ, or VOSO.--The Fifty-seventh Spirit is Oso, Osé, or Voso. He is a Great President, and appeareth like a Leopard at the first, but after a little time he putteth on the Shape of a Man. His Office is to make one cunning in the Liberal Sciences, and to give True Answers of Divine and Secret Things; also to change a Man into any Shape that the Exorcist pleaseth, so that he that is so changed will not think any other thing than that he is in verity that Creature or Thing he is changed into. He governeth 30[24] Legions of Spirits, and this is his Seal, etc.

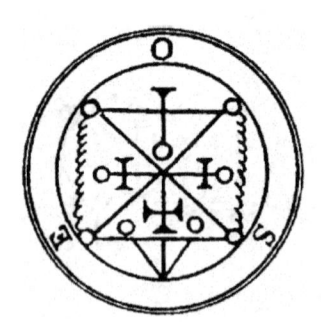

(58.) AMY, or AVNAS.--The Fifty-eighth Spirit is Amy, or Avnas. He is a Great President, and appeareth at first in the Form of a Flaming Fire; but after a while he putteth on the Shape of a Man. His office is to make one Wonderful Knowing[25] in Astrology and all the Liberal Sciences. He giveth Good Familiars, and can bewray Treasure that is kept by Spirits. He governeth 36 Legions of Spirits, and his Seal is this, etc.

---

[24] Should be 30. For these 72 Great Spirits of the Book Goetia are all Princes and Leaders of numbers.
[25] Thus in the actual Text.

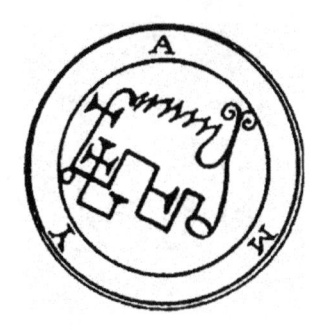

(59.) ORIAX, or ORIAS.--The Fifty-ninth Spirit is Oriax, or Orias. He is a Great Marquis, and appeareth in the Form of a Lion,[26] riding upon a Horse Mighty and Strong, with a Serpent's Tail;[27] and he holdeth in his Right Hand two Great Serpents hissing. His Office is to teach the Virtues of the Stars, and to know the Mansions of the Planets, and how to understand their Virtues. He also transformeth Men, and he giveth Dignities, Prelacies, and Confirmation thereof; also Favour with Friends and with Foes. He doth govern 30 Legions of Spirits; and his Seal is this, etc.

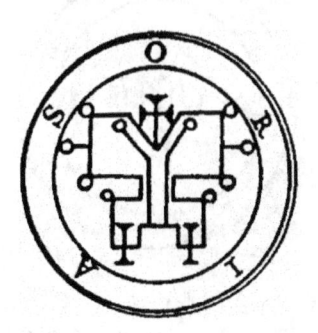

(60.) VAPULA, or NAPHULA.--The Sixtieth Spirit is Vapula, or Naphula. He is a Duke Great, Mighty, and Strong; appearing in the Form of a Lion with Gryphon's Wings. His Office is to make Men Knowing in all Handcrafts and Professions, also in Philosophy, and other Sciences. He governeth 36 Legions of Spirits, and his Seal or Character is thus made, and thou shalt wear it as aforesaid, etc.

---

[26] Or "with the Face of a Lion."
[27] The horse, or the Markist?--ED.

(61.) ZAGAN.--The Sixty-first Spirit is Zagan. He is a Great King and President, appearing at first in the Form of a Bull with Gryphon's Wings; but after a while he putteth on Human Shape. He maketh Men Witty. He can turn Wine into Water, and Blood into Wine, also Water into Wine. He can turn all Metals into Coin of the Dominion that Metal is of. He can even make Fools wise. He governeth 33 Legions of Spirits, and his Seal is this, etc.

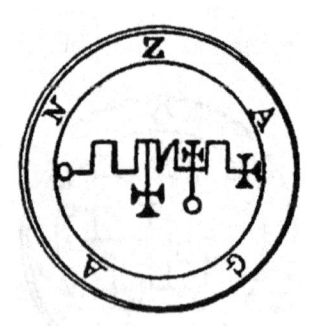

(62.) VOLAC, or VALAX, or VALU, or UALAC.--The Sixty-second Spirit is Volac, or Valak, or Valu. He is a President Mighty and Great, and appeareth like a Child with Angel's Wings, riding on a Two-headed Dragon. His Office is to give True Answers of Hidden Treasures, and to tell where Serpents may be seen. The which he will bring unto the Exorciser without any Force or Strength being by him employed. He governeth 38 Legions of Spirits, and his Seal is thus.

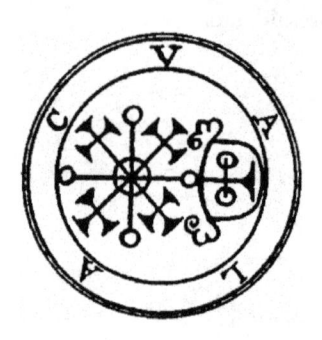

(63.) ANDRAS.--The Sixty-third Spirit is Andras. He is a Great Marquis, appearing in the Form of an Angel with a Head like a Black Night Raven, riding upon a strong Black Wolf, and having a Sharp and Bright Sword flourished aloft in his hand. His Office is to sow Discords. If the Exorcist have not a care, he will slay both him and his fellows. He governeth 30 Legions of Spirits, and this is his Seal, etc.

(64.) HAURES, or HAURAS, or HAVRES, or FLAUROS.--The Sixty-fourth Spirit is Haures, or Hauras, or Havres, or Flauros. He is a Great Duke, and appeareth at first like a Leopard, Mighty, Terrible, and Strong, but after a while, at the Command of the Exorcist, he putteth on Human Shape with Eyes Flaming and Fiery, and a most Terrible Countenance. He giveth True Answers of all things, Present, Past, and to Come. But if he be not commanded into a Triangle, Δ, he will Lie in all these Things, and deceive and beguile the Exorcist in these things, or in such and such business. He will, lastly, talk of the Creation of the World, and of Divinity, and of how he and other Spirits fell. He destroyeth and burneth up those who be the Enemies of the Exorcist should he so desire it; also he will not suffer him to be tempted by any other Spirit or otherwise. He governeth 36 Legions of Spirits, and his Seal is this, to be worn as a Lamen, etc.

(65.) ANDREALPHUS.--The Sixty-fifth Spirit is Andrealphus. He is a

Mighty Marquis, appearing at first in the form of a Peacock, with great Noises. But after a time he putteth on Human shape. He can teach Geometry perfectly. He maketh Men very subtle therein; and in all Things pertaining unto Mensuration or Astronomy. He can transform a Man into the Likeness of a Bird. He governeth 30 Legions of Infernal Spirits, and his Seal is this, etc.

(66.) CIMEJES, or CIMEIES, or KIMARIS.--The Sixty-sixth Spirit is Cimejes, or Cimeies, or Kimaris. He is a Marquis, Mighty, Great, Strong and Powerful, appearing like a Valiant Warrior riding upon a goodly Black Horse. He ruleth over all Spirits in the parts of Africa. His Office is to teach perfectly Grammar, Logic, Rhetoric, and to discover things Lost or Hidden, and Treasures. He governeth 20 Legions of Infernals; and his Seal is this, etc.

(67.) AMDUSIAS, or AMDUKIAS.--The Sixty-seventh Spirit is Amdusias, or Amdukias. He is a Duke Great and Strong, appearing at first like a Unicorn, but at the request of the Exorcist he standeth before him in Human Shape, causing Trumpets, and all manner of Musical Instruments to be heard, but not soon or immediately. Also he can cause Trees to bend and incline according to the Exorcist's Will. He giveth Excellent Familiars. He governeth 29 Legions of Spirits. And his Seal is this, etc.

(68.) BELIAL.--The Sixty-eighth Spirit is Belial. He is a Mighty and a Powerful King, and was created next after LUCIFER. He appeareth in the Form of Two Beautiful Angels sitting in a Chariot of Fire. He speaketh with a Comely Voice, and declareth that he fell first from among the worthier sort, that were before Michael, and other Heavenly Angels. His Office is to distribute Presentations and Senatorships, etc.; and to cause favour of Friends and of Foes. He giveth excellent Familiars, and governeth 50 Legions of Spirits. Note well that this King Belial. must have Offerings, Sacrifices and Gifts presented unto him by the Exorcist, or else he will not give True Answers unto his Demands. But then he tarrieth not one hour in the Truth, unless he be con. strained by Divine Power. And his Seal is this, which is to be worn as aforesaid, etc.

(69.) DECARABIA.--The Sixty-ninth Spirit is Decarabia. He appeareth in the Form of a Star in a Pentacle, at first; but after, at the command of the Exorcist, he putteth on the image of a Man. His Office is to discover the Virtues of Birds and Precious Stones, and to make the Similitude of all kinds of Birds to fly before the Exorcist, singing and drinking as natural Birds do. He governeth 30 Legions of Spirits, being himself a Great Marquis. And this is his Seal, which is to be worn, etc.

(70.) SEERE, SEAR, or SEIR.--The Seventieth Spirit is Seere, Sear, or Seir. He is a Mighty Prince, and Powerful, under AMAYMON, King of the East. He appeareth in the Form of a Beautiful Man, riding upon a Winged Horse. His Office is to go and come; and to bring abundance of things to pass on a sudden, and to carry or recarry anything whither thou wouldest have it to go, or whence thou wouldest have it from. He can pass over the whole Earth in the twinkling of an Eye. He giveth a True relation of all sorts of Theft, and of Treasure hid, and of many other things. He is of an indifferent Good Nature, and is willing to do anything which the Exorcist desireth. He governeth 26 Legions of Spirits. And this his Seal is to be worn, etc.

(71.) DANTALION.--The Seventy-first Spirit is Dantalion. He is a Duke Great and Mighty, appearing in the Form of a Man with many Countenances, all Men's and Women's Faces; and he hath a Book in his right hand. His Office is to teach all Arts and Sciences unto any; and to declare the Secret Counsel of any one; for he knoweth the Thoughts of all Men and Women, and can change them at his Will. He can cause Love, and show the Similitude of any person, and show the same by a Vision, let them be in what part of the World they Will. He governeth 36 Legions of Spirits; and this is his Seal, which wear thou, etc.

(72.) ANDROMALIUS.--The Seventy-second Spirit in Order is named Andromalius. He is an Earl, Great and Mighty, appearing in the Form of a Man holding a Great Serpent in his Hand. His Office is to bring back both a Thief, and the Goods which be stolen; and to discover all Wickedness, and Underhand Dealing; and to punish all Thieves and other Wicked People and also to discover Treasures that be Hid. He ruleth over 36 Legions of Spirits. His Seal is this, the which wear thou as aforesaid, etc.

THESE be the 72 Mighty Kings and Princes which King Solomon Commanded into a Vessel of Brass, together with their Legions. Of whom BELIAL, BILETH, ASMODAY, and GAAP, were Chief. And it is to be noted that Solomon did this because of their pride, for he never declared other reason why he thus bound them. And when he had thus bound them up and sealed the Vessel, he by Divine Power did chase them all into a deep Lake or Hole in Babylon. And they of Babylon, wondering to see such a thing, they did then go wholly into the Lake, to break the Vessel open, expecting to find great store of Treasure therein. But when they had broken it open, out flew the Chief Spirits immediately, with their Legions following them; and they were all restored to their former places except BELIAL, who entered into a certain Image, and thence gave answers unto those who did offer Sacrifices unto him, and did worship the Image as their God, etc.

OBSERVATIONS

FIRST, thou shalt know and observe the Moon's Age for thy working. The best days be when the Moon Luna is 2, 4, 6, 8, 10, 12, or 14 days old, as Solomon saith; and no other days be profitable. The Seals of the 72 Kings are to be made in Metals. The Chief Kings' in Sol (Gold); Marquises' in Luna (Silver); Dukes' in Venus (Copper); Prelacies' in Jupiter (Tin); Knights' in Saturn (Lead) Presidents' in Mercury (Mercury); Earls' in Venus (Copper), and Luna (Silver), alike equal, etc. THESE 72 Kings be under the Power of AMAYMON, CORSON, ZIMIMAY or ZIMINAIR, and GÖAP, who are the Four Great Kings ruling in the Four Quarters, or Cardinal Points,[28] viz.: East, West, North, and South, and are not to be called forth except it be upon Great Occasions; but are to be Invocated and Commanded to send such or such a Spirit that is under their Power and Rule, as is shown in the following Invocations or Conjurations. And the Chief Kings may be bound from 9 till 12 o'clock at Noon, and from 3 till Sunset; Marquises may be bound from 3 in the afternoon till 9 at Night, and from 9 at Night till Sunrise; Dukes may be bound from Sunrise till Noonday in Clear Weather; Prelates may be bound any hour of the Day; Knights may from Dawning of Day till Sunrise, or from 4 o'clock till Sunset; Presidents may be bound any time, excepting Twilight, at Night, unless the King whom they are under be Invocated; and Counties or Earls any hour of the Day, so it be in Woods, or in any other places whither men resort not, or where no noise is, etc.

---

[28] These four Great Kings are usually called Oriens, or Uriens, Paymon or Paymonia, Ariton or Egyn, and Amaymon or Amaimon. By the Rabbins they are frequently entitled: Samael, Azazel, Azäel, and Mahazael.

Classified List of the 72 Chief Spirits of the Goetia, According to Respective Rank

(Seal in Gold.) KINGS.--(1.) Bael; (9.) Paimon; (13.) Beleth; (20.) Purson; (32.) Asmoday; (45.) Viné; (51.) Balam; (61.) Zagan; (68.) Belial.

(Seal in Copper.) DUKES.--(2.) Agares; (6.) Valefor; (8.) Barbatos; (11.) Gusion;(15.) Eligos; (16.) Zepar; (18.) Bathim; (19.) Sallos; (23.) Aim; (26.) Buné; (28.) Berith; (29.) Astaroth; (41.) Focalor; (42.) Vepar; (47.) Vual; (49.) Crocell; (52.) Alloces; (54.) Murmur; (56.) Gremory; (60.) Vapula; (64.) Haures; (67.) Amdusias; (71.) Dantalion.

(Seal in Tin.) PRINCES AND PRELATES.--(3.) Vassago; (12.) Sitri; (22.) Ipos; (33.) Gäap; (36.) Stolas; (55.) Orobas; (70.) Seere.

(Seal in Silver.) MARQUISES.--(4.) Samigina; (7.) Amon; (14.) Leraje; (24.) Naberius; (27.) Ronové; (30.) Forneus; (35.) Marchosias; (37.) Phenex; (43.) Sabnock; (44.) Shax; (59.) Orias; (63.) Andras; (65.) Andrealphus; (66.) Cimeies; (69.) Decarabia.

(Seal in Mercury.) PRESIDENTS.-- (5.) Marbas; (10.) Buer; (17.) Botis; (21.) Marax; (25.) Glasya-Labolas; (31.) Foras; (33.) Gäap; (39.) Malphas; (48.) Häagenti; (53.) Caim; (57.) Ose; (58.) Amy; (61.) Zagan; (62.) Valac.

(Seal in Copper and Silver alike equal.) EARLS, or COUNTS.--(17.) Botis; (21.) Marax; (25.) Glasya-Labolas; (27.) Ronové; (34.) Furfur; (38.) Halphas; (40.) Räum; (45.) Viné; (46.) Bifrons; (72.) Andromalius.

(Seal in Lead.) KNIGHTS.--(50.) Furcas.

NOTE.--It will be remarked that several among the above Spirits possess two titles of different ranks; e.g., (45.) Viné is both King and Earl; (25.) Glasya-Labolas is both President and Earl, etc. "Prince" and "Prelate" are apparently used as interchangeable terms. Probably the Seals of Earls should be made of Iron, and those of Presidents in mixture either of Copper and Silver, or of Silver and Mercury; as otherwise the Metal of one Planet, Mars, is excluded from the List; the Metals attributed to the Seven Planets being: to Saturn, Lead; to Jupiter, Tin; to Mars, Iron; to the Sun, Gold; to Venus, Copper; to Mercury, Mercury and mixtures of Metals, and to Luna,

Silver.

IN a manuscript codex by Dr. Rudd, which is in the British Museum, Hebrew names of these 72 Spirits are given; but it appears to me that many are manifestly incorrect in orthography. The codex in question, though beautifully written, also contains many other errors, particularly in the Sigils. Such as they are, these names in the Hebrew of Dr. Rudd are here shown.

After the Hebrew of Dr. Rudd.

1. Bael בָּאֵל Figure 81.	2. Agares אגאראש Figure 82.	3. Vassago ושאגו Figure 83.	4. Gamigin גאמינין Figure 84.	5. Marbas מארבש Figure 85.	6. Valefor ואלפור Figure 86.
7. Amon אמון Figure 87.	8. Barbatos בארבטוש Figure 88.	9. Paimon פאימון Figure 89.	10. Buer בואר Figure 90.	11. Gusion גוסיון Figure 91.	12. Sitri שיטרי Figure 92.
13. Beleth בלאת Figure 93.	14. Leraje לראיך Figure 94.	15. Eligos אליגוש Figure 95.	16. Zepar זאפר Figure 96.	17. Botis בוטיש Figure 97.	18. Bathin באתין Figure 98.
19. Sallos שאלוש Figure 99.	20. Purson פורשון Figure 100.	21. Marax מאראס Figure 101.	22. Ipos יפוש Figure 102.	23. Aim אים Figure 103.	24. Naberius נבריוש Figure 104.
25. Glasya-Labolas נלאסיא-לב-ולש Figure 105.	26. Bimé בים Figure 106.	27. Ronove רונוג Figure 107.	28. Berith ברית Figure 108.	29. Astaroth אששארות Figure 109.	30. Forneus פהורנאוש Figure 110.
31. Foras פוראש Figure 111.	32. Asmoday אסמודי Figure 112.	33. Gaap גאאף Figure 113.	34. Furfur פהורפהור Figure 114.	35. Marchosias מרחושיאש Figure 115.	36. Stolas שטולרש Figure 116.
37. Phenex פאניס Figure 117.	38. Malthas מאלתש Figure 118.	39. Malphas מאלפש Figure 119.	40. Raum ראום Figure 120.	41. Focalor פהורכלור Figure 121.	42. Vepar ופאר Figure 122.
43. Sabnock שבנוך Figure 123.	44. Shax שאץ Figure 124.	45. Vine וינא Figure 125.	46. Bifrons ביפהרונש Figure 126.	47. Uvall וואל Figure 127.	48. Haagenti האגנטי Figure 128.
49. Crocell כרוכל Figure 129.	50. Furcas פהרכש Figure 130.	51. Balam בּאלאם Figure 131.	52. Alloces אלוכאס Figure 132.	53. Camio כאמיו Figure 133.	54. Murmus מורמוס Figure 134.
55. Orobas ורובש Figure 135.	56. Gamori גמורי Figure 136.	57. Voso ושו Figure 137.	58. Avnas אונש Figure 138.	59. Oriax וריאס Figure 139.	60. Naphula נפולא Figure 140.
61. Zagan זאגאן Figure 141.	62. Valu ואלו Figure 142.	63. Andras אנדראש Figure 143.	64. Haures האוראש Figure 144.	65. Andrealphus אנדראלפה-וש Figure 145.	66. Kimaris כימאריש Figure 146.
67. Amdukias אמדוכיאש Figure 147.	68. Belial בליאל Figure 148.	69. Decarabia דכאראביא Figure 149.	70. Seerë שאר Figure 150.	71. Dantalion דאנטאליון Figure 151.	72. Andromalius אנדרומאליוש Figure 152.

54

THE MAGICAL CIRCLE

This is the Form of the Magical Circle of King Solomon, the which he made that he might preserve himself therein from the malice of these Evil Spirits. This Magical Circle is to be made 9 feet across, and the Divine Names are to be written around it, beginning at EHYEH, and ending at LEVANAH, Luna.

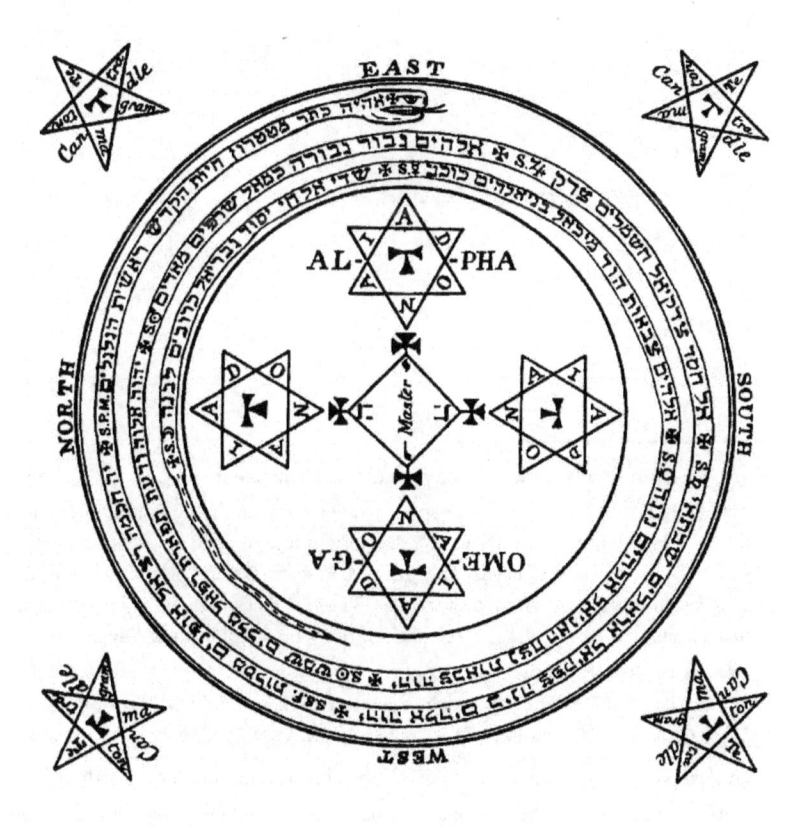

(Colours.--The space between the outer and inner circles, where the serpent is coiled, with the Hebrew names written along his body, is bright deep yellow. The square in the centre of the circle, where the word "Master" is written, is filled in with red. All names and letters are in black. In the Hexagrams the outer triangles where the letters A, D, O, N, A, I, appear are filled in with bright yellow, the centres, where the T-shaped crosses are, blue or green. In the Pentagrams outside the circle, the outer triangles where "Te, tra, gram, ma, ton," is written, are filled in bright yellow, and the centres with the T crosses written therein are red.[29])

---

[29] The coiled serpent is only shown in one private codex, the Hebrew names being in most cases simply written round in a somewhat spiral arrangement within the double circle. It is to be remembered that Hebrew is always written from right to left, p. 50 instead of from left to right like ordinary European languages. The small Maltese crosses are placed to mark the conclusion of each separate set of Hebrew names. These names are those of Deity Angels and Archangels allotted by the Qabalists to each of the 9 first Sephiroth or Divine Emanations. In English letters they run thus, beginning from the head of the serpent: ✠ Ehyeh Kether Metatron Chaioth Ha-Qadehs Rashith Ha-Galgalim S.P.M. (for "Sphere of the Primum Mobile") ✠ Iah Chokmah Ratziel Auphanim Masloth S.S.F (for "Sphere of the Fixed Stars," or S.Z. for "Sphere of the Zodiac") ✠ Iehovah Eolhim, Binah Tzadquiel Aralim Shabbathai S. (for "Sphere") of Saturn ✠ El Chesed Tzadquiel Chaschmalim Tzedeq S. of Jupiter ✠ Elohim Gibor Geburah Kamael Seraphim Madim S. of Mars ✠ Iehovah Eloah Va-Daäth Tiphereth Raphaêl Malakim Shemesh S. of the Sun ✠ Iehovah Tzabaoth Netzach Haniel Elohim Nogah S. of Venus. ✠ Elohim Tzabaoth Hod Michaêl Beni Elohim Kokav S. of Mercury ✠ Shaddaï El Chai Iesod Gabriel Cherubim Levanah S. of the Moon ✠.

THE MAGICAL TRIANGLE OF SOLOMON

This is the Form of the Magical Triangle, into the which Solomon did command the Evil Spirits. It is to be made at 2 feet distance from the Magical Circle and it is 3 feet across. Note that this triangle is to be placed toward that quarter whereunto the Spirit belongeth. And the base of the triangle is to be nearest unto the Circle, the apex pointing in the direction of the quarter of the Spirit. Observe thou also the Moon in thy working, as aforesaid, etc. Anaphaxeton is sometimes written Anepheneton.

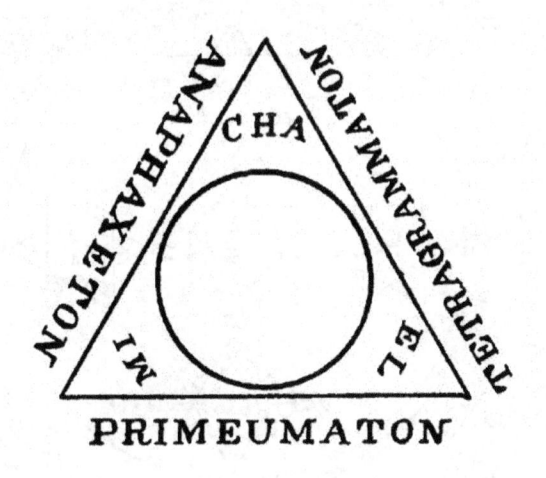

(Colours.--Triangle outlined in black; name of Michael black on white ground; the three Names without the triangle written in red; circle in centre entirely filled in in dark green.)

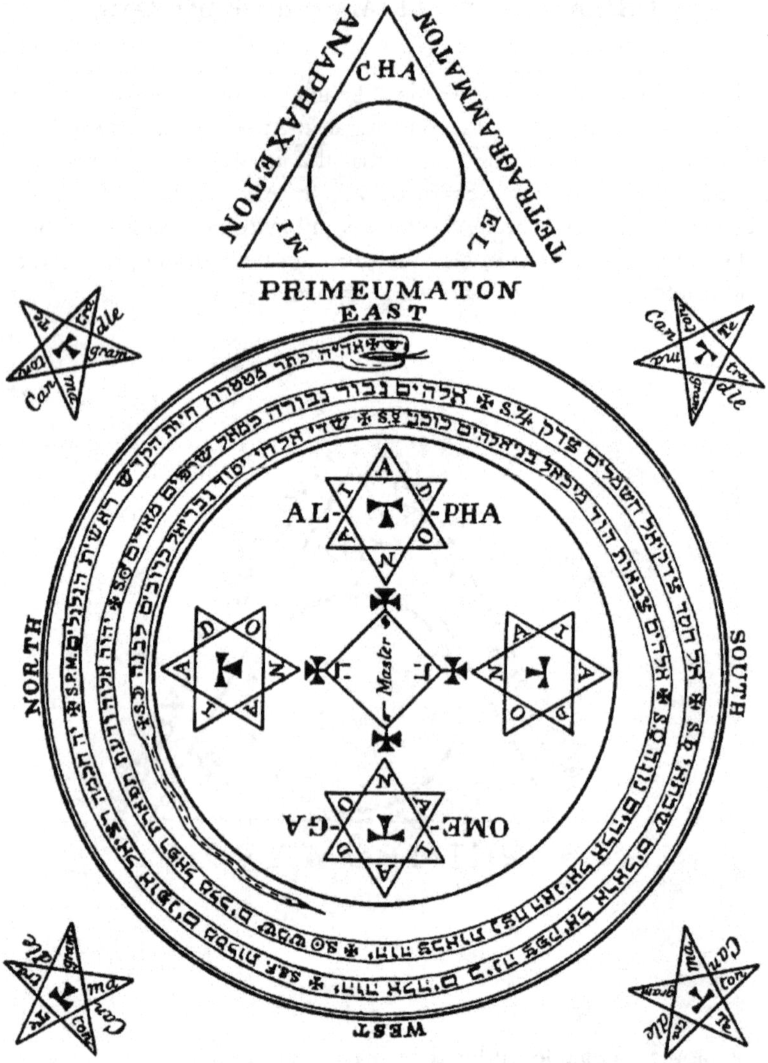
ANAPHAXETON
TETRAGRAMMATON
PRIMEUMATON
CHA
MI
EL
EAST
WEST
NORTH
SOUTH
AL-
-PHA
OME-
-GA
Master

THE HEXAGRAM OF SOLOMON

THIS is the Form of the Hexagram of Solomon, the figure whereof is to be made on parchment of a calf's skin, and worn at the skirt of thy white vestment, and covered with a cloth of fine linen white and pure, the which is to be shown unto the Spirits when they do appear, so that they be compelled to take human shape upon them and be obedient.

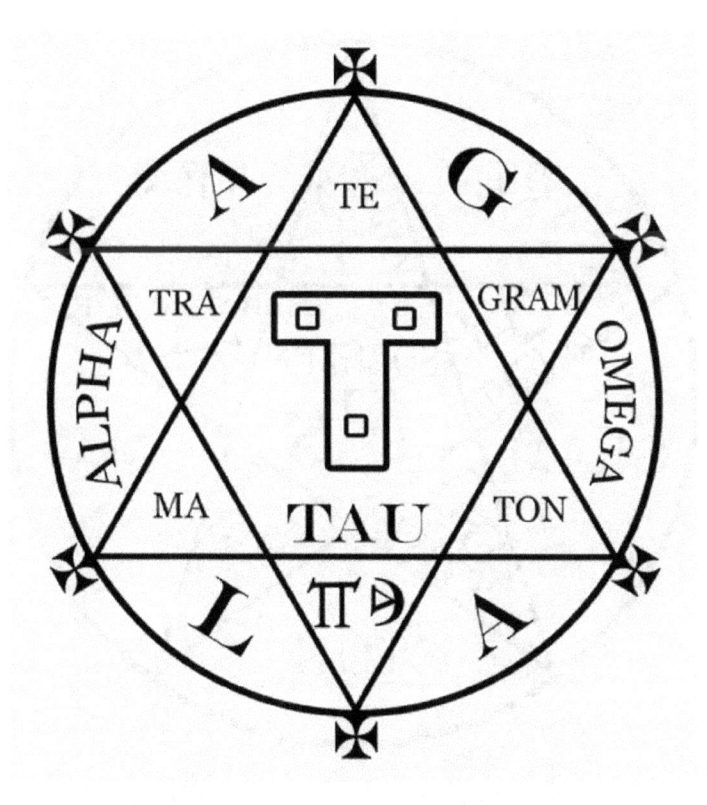

(Colours.--Circle, Hexagon, and T cross in centre outlined in black, Maltese crosses black; the five exterior triangles of the Hexagram where Te, tra, gram, ma, ton, is written, are filled in with bright yellow; the T cross in centre is red, with the three little squares therein in black. The lower exterior triangle, where the Sigil is drawn in black, is left white. The words "Tetragrammaton" and "Tau" are in black letters; and AGLA with Alpha and Omega in red letters.)

THE PENTAGRAM OF SOLOMON

THIS is the Form of Pentagram of Solomon, the figure whereof is to be made in Sol or Luna (Gold or Silver), and worn upon thy breast; having the Seal of the Spirit required upon the other side thereof. It is to preserve thee from danger, and also to command the Spirits by.

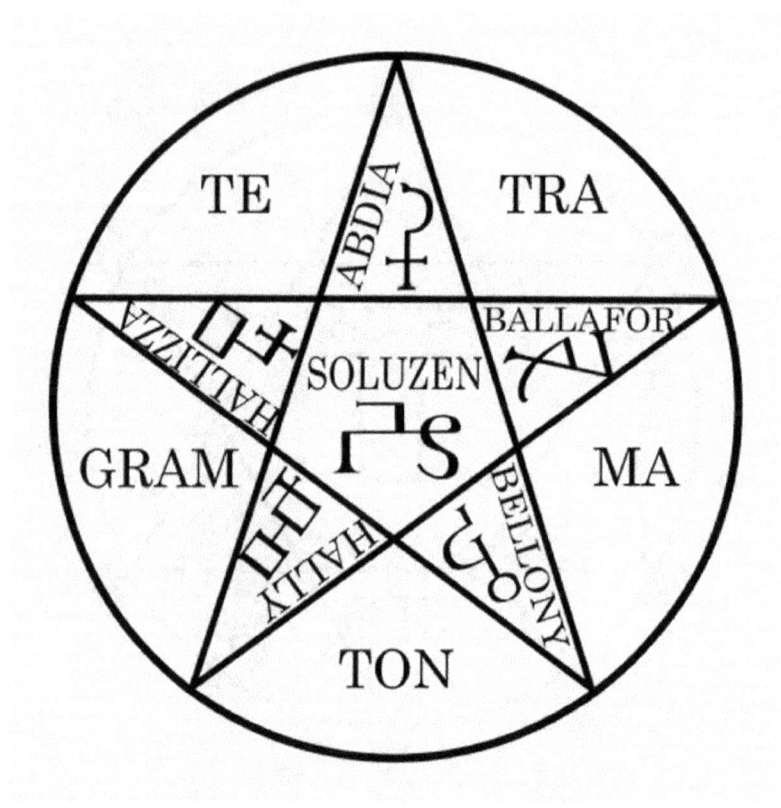

(Colours.--Circle and pentagram outlined in black. Names and Sigils within Pentagram black also. "Tetragrammaton" in red letters. Ground of centre of Pentagram, where "Soluzen" is written, green. External angles of Pentagram where "Abdia", "Ballaton," "Halliza," etc., are written, blue.)

The Magic Ring or Disc of Solomon

THIS is the Form of the Magic Ring, or rather Disc, of Solomon, the figure whereof is to be made in gold or silver. It is to be held before the face of the exorcist to preserve him from the stinking sulphurous fumes and flaming breath of the Evil Spirits.

(Colour.--Bright yellow. Letters, black.

THE VESSEL OF BRASS

THIS is the Form of the Vessel of Brass wherein King Solomon did shut up the Evil Spirits, etc. Somewhat different forms are given in the various codices. The seal was made in brass to cover this vessel with at the top. This history of the genii shut up in the brazen vessel by King Solomon recalls the story of "The Fisherman and the Jinni" in "The Arabian Nights." In this tale, however, there was only one jinni shut up in a vessel of yellow brass the which was covered at the top with a leaden seal. This jinni tells the fisherman that his name is Sakhr, or Sacar.)

THE LESSER KEY OF SOLOMON

(Colour.--Bronze. Letters.--Black on a red band.)

THE SECRET SEAL OF SOLOMON

THIS is the Form of the Secret Seal of Solomon, wherewith he did bind and seal up the aforesaid Spirits with their legions in the Vessel of Brass.

This seal is to be made by one that is clean both inwardly and outwardly, and that hath not defiled himself by any woman in the space of a month, but hath in prayer and fasting desired of God to forgive him all his sins, etc.

It is to be made on the day of Mars or Saturn (Tuesday or Saturday) at night at 12 o'clock, and written upon virgin parchment with the blood of a black cock that never trode hen. Note that on this night the moon must be increasing in light (i.e., going from new to full) and in the Zodiacal Sign of Virgo. And when the seal is so made thou shalt perfume it with alum, raisins dried in the sun, dates, cedar and lignum aloes.

Also, by this seal King Solomon did command all the aforesaid Spirits in the Vessel of Brass, and did seal it up with this same seal. He by it gained the love of all manner of persons, and overcame in battle, for neither weapons, nor fire, nor water could hurt him. And this privy seal was made to cover the vessel at the top withal, etc.

Note: The following figures are interesting as showing a marked resemblance to the central design of the Secret Seal. It will be observed that the evident desire is to represent hieroglyphically a person raising his or her hands in adoration. Nearly all are stone sepulchral steles, and the execution of them is rough and primitive in the extreme. Most are in the Musée du

THE LESSER KEY OF SOLOMON

Louvre at Paris.

Figures 162 and 163 are from the district of Constantine and show a figure raising its arms in adoration.

In Figure 164, also from Constantine, the person bears a palm branch in the right hand. Above is a hieroglyphic representing either the Lunar Disc or the Sun in the heavens; but more probably the former.

Figure 165 is a more complicated stele. Above is the symbol already mentioned, then comes the sign of the Pentagram, represented by a five-pointed star, towards which the person raises his or her hands. Besides the latter is a rude form of caduceus. A brief inscription follows in the Punic character. The Punic or Carthaginian language is usually considered to have been a dialect. of Phœnician, and Carthage was of course a colony of Tyre. Beneath the Tunic inscription is a horse's head in better drawing than the sculpture of the rest of the stele, which would seem to imply that the rudeness of the representation of the human figure is intentional. This and the following stele are also from Constantine.

In Figure 166 again, the horse is best delineated by far. In addition to the other symbols there is either a hand or a foot, for it is almost impossible to distinguish which, at the head of the stele, followed by an egg-and-tongue moulding. The figure of the person with the arms raised is treated as a pure hieroglyphic and is placed between two rude caducei. The Lunar or Solar Symbol follows.

Figure 167 , also from Constantine, shows the last-mentioned symbol above. The figure with the arms raised is simply a hieroglyph, and is placed between an arm and hand on the one side, and a rude caduceus on the other.

Figure 168 shows the person holding a rude caduceus in the right hand, and standing above a dolphin. This latter, as in the case of the horse in 165 and 166, is by far the best delineated.

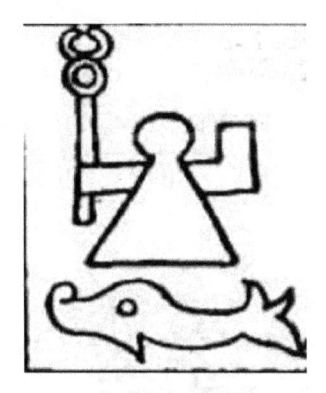

Figure 169, this also being from Constantine, shows the usual human hieroglyph between a caduceus and a crescent.

Figure 170 is from the site of ancient Carthage. It is very rough in workmanship, and the designs are mere scratchings on the stone. The ensemble has the effect of an evil Sigil.

Figure 171 is also from Carthage and the various symbols appear to have become compressed into and synthesised in the form of a peculiarly evil-looking caduceus.

THE LESSER KEY OF SOLOMON

Figure 172 is from the decoration of a sepulchral urn found at Oldenburgh in Germany. It is remarkable as showing the same hieroglyphic human form with the crescent above; the latter in the Secret Seal of Solomon has a flattened top, and is therefore more like a bowl, and is placed across the hieroglyph.

Figure 173 is an Egyptian design which would show an analogy between the symbol and the idea of the force of the creation.

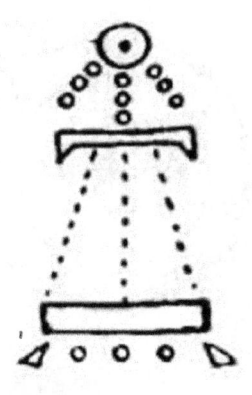

Figure 174 is a stele from Phœnicia somewhat similar to the others, except that the rudimentary caducei in Figures 166 and 170 are here replaced by two roughly drawn Ionic columns.

These last three designs are taken from the work of the Chevalier Emile Soldi-Colbert de Beaulieu, on the "Langue Sacrée."

In Figure 175 is given the Seal of the Spirit HALAHEL. This Spirit is said to be under the rule of BAEL, and to be of a mixed nature, partly good and partly evil, like the spirits of Theurgia-Goetia which follow in the second book of the Lemegeton

The Other Magical Requisites

THE other magical requisites are: a sceptre, a sword, a mitre, a cap, a long white robe of linen, and other garments for the purpose;[30] also a girdle of lion's skin three inches broad, with all the names written about it which he round the outmost part of the Magical Circle. Also perfumes, and a chafing-dish of charcoal kindled to put the fumes on, to smoke or perfume the place appointed for action; also anointing oil to anoint thy temples and thine eyes with; and fair water to wash thyself in. And in so doing, thou shalt say as David said:

---

[30] In many Codices it is written "a sceptre or sword, a mitre or cap." By the "other garments" would be meant not only undergarments, but also mantles of different colours.

THE ADORATION AT THE BATH

"Thou shalt purge me with hyssop, O Lord! and I shall be clean: Thou shalt wash me, and I shall be whiter than snow."

And at the putting on of thy garments thou shalt say: THE ADORATION AT THE INDUING OF THE VESTMENTS.

"By the figurative mystery of these holy vestures (or of this holy vestment) I will clothe me with the armour of salvation in the strength of the Most High, ANCHOR; AMACOR; AMIDES; THEODINIAS; ANITOR; that my desired end may be effected through Thy strength, O ADONAI! unto Whom the praise and glory will for ever and ever belong! Amen!"

After thou hast so done, make prayers unto God according unto thy work, as Solomon hath commanded.

The Conjuration to Call Forth Any of the Aforesaid Spirits

I DO invocate and conjure thee, O Spirit, N.[31]; and being with power armed from the SUPREME MAJESTY, I do strongly command thee, by BERALANENSIS, BALDACHIENSIS, PAUMACHIA, and APOLOGIAE SEDES; by the most Powerful Princes, Genii, Liachidæ, and Ministers of the Tartarean Abode; and by the Chief Prince of the Seat of Apologia in the Ninth Legion, I do invoke thee, and by invocating conjure thee. And being armed with power from the SUPREME MAJESTY, I do strongly command thee, by Him Who spake and it was done, and unto whom all creatures be obedient. Also I, being made after the image of GOD, endued with power from GOD and created according unto His will, do exorcise thee by that most mighty and powerful name of GOD, EL, strong and wonderful; O thou Spirit N. And I command thee and Him who spake the Word and His FIAT was accomplished, and by all the names of God. Also by the names ADONAI, EL, ELOHIM, ELOHI, EHYEH, ASHER EHYEH, ZABAOTH, ELION, IAH, TETRAGRAMMATON, SHADDAI, LORD GOD MOST HIGH, I do exorcise thee and do powerfully command thee, O thou Spirit N., that thou dost forthwith appear unto me here before this Circle in a fair human shape, without any deformity or tortuosity. And by this ineffable name, TETRAGRAMMATON IEHOVAH, do I command thee, at the which being heard the elements are overthrown, the air is shaken, the sea runneth back, the fire is quenched, the earth trembleth, and all the hosts of the celestials, terrestrials, and infernals, do tremble together, and are troubled and confounded. Wherefore come thou, O Spirit N., forthwith, and without delay, from any or all parts of the world wherever thou mayest be, and make rational answers unto all things that I shall demand of thee. Come thou peaceably, visibly, and affably, now, and without delay, manifesting that which I shall desire. For thou art conjured by the name of the LIVING and TRUE GOD, HELIOREN, wherefore fulfil thou my commands, and persist thou therein unto the end, and according unto mine interest, visibly and

---

[31] Here interpolate the name of the Spirit desired to be invocated. In some of the Codices there are faint variations in the form of wording of the conjurations, but not sufficient to change the sense, e. g., "Tartarean abode" for "Tartarean seat," etc.

affably speaking unto me with a voice clear and intelligible without any ambiguity.

REPEAT this conjuration as often as thou pleasest, and if the Spirit come not yet, say as followeth:

The Second Conjuration

I DO invoke, conjure, and command thee, O thou Spirit N., to appear and to show thyself visibly unto me before this Circle in fair and comely shape, without any deformity or tortuosity; by the name and in the name IAH and VAU, which Adam heard and spake; and by the name Of GOD, AGLA, which Lot heard and was saved with his family; and by the name IOTH, which Jacob heard from the angel wrestling with him, and was delivered from the hand of Esau his brother; and by the name ANAPHAXETON which Aaron heard and spake and was made wise; and by the name ZABAOTH, which Moses named and all the rivers were turned into blood; and by the name ASHER EHYEH ORISTON, which Moses named, and all the rivers brought forth frogs, and they ascended into the houses, destroying all things; and by the name ELION, which Moses named, and there was great hail such as had not been since the beginning of the world; and by the name ADONAI, which Moses named, and there came up locusts, which appeared upon the whole land, and devoured all which the hail had left; and by the name SCHEMA AMATHIA which Ioshua called upon, and the sun stayed his course; and by the name ALPHA and OMEGA, which Daniel named, and destroyed Bel, and slew the Dragon; and in the name EMMANUEL, which the three children, Shadrach, Meshach and Abed-nego, sang in the midst of the fiery furnace, and were delivered; and by the name HAGIOS; and by the SEAL[32] OF ADONI; and by ISCHYROS, ATHANATOS, PARACLETOS; and by O THEOS, ICTROS, ATHANATOS; and by these three secret names, AGLA, ON, TETRAGRAMMATON, do I adjure and constrain thee. And by these names, and by all the other names of the LIVING and TRUE GOD, the LORD ALMIGHTY, I do exorcise and command thee, O Spirit N., even by Him Who spake the Word and it was done, and to Whom all creatures are obedient; and by the dreadful judgments of GOD; and by the uncertain Sea of Glass, which is before the DIVINE MAJESTY, mighty and powerful; by the four beasts before the throne, having eyes before and behind; by the fire round about the throne; by the holy angels of Heaven; and by the mighty wisdom of GOD; I do potently exorcise thee, that thou appearest here before this Circle, to fulfil my will in all things which shall seem good unto me; by the Seal of BASDATHEA BALDACHIA; and by

---

[32] In some "By the Seat of Adonai" or "By the Throne of Adonai." In these conjurations and elsewhere in the body of the text I have given the divine names correctly.

this name PRIMEUMATON, which Moses named, and the earth opened, and did swallow up Kora, Dathan, and Abiram. Wherefore thou shalt make faithful answers unto all my demands, O Spirit N., and shalt perform all my desires so far as in thine office thou art capable hereof. Wherefore, come thou, visibly, peaceably, and affably, now without delay, to manifest that which I desire, speaking with a clear and perfect voice, intelligibly, and to mine understanding.

IF HE come not yet at the rehearsal of these two first conjurations (but without doubt he will), say on as followeth; it being a constraint:

The Constraint

I Do conjure thee, O thou Spirit N., by all the most glorious and efficacious names of the MOST GREAT AND INCOMPREHENSIBLE LORD GOD op HOSTS, that thou comest quickly and without delay from all parts and places of the earth and world wherever thou mayest be, to make rational answers unto my demands, and that visibly and affably, speaking with a voice intelligible unto mine understanding as aforesaid. I conjure and constrain thee, O thou Spirit N., by all the names aforesaid; and in addition by these seven great names wherewith Solomon the Wise bound thee and thy companions in a Vessel of Brass, ADONAI, PREYAI or PRERAI, TETRAGRAMMATON, ANAPHAXETON or ANEPHENETON, INESSENFATOAL or INESSENFATALL, PATHTUMON or PATHATUMON, and ITEMON; that thou appearest, here before this Circle to fulfil my will in all things that seem good unto me. And if thou be still so disobedient, and refusest still to come, I will in the power and by the power of the name of the SUPREME AND EVERLASTING LORD GOD WHO created both thee and me and all the world in six days, and what is contained therein, EIE, SARAYE, and by the power of this name PRIMEUMATON which commandeth the whole host of Heaven, curse thee, and deprive thee of thine office, joy, and place, and bind thee in the depths of the Bottomless Pit or Abyss, there to remain unto the Day of the Last Judgment. And I will bind thee in the Eternal Fire, and into the Lake of Flame and of Brimstone, unless thou comest quickly and appearest here before this Circle to do my will. Therefore, come thou! in and by the holy names ADONAI, ZABAOTH, ADONAI, AMIORAN. Come thou! for it is ADONAI who commandest thee.

IF THOU hast come thus far, and yet he appeareth not, thou mayest be sure that he is sent unto some other place by his King, and cannot come; and if it be so, invocate the King as here followeth, to send him. But if he do not come still, then thou mayest be sure that he is bound in chains in hell, and that he is not in the custody of his King. If so, and thou still hast a desire to call him even from thence, thou must rehearse the general curse which is called the Spirits' Chain.

Here followeth, therefore, the Invocation of the King:

THE INVOCATION OF THE KING

O THOU great, powerful, and mighty KING AMAIMON, who bearest rule by the power of the SUPREME GOD EL over all spirits both superior and inferior of the Infernal Orders in the Dominion of the East; I do invocate and command thee by the especial and true name Of GOD; and by that God that Thou Worshippest; and by the Seal of thy creation; and by the most mighty and powerful name Of GOD, IEHOVAH TETRAGRAMMATON who cast thee out of heaven with all other infernal spirits; and by all the most powerful and great names of GOD who created Heaven, and Earth, and Hell, and all things in them contained; and by their power and virtue; and by the name PRIMEUMATON who commandeth the whole host of Heaven; that thou mayest cause, enforce, and compel the Spirit N. to come unto me here before this Circle in a fair and comely shape, without harm unto me or unto any other creature, to answer truly and faithfully unto all my requests; so that I may accomplish my will and desire in knowing or obtaining any matter or thing which by office thou knowest is proper for him to perform or accomplish, through the power of GOD, EL, Who created and doth dispose of all things both celestial, aërial, terrestrial, and infernal.

AFTER thou shalt have invocated the King in this manner twice or thrice over, then conjure the spirit thou wouldst call forth by the aforesaid conjurations, rehearsing them several times together, and he will come without doubt, if not at the first or second time of rehearsing. But if he do not come, add the "Spirits' Chain" unto the end of the aforesaid conjurations, and he will be forced to come, even if he be bound in chains, for the chains must break off from him, and he will be at liberty:

The General Curse, Called the Spirits' Chain, Against All Spirits That Rebel

O THOU wicked and disobedient spirit N., because thou hast rebelled, and hast not obeyed nor regarded my words which I have rehearsed; they being all glorious and incomprehensible names of the true GOD, the maker and creator of thee and of me, and of all the world; I DO by the power of these names the which no creature is able to resist, curse thee into the depth of the Bottomless Abyss, there to remain unto the Day of Doom in chains, and in fire and brimstone unquenchable, unless thou forthwith appear here before this Circle, in this triangle to do my will. And, therefore, come thou quickly and peaceably, in and by these names of GOD, ADONAI, ZABAOTH, ADONAI, AMIORAN; come thou! come thou! for it is the King of Kings, even ADONAI, who commandeth thee.

WHEN thou shalt have rehearsed thus far, but still be cometh not, then write thou his seal on parchment and put thou it into a strong black box;[33] with brimstone, assafœtida, and such like things that bear a stinking smell; and then bind the box up round with an iron wire, and bang it upon the point of thy sword, and hold it over the fire of charcoal; and say as followeth unto the fire first, it being placed toward that quarter whence the Spirit is to come:

---

[33] This BOX should evidently be in metal or in something which does not take fire easily.

The Conjuration of the Fire

I CONJURE thee, O fire, by him who made thee and all other creatures for good in the world, that thou torment, burn, and consume this Spirit N., for everlasting. I condemn thee, thou Spirit N., because thou art disobedient and obeyest not my commandment, nor keepest the precepts of the LORD THY GOD, neither wilt thou obey me nor mine invocations, having thereby called thee forth, 1, who am the servant of the MOST HIGH AND IMPERIAL LORD GOD OF HOSTS, IEHOVAH, I who am dignified and fortified by His celestial power and permission, and yet thou comest not to answer these my propositions here made unto thee. For the which thine averseness and contempt thou art guilty of great disobedience and rebellion, and therefore shall I excommunicate thee, and destroy thy name and seal, the which I have enclosed in this box; and shall burn thee in the immortal fire and bury thee in immortal oblivion; unless thou immediately come and appear visibly and affably, friendly and courteously here unto me before this Circle, in this triangle, in a form comely and fair, and in no wise terrible, hurtful, or frightful to me or any other creature whatsoever upon the face of earth. And thou shalt make rational answers unto my requests, and perform all my desires in all things, that I shall make unto thee.

AND if he come not even yet, thou shalt say as followeth:

The Greater Curse[34]

Now, O thou Spirit N., since thou art still pernicious and disobedient, and wilt not appear unto me to answer unto such things as I would have desired of thee, or would have been satisfied in; I do in the name, and by the power and dignity of the Omnipresent and Immortal Lord God of Hosts IEHOVAH TETRAGRAMMATON, the only creator of Heaven, and Earth, and Hell, and all that is therein, who is the marvellous Disposer of all things both visible and invisible, curse thee, and deprive thee of all thine office, joy, and place; and I do bind thee in the depths of the Bottomless Abyss there to remain until the Day of Judgment, I say into the Lake of Fire and Brimstone which is prepared for all rebellious, disobedient, obstinate, and pernicious spirits. Let all the company of Heaven curse thee! Let the sun, moon, and all the stars curse thee! Let the LIGHT and all the hosts of Heaven curse thee into the fire unquenchable, and into the torments unspeakable. And as thy name and seal contained in this box chained and bound up, shall be choken in sulphurous stinking substances, and burned in this material fire; so in the name IEHOVAH and by the power and dignity of these three names, TETRAGRAMMATON, ANAPHAXETON, and PRIMEUMATON, I do cast thee, O thou wicked and disobedient Spirit N., into the Lake of Fire which is prepared for the damnéd and accurséd spirits, and there to remain unto the day of doom, and never more to be remembered before the face of GOD, who shall come to judge the quick, and the dead, and the world, by fire.

THEN the exorcist must put the box into the fire, and by-and-by the Spirit will come, but as soon as he is come, quench the fire that the box is in, and make a sweet perfume, and give him welcome and a kind entertainment, showing unto him the Pentacle that is at tile bottom of your vesture covered with a linen cloth, saying:

---

[34] In some codices this is called "the Curse" only; but in one or two the "Spirits' Chain" is called "the Lesser Curse," and this the "Greater Curse."

THE ADDRESS UNTO THE SPIRIT UPON HIS COMING

BEHOLD thy confusion if thou refusest to be obedient! Behold the Pentacle of Solomon which I have brought here before thy presence! Behold the person of the exorcist in the midst of the exorcism; him who is arméd by GOD and without fear; him who potently invocateth thee and calleth thee forth unto appearance; even him, thy master, who is called OCTINIMOS. Wherefore make rational answer unto my demands, and prepare to be obedient unto thy master in the name of the Lord:

BATHAL OR VATHAT RUSHING UPON ABRAC!
ABEOR COMING UPON ABERER[35]

THEN he or they will be obedient, and bid thee ask what thou wilt, for he or they be subjected by God to fulfil our desires and commands. And when he or they shall have appeared and showed himself or themselves humble and meek, then shalt thou rehearse:

---

[35] In the Latin, "Bathal vel Vathat super Abrac ruens! Absor veniens super Aberer!"

The Welcome Unto the Spirit

WELCOME Spirit N., O most noble king[36] (or kings)! I say thou art welcome unto me, because I have called thee through Him who has created Heaven, and Earth, and Hell, and all that is in them contained, and because also thou hast obeyed. By that same power by the which I have called thee forth, I bind thee, that thou remain affably and visibly here before this Circle (or before this Circle and in this triangle) so constant and so long as I shall have occasion for thy presence; and not to depart without my license until thou hast duly and faithfully performed my will without any falsity.

THEN standing in the midst of the Circle, thou shall stretch forth thine hand in a gesture of command and say:

"BY TIME PENTACLE OF SOLOMON HAVE I CALLED THEE! GIVE UNTO ME A TRUE ANSWER."

Then let the exorcist state his desires and requests.

And when the evocation is finished thou shalt license the Spirit to depart thus:

---

[36] Or whatever his dignity may be.

THE LICENSE TO DEPART

O THOU Spirit N., because thou hast-diligently answered unto my demands, and hast been very ready and willing to come at my call, I do here license thee to depart unto thy proper place; without causing harm or danger unto man or beast. Depart, then, I say, and be thou very ready to come at my call, being duly exorcised and conjured by the sacred rites of magic. I charge thee to withdraw peaceably and quietly, and the peace of GOD be ever continued between thee and me I AMEN!

AFTER thou hast given the Spirit license to depart, thou art not to go out of the circle until he or they be gone, and until thou shalt have made prayers and rendered thanks unto God for the great blessings He hath bestowed upon thee in granting thy desires, and delivering thee from all the malice of the enemy the devil.

Also note! Thou mayest command these spirits into the Vessel of Brass in the same manner as thou dost into the triangle, by saying: "that thou dost forthwith appear before this Circle, in this Vessel of Brass, in a fair and comely shape," etc., as hath been shown in the foregoing conjurations.

Part Two

Explanation of Certain Names Used in This Book Lemegeton

Explanation of Certain Names Used in this Book Lemegeton

Eheie. Kether.--Almighty God, whose dwelling is in the highest Heavens:

Haioth.--The great King of Heaven, and of all the powers therein:

Methratton.--And of all the holy hosts of Angels and Archangels:

Reschith.--Hear the prayers of Thy servant who putteth his trust in Thee:

Hagalgalim.--Let thy Holy Angels be commanded to assist me at this time and at all times.

Iehovah.--God Almighty, God Omnipotent, hear my prayer:

Hadonat.--Command Thy Holy Angels above the fixed stars:

Ophanim.--To be assisting and aiding Thy servant:

Iophiel.--That I may command all spirits of air, water, fire, earth, and hell:

Masloth.--So that it may tend unto Thy glory and unto the good of man.

Iehovah.--God Almighty, God Omnipotent, hear my prayer:

Elohim.--God with us, God be always present with us.

Binah.--Strengthen us and support us, both now and for ever:

Aralim.--In these our undertakings, which we perform but as instruments in Thy hands:

Zabbathi (should be Shabbathii).--In the hands of Thee, the great God of Sabäoth.

Hesel (should be Chesed).--Thou great God, governor and creator of the planets, and of the Host of Heaven:

Hasmalim (should be Chashmalim).--Command them by Thine almighty power:

Zelez (should be Zedeq).--To be now present and assisting to us Thy poor servants, both now and for ever.

Elohim Geber (should be Gibor).--Most Almighty and eternal and ever living Lord God:

Seraphim.--Command Thy seraphim:

Camael, Madim.--To attend on us now at this time, to assist us, and to defend us from all perils and dangers.

Eloha.--O Almighty God! be present with us both now and for ever:

Tetragrammaton.--And let thine Almighty power and presence ever guard and protect us now and for ever:

Raphael.--Let thy holy angel Raphael wait upon us at this present and for ever:

Schemes (or Shemesh).--To assist us in these our undertakings.

Iehovah.--God Almighty, God Omnipotent, hear my prayer:

Sabäoth.--Thou great God of Sabäoth:

Netzah (or Netzach).--All-seeing God:

Elohim.--God be present with us, and let thy presence be now and always present with us:

Haniel.--Let thy holy angel Haniel come and minister unto us at this present.

Sabäoth.--O thou great God of Sabäoth, be present with us at this time and for ever:

Hodben (should be Hod simply).--Let Thine Almighty power defend us and protect us, both now and for ever:

Michael.--Let Michael, who is, under Thee, general of thy heavenly host:

Cochab.--Come and expel all evil and danger from us both now and for ever.

Sadai.--Thou great God of all wisdom and knowledge:

Jesal (should be Iesod).--Instruct Thy poor and most humble servant:

Cherubim.--By Thy holy cherubim:

Gabriel.--By Thy Holy Angel Gabriel, who is the Author and Messenger of good tidings:

Levanah.--Direct and support us at this present and for ever.

The Explanation of the Two Triangles[37] in the Parchment

Alpha And Omega.--Thou, O great God, Who art the beginning and the end:

Tetragrammaton.--Thou God of Almighty power, be ever present with us to guard and protect us, and let Thy Holy Spirit and presence be now and always with us:

Soluzen.--I command thee, thou Spirit of whatsoever region thou art, to come unto this circle:

Halliza.--And appear in human shape:

Bellator (or Ballaton).--And speak unto us audibly in our mother-tongue:

Bellonoy (or Bellony).--And show, and discover unto us all treasure that thou knowest of, or that is in thy keeping, and deliver it unto us quietly:

Hallii. Hra.--And answer all such questions as we may demand without any defect now at this time.

---

[37] Evidently meaning both the Hexagram and the Pentagram of Solomon.

An Explanation of Solomon's Triangle

Anephezeton.--Thou great God of all the Heavenly Host:

Primeumaton.--Thou Who art the First and Last, let all spirits be subject unto us, and let the Spirit be bound in this triangle, which disturbs this place:

Michael.--By Thy Holy Angel Michael, until I shall discharge him.

(HERE ENDETH THIS FIRST BOOK OF THE LEMEGETON, WHICH IS CALLED THE GOETIA.)

PART THREE

CONJURATIONS

Preamble

Y^{se} Conjuratiouns of ye Books Goetia in ye Lemegeton which Solomoun ye Kynge did give unto Lemuel hys sonne rendered into ye Magicall or Angelike Language by our Illustrious and ever Glorious Frater, ye Wise Perdurabo, that Myghtye Chiefe of ye Rosy-Cross Fraternitye, now sepulchred in ye Vault of ye Collegium S.S. And soe may we doe alle!

ATTE YE BATHES OF ART

Asperges me, Domine, hyssopo, et mundabor:
Lavabis me, et super nivem dealbabor.

Atte Ye Induynge of Ye Holy Vestures

In the mystery of these vestures of the Holy Ones, I gird up my power in the girdles of righteousness and truth in the power of the Most High: Ancor: Amacor: Amides: Theodonias: Anitor: let be mighty my power: let it endure for ever: in the power of Adonai, to whom the praise and the glory shall be; whose end cannot be.

Ye Fyrste Conjouratioun

I invoke and move thee, O thou, Spirit N.: and being exalted above ye in the power of the Most High, I say unto thee, Obey! in the name Beralensis, Baldachiensis, Paumachia, and Apologiae Sedes: and of the mighty ones who govern, spirits, Liachidae and ministers of the House of Death: and by the Chief Prince of the seat of Apologia in the Ninth Legion, I do invoke. thee and by invoking conjure thee. And being exalted above ye in the power of the, Most High., I say unto thee, Obey! in the name of him who spake and it was, to whom all creatures and things obey. Moreover I, whom God made in the likeness of God, who is the. creator according to his living breath, stir thee up in the name which is the voice of wonder of the mighty God, El, strong and unspeakable, O thou Spirit N. And I say to thee obey, in the name of him who spake and it was; and in every one of ye, O ye names of God! Moreover in the names Adonai, El., Elohim., Elohi, Ehyeh Asher Ehyeh, Zabaoth, Elion, Iah, Tetragrammaton, Shaddai, Lord God Most High, I stir thee up; and in our strength I say Obey! O Spirit N. Appear unto His servants in a moment; before the circle in the likeness of a man; and visit me in peace. And in the ineffable name Tetragrammaton Iehovah, I say, Obey! whose mighty sound being exalted in power the pillars are divided, the winds of the firmament groan aloud; the fire burns not; the earth moves in earthquakes; and all things of the house of heaven and earth and the dwelling-place of darkness are as earthquakes, and are in torment, and are confounded in thunder. Come forth, O Spirit N. in. a moment: let thy dwelling-place be empty, apply unto us the secrets of Truth and obey my power. Come forth, visit us in peace, appear unto my eyes; be friendly: Obey the living breath! For I stir thee up in the name of the God of Truth who liveth for ever, Helioren. Obey the living breath, therefore continually unto the end as my thoughts appear to my eyes: therefore be friendly: speaking the secrets of Truth in voice and in understanding.

YE SECOUNDE CONJOURATIOUN

I invoke thee, and move thee, and stir thee up O Spirit N. appear unto my eyes before the circle in the likeness of a man in the names and by the name Iah and Vau, which Adam spake and in the name of God, Agla, which Lot spake: and it was as pleasant deliverers unto him and his house and in the name Ioth which Iacob spake in the voice of the Holy ones who cast him down, and it was also as pleasant deliverers in the anger of his brother and in the name Anaphaxeton, which Aaron spake and it was as the Secret Wisdom and in the name Zabaoth which Mosheh spake, and all things of water were as blood; and in the name Asher Ehyeh Oriston, which Mosheh spake, and all waters were bringing forth creatures who wax strong, which lifted up unto the houses, which destroy all things and in the name of Elion which Mosheh spake, and it was as stones from the firmament of wrath, such as was not in the ages of Time the beginning of the Earth and in the name of Adni, which Mosheh spake and there appeared creatures of earth who destroyed what the big stones did not: and in the name Schema Amathia, which Ioshua invoked, and the Sun remained over ye, O ye hills the seats of Gibeon, and in the names Alpha and Omega which Daniel spake, and destroyed Bel and the Dragon: and in the name Emmanuel which the sons of God sang praises in the midst of the burning plain, and flourished in conquest: and in the name Hagios, and by the Throne of Adni, and in Ischyros, Athanatos, Paracletos: and in O Theos, Ictros, Athanatos. And in these names of secret truth, Agla, On, Tetragrammaton, do I invoke and move thee. And in these names, and all things that are the names of the God of Secret Truth who liveth for ever, the All-Powerful. I invoke and stir thee up, O spirit N. Even by him who spake it was, to whom all creatures are obedient and in the Extreme Justice and Anger of God; and by the veil(?) that is before the glory of God, mighty; and by the creatures of living breath before the Throne whose eyes are east and west; by the fire in the fire of just Glory of the Throne; by the Holy ones of Heaven; and by the secret wisdom of God, I, exalted in power, stir thee up. Appear before this circle; obey in all things that I say; in the seal Basdathea Baldachia; and in this Name Primeumaton, which Mosheh spake, and the earth was divided, and Korah, Dathan, and Abiram fell in the depth. Therefore obey in all things, O spirit N., obey thy creation. Come thou forth: appear unto my eyes; visit us in peace, be friendly; come forth in the 24th of a moment; obey my power, speaking the secrets of Truth in voice and in understanding!

Ye Constraynte

I stir thee up, O spirit N. in all things that are the names of glory and power of God the Great One who is greater than understanding, Adni Ihvh Tzabaoth, come forth in the 24th of a moment, let Thy dwelling-place be empty; apply thyself unto the secret truth and obey my power: appear unto my eyes, visit us in peace, speaking the secrets of truth in voice and understanding. I stir thee up and move thee, O spirit N., in all the names that I have said, and I add these one and six names wherein Solomon, the lord of the secret wisdom, placed yourselves, spirits of wrath, in a vessel, Adonai,. Preyai Tetragrammaton, Anaphaxeton Inessenfatoal, Pathomon and Itemon: appear before this circle; obey in all things my power. And as thou art he that obeys not and comes not I shall be in thy power, O God Most High that liveth for ever, who is the creator of all things in six days Eie, Saraye, and in my power in the name Prieumaton that ruleth over the palaces of heaven, Curse Thee, and destroy thy seat, joy, and power; and I bind thee in the depth of Abaddon, to remain until the day of judgment whose end cannot be. And I bind thee in the fire of sulphur mingled with poison and the seas of fire and sulphur: come, forth, therefore, obey my power and appear before, this circle. Therefore come forth in the name of the Holy Ones Zabaoth, Adonai, Amioran. Come! for I am Adonai who stir thee up.

YE POTENT INVOCATIOUN OF HYS KYNGE

O thou great powerful governor Amaimon, who reigneth exalted in the power of the only El above all spirits in the kingdoms of the East, (South, West, North), I invoke and move thee in the name of the true God, and in God whom thou worshippest: and in the, seal of thy creation: and in the mighty names of God, Iehevohe Tetragrammaton, who cast thee down from Heaven, thou and the spirits of darkness, and in all the names of the mighty God who is the creator of Heaven and earth, and the dwelling of darkness, and all things and in their power and brightness; and in the name Primeumaton who reigns over the palaces of Heaven. Bring forth, I say, the spirit N.; bring him forth in the 24th of a moment let his dwelling be, empty until he visits us in peace, speaking the secrets of truth; until he obey my power and his creation in the power of God, El, who is the Creator and doth dispose of all things, heaven, firmament, earth, and the dwelling of darkness.

Ye Generall Curse

Yclept Ye Spirits' Chayne, Against All Spirits Yt Rebelle.

O thou wicket spirit N. that obeyeth not, because I made a law and invoked the names of the glorious and ineffable God of Truth, the creator of all, and thou obeyest not the mighty sounds that I make: therefore I curse thee in the depth of Abaddon to remain until the day of judgment in torment in fire and in sulphur without end, until thou appear before our will and obey my power. Come, therefore, in the 24th of a moment, before the circle in the triangle in this name and by this name of God, Adni, Tzabaoth, Adonai, Amioran. Come! Come! for it is the Lord of Lords Adni, that stirreth thee up.

YE CONJOURATIOUN OF YE FYRE

I stir thee up, O thou fire, in him who is thy Creator and of all creatures. Torment, burn, destroy the spirit N. always whose end cannot be, I judge thee in judgment and in extreme justice, O spirit N., because thou art he that obeyeth not my power and obeyeth not that law which the Lord God made, and obeyeth not the Mighty Sounds and the Living Breath which I invoke, which I send: Come forth, I, who am the Servant of the game Most High governor Lord God powerful, Iehovohe, I who am exalted in power and am mighty in his power above ye, O thou who comest not giving obedience and faith to him that liveth and triumpheth. Therefore I say the judgment: I curse thee and destroy the name N. and the seal N., which I have placed in this dwelling of poison, and I burn thee in fire whose end cannot be; and I cast thee down unto the seas of torment, out of which thou shalt not rise until thou come to my eyes: visit me in peace: be friendly before the circle in the Δ in the 24th of a moment in the likeness of a man not unto the terror of the sons of men the creatures or all things on the face of the earth. Obey my power like reasoning creatures; obey the living breath, the law which I speak.

YE GRETER CURSE

Hearken to me, O ye Heavens! O thou Spirit N. because thou art the disobedient one who is wicked and appearest not, speaking the secrets of truth according to the, living breath; I, exalted in the power of God, the All powerful, the center of the circle, powerful God who liveth, whose end cannot be., Iehevohe Tetragrammaton,, the only creator of heaven, earth, and dwelling of darkness and, all that is in their palaces; who disposeth in secret wisdom of all things in darkness and light: Curse thee and cast thee down and destroy thy seat, joy and power, and I bind thee in the depths of Abaddon, to remain until the day of judgment whose end cannot be, I say, unto the seas of fire and sulphur which I have prepared for the wicked spirits that obey not; the sons of iniquity.

Let the company of heaven curse thee!

Let the sun, moon, all the stars curse thee!

Let the light and all the Holy Ones of Heaven curse thee unto the burning flame that liveth for ever, and unto the torment unspeakable!

And even as thy name and seal, which I have put in this dwelling of poison, shall be in torment among creatures of sulphur and bitter sting, burning in fire of earth, in them Iehevohe and exalted in power in these three names, Tetragrammaton Anaphaxeton, Primeumaton, I cast thee down, O wicked spirit N. unto the seas of fire and sulphur which are prepared for the wicked spirits that obey not, the sons of iniquity, to remain until the day of judgment; let the Mercies of God forget thee; let the face of God forget the face of N. who will not see light: let God forget, I say that shall be the balance of justice over the sons of living breath and death and the world, by fire.

YE ADDRESSE UNTO YE SPIRIT ON HYS COMING

Behold! I confound thee as thou art he that obeys not! Behold the mysteries of the seal of Solomon which I bring forth unto thy power and presence! Behold the creator, the centre of the circle of the living breath; he that is exalted in the power of God and shall not see unto the terror: he that powerfully invoketh and stirreth thee up unto visible appearance: he, the lord of thy governments whose Name is called Octinomos.

Obey, therefore, my power as a reasoning creature -in the name of the Lord.

Ye Welcome Unto Yᴱ Spirit Dygnytie

I am he that is looking with gladness upon thee, O thou spirit . . . N. beautiful and praiseworthy! with gladness I say, because thou art called in him who is creator of Heaven and earth and the dwelling of darkness, and all things that are in their palaces, and because thou art the servant of obedience. In these the power by which thou art obedient to the living breath, I bind thee to remain visible to our eyes in power and presence as the servant of fealty before the circle until I say "Descend unto thy dwelling" until the living breath of the voice of the Lord is according to the law which shall be given unto thee.

By the seal of the secret wisdom of Solomon thou art called! Obey the mighty sounds! obey the living breath of the voice of the Lord!

Follows ye charge.

Ye License To Ye Spirit Y^T He Maye Depart

O thou Spirit N. because thou art the servant of fealty and obedience, and because thou art he that obeyeth my power and thy creation; therefore I say Descend unto thy dwelling, obey the law which I have made, without terror to the sons of men, creatures, all things upon the surface of the earth.

Descend therefore I say, and be thou as stewards of Time; come forth in a moment, even as servants that hearken to the voice of the Lord; in the moment in which I invoke thee and stir thee up and move thee in the, mysteries of the secret wisdom of the Creator!

Descend unto thy dwelling place in pleasure: let there be the mercies of God upon thee: be friendly in continuing; whose long continuance shall be comforters unto all creatures. Amen.

THE GREATER KEY OF SOLOMON THE KING

(CLAVICULA SALOMONIS)

NOW FIRST TRANSLATED AND EDITED FROM ANCIENT MANUSCRIPTS IN THE BRITISH MUSEUM

BY

S. L. MacGregor Mathers

[1888]

Book One

PREFACE

IN presenting this celebrated magical work to the student of occult science some few prefatory remarks are necessary.

The Key of Solomon, save for a curtailed and incomplete copy published in France in the seventeenth century, has never yet been printed, but has for centuries remained in Manuscript form inaccessible to all but the few fortunate scholars to whom the inmost recesses of the great libraries were open. I therefore consider that I am highly honoured in being the individual to whose lot it has fallen to usher it into the light of day.

The fountain-head and storehouse of Qabalistical Magic, and the origin of much of the Ceremonial Magic of mediaeval times, the 'Key' has been ever valued by occult writers as a work of the highest authority; and notably in our own day Eliphaz Lévi has taken it for the model on which his celebrated 'Dogme et Rituel de la Haute Magie' was based. It must be evident to the initiated reader of Levi, that the Key of Solomon was his text book of study, and at the end of this volume I give a fragment of an ancient Hebrew manuscript of the 'Key of Solomon,' translated and published in the 'Philosophie Occulte,' as well as an Invocation called the 'Qabalistical Invocation of Solomon,' which bears close analogy to one in the First Book, being constructed in the same manner on the scheme of the Sephiroth.

The history of the Hebrew original of the 'Key of Solomon' is given in the Introductions, but there is every reason to suppose that this has been entirely lost, and Christian, the pupil of Lévi, says as much in his 'Histoire dc la Magie.'

I see no reason to doubt the tradition which assigns the authorship of the 'Key' to King Solomon, for among others Josephus, the Jewish historian, especially mentions the magical works attributed to that monarch; this is confirmed by many Eastern traditions, and his magical skill is frequently mentioned in the Arabian Nights.

There are, however, two works on Black Magic, the 'Grimorium Verum,' and the 'Clavicola di Salomone ridolta,' which have been attributed to Solomon, and which have been in some cases especially mixed up with the present work; but which have nothing really to do therewith; they are full of evil magic, and I cannot caution the practical student too strongly against them.

There is also another work called 'Lemegeton or the Lesser Key of Solomon the King,' which is full of seals of various Spirits, and is not the same as the present book, though extremely valuable in its own department.

In editing this volume I have omitted one or two experiments partaking largely of Black Magic, and which had evidently been derived from the two

Goetic works mentioned above I must further caution the practical worker against the use of blood the prayer, the pentacle, and the perfumes, rightly used, are sufficient and the former verges dangerously on the evil path. Let him who, in spite of the warnings of this volume determines to work evil, be assured that that evil will recoil on himself and that he will be struck by the reflex current.

This work is edited from several ancient MSS. in the British Museum, which all differ from each other in various points, some giving what is omitted by the others, but all unfortunately agreeing in one thing, which is the execrable mangling of the Hebrew words through the ignorance of the transcribers. But it is in the Pentacles that the Hebrew is worst, the letters being so vilely scribbled as to be actually undecipherable in some instances, and it has been part of my work for several years to correct and reinstate the proper Hebrew and Magical characters in the Pentacles. The student may therefore safely rely on their being now as nearly correct in their present reproduction as it is possible for them to be. I have therefore, wherever I could, corrected the Hebrew of the Magical Names in the Conjurations and Pentacles; and in the few instances where it was not possible- to do so, I have put them in the most usual form; carefully collating throughout one MS. with another. The Chapters are a little differently classed in the various MSS., in some instances the matter contained in them being transposed, etc. I have added notes wherever necessary.

The MSS. from which this work is edited are:--Add. MSS., 10,862; Sloane MSS., 1307 and 3091; Harleian MSS., 3981; King's MSS., 288; and Lansdowne MSS., 1202 and 1203; seven codices in all.

Of all these 10,862 Add. MSS. is the oldest, its date being about the end of the sixteenth century; 3981 Harleian is probably about the middle of the seventeenth century; the others of rather later date.

Add. MSS. 10,862 is written in contracted Latin, and is hard to read, but it contains Chapters which are omitted in the others and also an important Introduction. It is more concise in its wording. Its title is short, being simply 'The Key of Solomon, translated from the Hebrew language into the Latin.' An exact copy of the signature of the writer of this MS. is given in Figure 93. The Pentacles are very badly drawn.

3981 Harleian MSS.; 288 King's MSS.; and 3091 Sloane MSS., are similar, and contain the same matter and nearly the same wording; but the latter MS. has many errors of transcription. They are all in French. The Conjurations and wording of these are much fuller than in 10,867 Add. MSS. and 1202 Lansdowne MSS. The title is 'The Key of Solomon King of the Hebrews, translated from the Hebrew Language into Italian by Abraham Colorno, by the order of his most Serene Highness of Mantua; and recently put into French.' The Pentacles are much better drawn, are in coloured inks, and in the case of 3091 Sloane MSS., gold and silver are employed.

1307 Sloane MSS. is in Italian; its Title is 'La Clavicola di Salomone Redotta et epilogata nella nostra materna lingua del dottissimo Gio Peccatrix.' It is full of Black Magic, and is a jumble of the Key of Solomon proper, and the two Black Magic books before mentioned. The Pentacles are badly drawn. It, however, gives part of the Introduction to 10,862 Add. MSS., and is the only other MS. which does, save the beginning of another Italian version which is bound up with the former MS., and bears the title 'Zecorbenei.'

1202 Lansdowne MSS. is 'The True Keys of King Solomon, by Armadel.' It is beautifully written, with painted initial letters, and the Pentacles are carefully drawn in coloured inks. It is more concise in style, but omits several Chapters. At the end are some short extracts from the Grimorium Verum with the Seals of evil spirits, which, as they do not belong to the 'Key of Solomon' proper, I have not given. For the evident classification of the 'Key' is in two books and no more.

1203 Lansdowne MSS. is 'The Veritable Keys of Solomon translated from the Hebrew into the Latin language by the Rabbin Abognazar (?Aben Ezra).' It is in French, exquisitely written in printing letters, and the Pentacles are carefully drawn in coloured inks. Though containing similar matter to the others, the arrangement is utterly different being all in one book, and not even divided into chapters.

The antiquity of the Planetary sigils is shown by the fact that, among the Gnostic talismans in the British Museum, there is a ring of copper with the sigils of Venus, which are exactly the same as those given by the mediaeval writers on Magic.

Where Psalms are referred to I have in all instances given the English and not the Hebrew numbering of them.

In some places I have substituted the word AZOTH for 'Alpha and Omega,' e.g., on the blade of the Knife with the Black Hilt, Figure 62. I may remark that the Magical Sword may, in many cases, be used instead of the Knife.

In conclusion I will only mention, for the benefit of non-Hebraists, that Hebrew is written from right to left, and that from the consonantal nature of the Hebrew Alphabet, it will require fewer letters than in English to express the same word.

I take this opportunity of expressing my obligations to Dr. Wynn Westcott for the valuable assistance he has given me in the reconstruction of the Hebrew of the Pentacles.

S. LIDDELL MACGREGOR MATHERS.
LONDON, October, 1888.

Book One

Preliminary Discourse

From Lansdowne MSS. 1203, 'The Veritable Clavicles of Solomon, Translated from the Hebrew Into the Latin Language by the Rabbi Abognazar.[38]

EVERY one knoweth in the present day that from time immemorial Solomon possessed knowledge inspired by the wise teachings of an angel, to which he appeared so submissive and obedient, that in addition to the gift of wisdom, which he demanded, he obtained with profusion all the other virtues; which happened in order that knowledge worthy of eternal preservation might not be buried with his body. Being, so to speak, near his end, he left to his son Roboam a Testament which should contain all (the Wisdom) he had possessed prior to his death. The Rabbins, who were careful to cultivate (the same knowledge) after him, called this Testament the Clavicle or Key of Solomon, which they caused to be engraved on (pieces of) the bark of trees, while the Pentacles were inscribed in Hebrew letters on plates of copper, so that they might be carefully preserved in the Temple which that wise king had caused to be built.

This Testament was in ancient time translated from the Hebrew into the Latin language by Rabbi Abognazar, who transported it with him into the town of Arles in Provence, where by a notable piece of good fortune the ancient Hebrew Clavicle, that is to say this precious translation of it, fell into the hands of the Archbishop of Arles, after the destruction of the Jews in that city; who, from the Latin, translated it into the vulgar tongue, in the same terms which here follow, without having either changed or augmented the original translation from the Hebrew.

---

[38] I fancy this Must be a corruption of 'Aben Ezra.'

Introduction

From Add. MSS. 10862., 'The Key of Solomon, Translated Into Latin from the Hebrew Idiom.'

TREASURE Up, O my son Roboam! the wisdom of my words, seeing that I, Solomon, have received it from the Lord.

Then answered Roboam, and said: How have I deserved to follow the example of my father Solomon in such things, who hath been found worthy to receive the knowledge of all living things through (the teaching of) an Angel of God?

And Solomon said: Hear, O my son, and receive my sayings, and learn the wonders of God. For, on a certain night, when I laid me down to sleep, I called upon that most holy Name of God, IAH, and prayed for the Ineffable Wisdom, and when I was beginning to close mine eyes, the Angel of the Lord, even Homadiel, appeared unto me, spake many things courteously unto me, and said: Listen, O Solomon! thy prayer before the Most High is not in vain, and since thou hast asked neither for long life, nor for much riches, nor for the souls of thine enemies, but hast asked for thyself wisdom to perform justice. Thus saith the Lord: According to thy word have I given unto thee a wise and understanding heart, so that before thee was none like unto thee, nor ever shall arise.

And when I comprehended the speech which was made unto me, I understood that in me was the knowledge of all creatures, both things which are in the heavens and things which are beneath the heavens; and I saw that all the writings and wisdom of this present age were vain and futile, and that no man was perfect. And I composed a certain work wherein I rehearsed the secret of secrets, in which I have preserved them hidden, and I have also therein concealed all secrets whatsoever of magical arts of any masters; any secret or experiments, namely, of these sciences which is in any way worth being accomplished. Also I have written them in this Key, so that like as a key openeth a treasure-house, so this (Key) alone may open the knowledge and understanding of magical arts and sciences.

Therefore, O my son! thou mayest see every experiment of mine or of others, and let everything be properly prepared for them, as thou shalt see properly set down by me, both day and hour, and all things necessary for without this there will be but falsehood and vanity in this my work; wherein are hidden all secrets and mysteries which can be performed; and that which is (set down) concerning a single divination or a single experiment, that same I think concerning all things which are in the Universe, and which have been, and which shall be in future time.

Therefore, O my son Roboam, I command thee by the blessing which thou expectest from thy father, that thou shall make an Ivory Casket, and therein place, keep, and hide this my Key; and when I shall have passed away unto my fathers, I entreat thee to place the same in my sepulchre beside me, lest at another time it might fall into the hands of the wicked. And as Solomon commanded, so was it done.

And when, therefore (men) had waited for a long time, there came unto the Sepulchre certain Babylonian Philosophers; and when they had assembled they at once took counsel together that a certain number of men should renew the Sepulchre in his (Solomon's) honour; and when the Sepulchre was dug out and repaired the Ivory Casket was discovered, and therein was the Key of Secrets, which they took with joyful mind, and when they had opened it none among them could understand it on account of the obscurity of the words and their occult arrangement, and the hidden character of the sense and knowledge, for they were not worthy to possess this treasure.

Then, therefore, arose one among them, more worthy (than the others), both in the sight of the gods, and by reason of his age, who was called Iohé Grevis,[39] and said unto the others: Unless we shall come and ask the interpretation from the Lord, with tears and entreaties, we shall never arrive at the knowledge of it.

Therefore, when each of them had retired to his bed, Iohé indeed falling upon his face on the earth, began to weep, and striking his breast, said:

What have I deserved (above others), seeing that so many men can neither understand nor interpret this knowledge, even though there were no secret thing in nature which the Lord hath hidden from me! Wherefore are these words so obscure? Wherefore am I so ignorant?

And then on his bended knees, stretching his hands to heaven, he said:

O God, the Creator of all, Thou Who knowest all things, Who gavest so great Wisdom unto Solomon the Son of David the King; grant unto me, I beseech Thee, O Holy Omnipotent and Incffable Father, to receive the virtue of that wisdom, so that I may become worthy by Thine aid to attain unto the understanding of this Key of Secrets.

And immediately there appeared unto me,[40] the Angel of the Lord, saying:

Do thou remember if the secrets of Solomon appear hidden and obscure unto thee, that the Lord hath wished it, so that such wisdom may not fall into the hands of wicked men; wherefore do thou promise unto me, that thou art not willing that so great wisdom should ever come to any living creature, and that which thou revealest unto any let them know that they must keep it unto

---

[39] I think this is correct, but the name is very indistinctly written in the MS., which is difficult to decipher. In another copy of the Clavicle it is written Iroe Grecis, but I think this is an error.

[40] 'Mihi' in MS., probably a slip for 'unto him,' 'ei.'

themselves, otherwise the secrets are profaned and no effect can follow?

And Iohé answered: I promise unto thee that to none will I reveal (them), save to the honour of the Lord, and with much discipline, unto penitent, secret, and faithful (persons).

Then answered the Angel: Go and read the Key, and its words which were obscure throughout shall be manifest unto thee.

And after this the Angel ascended into Heaven in a Flame of Fire.

Then Iohé was glad, and labouring with a clear mind, understood that which the Angel of the Lord had said, and he saw that the Key of Solomon was changed, so that it appeared quite clear unto him plainly in all parts. And Iohé understood that this Work might fall into the hands of the ignorant, and he said: I conjure him into whose hands this secret may come, by the Power of the Creator, and His Wisdom, that in all things he may, desire, intend and perform, that this Treasure may come unto no unworthy (person), nor may he manifest it unto any who is unwise, nor unto one who feareth not God. Because if he act otherwise, I pray God that he may never be worthy to attain unto the desired effect.

And so he deposited the Key, which Solomon preserved, in the Ivory Casket. But the Words of the Key are as follows, divided into two books, and shown in order.

Book One

Introduction

From Lansdowne MSS. 1203, 'The Veritable Clavicles of Solomon, translated from the Hebrew into the Latin language by the Rabbi Abognazar.'

O my Son Roboam! seeing that of all Sciences there is none more useful than the knowledge of Celestial Movements, I have thought it my duty, being at the point of death, to leave thee an inheritance more precious than all the riches which I have enjoyed.' And in order that thou mayest understand how I have arrived at this degree (of wisdom), it is necessary to tell thee that one day, when I was meditating upon the power of the Supreme Being, the Angel of the Great God appeared before me as I was saying, O how wonderful are the works of God! I suddenly beheld, at the end of a thickly-shaded vista of trees, a Light in the form of a blazing Star, which said unto me with a voice of thunder: Solomon, Solomon, be not dismayed; the Lord is willing to satisfy thy desire by giving thee knowledge of whatsoever thing is most pleasant unto thee. I order thee to ask of Him whatsoever thou desirest. Whereupon, recovering from my surprise, I answered unto the Angel, that according to the Will of the Lord, I only desired the Gift of Wisdom, and by the Grace of God I obtained in addition the enjoyment of all the Celestial treasures and the knowledge of all natural things.

It is by this means, my Son, that I possess all the virtues and riches of which thou now seest me in the enjoyment, and in order that thou mayest be willing to be attentive to all which I am about to relate to thee, and that thou mayest retain with care all that I am about to tell thee, I assure thee that the Graces of the Great God will be familiar unto thee, and that the Celestial and Terrestrial Creatures will be obedient unto thee, and a science which only works by the strength and power of natural things, and by the pure Angels which govern them. Of which latter I will give thee the names in order, their exercises and particular employments to which they are destined, together with the days over which they particularly preside, in order that thou mayest arrive at the accomplishment of all, which thou wilt find in this my Testament. In all which I promise thee success, provided that all thy works only tend unto the honour of God, Who hath given me the power to rule, not only over Terrestrial but also over Celestial things, that is to say, over the Angels, of whom I am able to dispose according to my will, and to obtain from them very considerable services.

Firstly. It is necessary for thee to understand that God, having made all things, in order that they may be submitted unto Him, hath wished to bring His works to perfection, by making one which participates of the Divine and of the Terrestrial, that is to say, Man; whose body is gross and terrestrial, while his soul is spiritual and celestial, unto whom He hath made subject the whole earth and its inhabitants, and hath given unto Him means by which He may render the Angels familiar, as I call those Celestial creatures who are destined: some to regulate the motion of the Stars, others to inhabit the Elements, others to aid and direct men, and others again to sing continually the praises of the Lord. Thou mayest then, by the use of their seals and characters, render them familiar unto thee, provided that thou abusest not this privilege by demanding from them things which are contrary to their nature; for accursed be he who will take the Name of God in vain, and who will employ for evil purposes the knowledge and good wherewith He hath enriched us.

I command thee, my Son, to carefully engrave in thy memory all that I say unto thee, in order that it may never leave thee. If thou dost not intend to use for a good purpose the secrets which I here teach thee, I command thee rather to cast this Testament into the fire, than to abuse the power thou wilt have of constraining the Spirits, for I warn thee that the beneficent Angels, wearied and fatigued by thine illicit demands, would to thy sorrow execute the commands of God, as well as to that of all such who, with evil intent, would abuse those secrets which He hath given and revealed unto me. Think not, however, O my Son, that it would not be permitted thee to profit by the good fortune and happiness which the Divine Spirits can bring thee; on the contrary, it gives them great pleasure to render service to Man for whom many of these Spirits have great liking and affinity, God having destined them for the preservation and guidance of those Terrestrial things which are submitted to the power of Man.

There are different kinds of Spirits, according to the things over which they preside; some of them govern the Empyrean Heaven, others the Primum Mobile, others the First and Second Crystalline, others the Starry Heaven there are also Spirits of the Heaven of Saturn, which I call Saturnites there are jovial, Martial, Solar, Venerean, Mercurial . and Lunar Spirits there are also (Spirits) in the Elements as well as in the Heavens, there are some in the Fiery Region, others in the Air, others in the Water, and others upon the Earth, which can all render service to that man who shall have the good fortune to understand their nature, and to know how to attract them.

Furthermore, I wish to make thee understand that God hath destined to each one of us a Spirit, which watches over us and takes care of our preservation; these are called Genii, who are elementary like us, and who are more ready to render service to those whose temperament is conformed to the Element which these Genii inhabit; for example, shouldest thou be of a fiery temperament, that is to say sanguine, thy genius would be fiery and submitted to the Empire of Baël. Besides this, there are special times reserved for the invocation of these Spirits, in the days and hours when they have power and absolute empire. It is for this reason that thou wilt see in the following tables to what Planet and to what Angel each Day and Hour is submitted, together with the Colours which belong unto them, the Metals, Herbs, Plants, Aquatic, Aërial, and Terrestrial Animals, and Incense, which are proper to each of them, as also in what quarter of the Universe they ask to be invoked. Neither are omitted, the Conjurations, Seals, Characters, and Divine Letters, which belong to them, by means of which we receive the power to sympathise with these Spirits.

Table of the Planetary Hours

Sund.	Mon.	Tue.	Wed.	Hours from Sunset to Sunset	Hours from Midnight to Midnight	Thur.	Fri.	Sat.
Merc.	Jup.	Ven.	Satn.	8	1	Sun	Mn.	Mars
Mn.	Mars	Mer.	Jup.	9	2	Ven.	Satn.	Sun
Satn.	Sun	Mn.	Mars	10	3	Mer.	Jup.	Ven.
Jup.	Ven.	Satn.	Sun	11	4	Mn.	Mars	Mer.
Mars	Mer.	Jup.	Ven.	12	5	Satn.	Sun	Mn.
Sun	Mn.	Mars	Mer.	1	6	Jup.	Ven.	Satn.
Ven.	Satn.	Sun	Mn.	2	7	Mars	Mer.	Jup.
Mer.	Jup.	Ven.	Satn.	3	8	Sun	Mn.	Mars
Mn.	Mars	Mer.	Jup.	4	9	Ven.	Satn.	Sun
Satn.	Sun	Mn.	Mars	5	10	Mer.	Jup.	Ven.
Jup.	Ven.	Satn.	Sun	6	11	Mn.	Mars	Mer.
Mars	Mer.	Jup.	Ven.	7	12	Satn.	Sun	Mn.
Sun	Mn.	Mars	Mer.	8	1	Jup.	Ven.	Satn.
Ven.	Satn.	Sun	Mn.	9	2	Mars	Mer.	Jup.
Mer.	Jup.	Ven.	Satn.	10	3	Sun.	Mn.	Mars
Mn.	Mars	Mer.	Jup.	11	4	Ven.	Satn.	Sun
Satn.	Sun	Mn.	Mars	12	5	Mer.	Jup.	Ven.
Jup.	Ven.	Satn.	Sun	1	6	Mn.	Mars	Mer.
Mars	Mer.	Jup.	Ven.	2	7	Satn.	Sun	Mn.
Sun	Mn.	Mars	Mer.	3	8	Jup.	Ven.	Satn.
Ven.	Satn.	Sun	Mn.	4	9	Mars	Mer.	Jup.
Mer.	Jup.	Ven.	Satn.	5	10	Sun	Mn.	Mars
Mn.	Mars	Mer.	Jup.	6	11	Ven.	Satn.	Sun
Satn.	Sun	Mn.	Mars	7	12	Mer.	Jup.	Ven.

BOOK ONE

Table of the Magical Names of the Hours and of the Angels who Rule them, Commencing at the First Hour After Midnight of Each Day, and Ending at the Ensuing Midnight

Hours.	Sun..	Mon.	Tues.	Wed.	Thur.	Fri.	Sat.
1.Yayn	Raphael	Sachiel	Anael	Cassiel	Michael	Gabriel	Zamael
2.Yanor	Gabriel	Zamael	Raphael	Sachiel	Anael	Cassiel	Michael
3.Nasnia	Cassiel	Michael	Gabriel	Zamael	Raphael	Sachiel	Anael
4.Salla	Sachiel	Anael	Cassiel	Michael	Gabriel	Zamael	Raphael
5.Sadedali	Zamael	Raphael	Sachiel	Anael	Cassiel	Michael	Gabriel
6.Thamur	Michael	Gabriel	Zamael	Raphael	Sachiel	Anael	Cassiel
7.Ourer	Anael	Cassiel	Michael	Gabriel	Zasnael	Raphael	Sachiel
8.Thainé	Raphael	Sachiel	Anael	Cassiel	Michael	Gabriel	Zamael
9.Neron	Gabriel	Zamael	Raphael	Sachiel	Anael	Cassiel	Michael
10.Yayon	Cassiel	Michael	Gablriel	Zamael	Raphael	Sachiel	Anael
11.Abai	Sachiel	Anael	Caiel	Michael	Gabriel	Zamael	Raphael
12.Nathalon	Zamael	Raphael	Sachiel	Anael	Cassiel	Michael	Gabriel
1.Beron	Michael	Gabriel	Zamael	Raphael	Sachiel	Anael	Cassiel
2.Barol	Anael	Cassiel	Michael	Gabriel	Zamael	Raphael	Sachiel
3.Thanu	Raphael	Sachiel	Anael	Cassiel	Michael	Gabriel	Zamael
4.Athor	Gabriel	Zamael	Raphael	Sachiel	Anael	Cassiel	Michael
5.Mathon	Cassiel	Michael	Gabriel	Zamael	Raphael	Sachiel	Anael
6.Rana	Sachiel	Anael	Cassiel	Michael	Gabriel	Zamael	Raphael
7.Netos	Zamael	Raphael	Sachiel	Anael	Cassiel	Michael	Gabriel
8.Tafrac	Michael	Gabriel	Zamael	Raphael	Sachiel	Anael	Cassiel
9.Sassur	Anael	Cassiel	Michael	Gabriel	Zamael	Raphael	Sachiel
10.Agla	Raphael	Sachiel	Anael	Cassiel	Michael	Gabriel	Zamael
11.Cäerra	Gabriel	Zamael	Raphael	Sachiel	Anael	Cassiel	Michael
12.Salam	Cassiel	Michael	Gabriel	Zamael	Raphael	Sachiel	Anael

The Key of Solomon the King

Table of the Archangels, Angels, Metals, Days of the Week, and Colours attributed to each Planet.

Days.	Saturday.	Thursday.	Tuesday.	Sunday.	Friday.	Wednesday.	Monday.
Archangel	Tzaphqiel	Tzadiqel	Khaniael	Raphael	Haniel	Michael	Gabriel
Angel	Cassiel	Sachiel	Zamael	Michael	Anael	Raphael	Gabriel
Planet	Saturn	Jupiter	Mars	Sun	Venus	Mercury	Moon
Metal	Lead	Tin	Iron	Gold	Copper	Mercury	Silver
Colour	Black	Blue	Red	Yellow	Green	Purple or Mixed Colours	White

NOTE BY EDITOR

These Tables have been collated and compared with various examples of them both MS. and printed. They are to be used thus:--Supposing the student wishes to discover the properties of the hour from 12 to 1 O'clock p.m. on a Tuesday, let him look in the 'Table of the Planetary Hours,' and having found the hour marked 1 in the column headed 'Hours from Midnight to Midnight,' he will see in the column headed 'Hours from Sunset to Sunset,' on the same line the figure 8, showing it to be the eighth hour of the day; and in the column headed Tuesday, the name Mars, showing that it is under the dominion of the planet Mars. On consulting the 'Table of the Magical Names of the Hours,' etc., he will find under the number 1, the name Beron, and in the column 'Tuesday,' the name of the Angel Zamael over against it on the same line, showing that the ruler of the hour is the Angel Zamael, and that its Magical Name is Beron. Further, on referring to the third Table he will see that Tuesday is under the rule of the planet Mars, whose Archangel is Khamael, Angel Zamael, Metal Iron, and Colour Red. Similarly it will be found that the hour from 10 to 11 p.m. on Saturday is the sixth hour of the night, under the dominion of the Sun, that its Magical Name is Cäerra, and that the Angel Michael rules it; while Saturday itself is under the dominion of the Archangel Tzaphqiel, of the Angel Cassiel, of the Planet Saturn, and that the Metal Lead and the Colour Black are applicable to it.

The ensuing Text is taken from the following MSS., collated and compared with each other.

Sloane MSS. 1307; Sloane MSS. 3091; Harleian MSS. 3981; Add. MSS. 10862; King's MSS. 288; Lansdowne MSS. 1202.

Extracts have also been made from Lansdowne MSS. 1203, which differs considerably from the others in general arrangement, though containing very similar matter.

In cases where the MSS. varied from each other I have taken the version which seemed most likely to be correct, in some cases mentioning the variant readings in footnotes. I have also, wherever it was possible to do so, corrected the Hebrew names in the Incantations, for these were in some cases so marred as to be hardly recognisable; e.g. Zenard, written for Tzabaoth, etc.

Chapter I

Concerning the Divine Love Which Ought to Precede the Acquisition of this Knowledge

SOLOMON, the Son of David, King of Israel, hath said that the beginning of our Key is to fear God, to adore Him, to honour Him with contrition of heart, to invoke Him[41] in all matters which we wish to undertake, and to operate with very great devotion, for thus God will lead us in the right way. When, therefore, thou shalt wish to acquire the knowledge of Magical Arts and Sciences, it is necessary to have prepared the order of hours and of days, and of the position of the Moon, without the operation of which thou canst effect nothing; but if thou observest them with diligence thou mayest easily and thoroughly arrive at the effect and end which thou desirest to attain.

---

[41] 1202 Lansdowne MSS. omits the concluding part of this sentence.

Chapter II

Of the Days, and Hours, and of the Virtues of the Planets

WHEN[42] thou wishest to make any experiment or operation, thou must first prepare, beforehand, all the requisites which thou wilt find described in the following Chapters: observing the days, the hours, and the other effects of the Constellations which may be found in this Chapter.

It is, therefore, advisable to know that the hours of the day and of the night together, are twenty-four in number, and that each hour is governed by one of the Seven Planets in regular order, commencing at the highest and descending to the lowest. The order of the Planets is as follows: ShBThAI, Shabbathai, Saturn; beneath Saturn is TzDQ, Tzedeq, Jupiter; beneath Jupiter is MADIM, Madim, Mars; beneath Mars is ShMSh, Shemesh, the Sun; beneath the Sun is NVGH, Nogah, Venus; beneath Venus is KVKB, Kokav, Mercury; and beneath Mercury is LBNH, Levanah, the Moon, which is the lowest of all the Planets.

It must, therefore, be understood that the Planets have their dominion over the day which approacheth nearest unto the name which is given and attributed unto them--viz., over Saturday, Saturn; Thursday, Jupiter; Tuesday, Mars; Sunday, the Sun; Friday, Venus; Wednesday, Mercury; and Monday, the Moon.

The rule of the Planets over each hour begins from the dawn at the rising of the Sun on the day which takes its name from such Planet, and the Planet which follows it in order, succeeds to the rule over the next hour. Thus (on Saturday) Saturn rules the first hour, Jupiter the second, Mars the third, the Sun the fourth, Venus the fifth, Mercury the sixth, the Moon the seventh, and Saturn returns in the rule over the eighth, and the others in their turn, the Planets always keeping the same relative order.

Note that each experiment or magical operation should be performed under the Planet, and usually in the hour, which refers to the same. For example:--In the Days and Hours of Saturn thou canst perform experiments to summon the Souls from Hades, but only of those who have died a natural death. Similarly on these days and hours thou canst operate to bring either good or bad fortune to buildings; to have familiar Spirits attend thee in sleep; to cause good or ill success to business, possessions, goods, seeds, fruits, and similar things, in order to acquire learning; to bring destruction and to give death, and to sow hatred and discord.

The Days and Hours of Jupiter are proper for obtaining honours,

---

[42] This first paragraph is omitted in 1307 Sloane MSS., and in 10862 Add. MSS.

acquiring riches; contracting friendships, preserving health; and arriving at all that thou canst desire.

In the Days and Hours of Mars thou canst make experiments regarding War; to arrive at military honour; to acquire courage; to overthrow enemies; and further to cause ruin, slaughter, cruelty, discord; to wound and to give death.

The Days and Hours of the Sun are very good for perfecting experiments regarding temporal wealth, hope, gain, fortune, divination, the favour of princes, to dissolve hostile feeling, and to make friends.

The Days and Hours of Venus are good for forming friendships; for kindness and love; for joyous and pleasant undertakings, and for travelling.

The Days and Hours of Mercury are good to operate for eloquence and intelligence; promptitude in business; science and divination; wonders; apparitions; and answers regarding the future. Thou canst also operate under this Planet for thefts; writings; deceit; and merchandise.

The Days and Hours of the Moon are good for embassies; voyages envoys; messages; navigation; reconciliation; love; and the acquisition of merchandise by water.[43]

Thou shouldest take care punctually to observe all the instructions contained in this chapter, if thou desirest to succeed, seeing that the truth of Magical Science dependeth thereon.

The Hours of Saturn, of Mars, and of the Moon are alike good for communicating and speaking with Spirits; as those of Mercury are for recovering thefts by the means of Spirits.

The Hours of Mars serve for summoning Souls from Hades,[44] especially of those slain in battle.

The Hours of the Sun, of Jupiter, and of Venus, are adapted for preparing any operations whatsoever of love, of kindness, and of invisibility, as is hereafter more fully shown, to which must be added other things of a similar nature which are contained in our work.

The Hours of Saturn and Mars and also the days on which the Moon is conjunct[45] with them, or when she receives their opposition or quartile aspect, are excellent for making experiments of hatred, enmity, quarrel, and discord; and other operations of the same kind which are given later on in this work.

The Hours of Mercury are good for undertaking experiments relating to games, raillery, jests, sports, and the like.

---

[43] Much of these foregoing instructions is omitted in the 10862 Add. MSS., but given in a different way in the ensuing paragraphs.
[44] In the French 'des Enfers,' in the Latin 'Inferis.'
[45] Conjunction means being in the same degree of the Zodiac; opposition is being 180 degrees, and quartile 90 degrees apart from each other.

The Hours of the Sun, of Jupiter, and of Venus, particularly on the days which they rule, are good for all extraordinary, uncommon, and unknown operations.

The Hours of the Moon are proper for making trial of experiments relating to recovery of stolen property, for obtaining nocturnal visions, for summoning Spirits in sleep, and for preparing anything relating to Water.

The Hours of Venus are furthermore useful for lots, poisons, all things of the nature of Venus, for preparing powders provocative of madness and the like things.

But in order to thoroughly effect the operations of this Art, thou shouldest perform them not only on the Hours but on the Days of the Planets as well, because then the experiment will always succeed better, provided thou observest the rules laid down later on, for if thou omittest one single condition thou wilt never arrive at the accomplishment of the Art.

For those matters then which appertain unto the Moon, such as the Invocation of Spirits, the Works of Necromancy, and the recovery of stolen property, it is necessary that the Moon should be in a Terrestrial Sign, viz.:-- Taurus, Virgo, or Capricorn.

For love, grace, and invisibility, the Moon should be in a Fiery Sign, viz.:--Aries, Leo, or Sagittarius.

For hatred, discord, and destruction, the Moon should be in a Watery Sign, viz.:--Cancer, Scorpio, or Pisces.

For experiments of a peculiar nature, which cannot be classed under any certain head, the Moon should be in an Airy Sign, viz.:--Gemini, Libra, or Aquarius.

But if these things seem unto thee difficult to accomplish, it will suffice thee merely to notice the Moon after her combustion, or conjunction with the Sun, especially just when she[46] quits his beams and appeareth visible. For then it is good to make all experiments for the construction and operation of any matter. That is why the time from the New unto the Full Moon is proper for performing any of the experiments of which we have spoken above. But in her decrease or wane it is good for War, Disturbance, and Discord. Likewise the period when she is almost deprived of light, is proper for experiments of invisibility, and of Death.

But observe inviolably that thou commence nothing while the Moon is in conjunction with the Sun, seeing that this is extremely unfortunate, and that thou wilt then be able to effect nothing; but the Moon quitting his beams and increasing in Light, thou canst perform all that thou desirest, observing nevertheless the directions in this Chapter.

Furthermore, if thou wishest to converse with Spirits it should be

---

[46] *i.e.* New Moon.

especially on the day of Mercury and in his hour, and let the Moon be in an Airy Sign,[47] as well as the Sun.

Retire[48] thou then unto a secret place, where no one may be able to see thee or to hinder thee, before the completion of the experiment, whether thou shouldest wish to work by day or by night. But if thou shouldest wish to work by night, perfect thy work on the succeeding night; if by day, seeing that the day beginneth with the rising of the Sun (perfect thy work on) the succeeding day. But the Hour of Inception is the Hour of Mercury.

Verily, since no experiments for converse with Spirits can be done without a Circle being prepared, whatsoever experiments therefore thou wishest to undertake for conversing with Spirits, therein thou must learn to construct a certain particular Circle; that being done surround that Circle with a Circle of Art for better caution and efficacy.

---

[47] In Add. MSS. 10862; 'or in an Earthy Sign, as hath been before said.'
[48] The following paragraphs to the end of this Chapter are only found in the Latin version, Add. MSS. 10862.

Chapter III

Concerning the Arts

IF thou wishest to succeed, it is necessary to make the following Experiments and Arts in the appropriate Days and Hours, with the requisite solemnities and ceremonies contained and laid down in the following Chapters.

Experiments, then, are of two kinds; the first is to make trial of what, as I have said, can be easily performed without a Circle, and in this case it is not necessary to observe anything but what thou wilt find in the proper Chapters. The second can in no way be brought to perfection without the Circle; and in order to accomplish this perfectly it is necessary to take note of all the preparations which the Master of the Art and his Disciples must undertake before constructing[49] the Circle.

Before commencing operations both the Master and his Disciples must abstain with great and thorough continence during the space of nine days from sensual pleasures and from vain and foolish conversation; as plainly appeareth in the Second Book, Chapter 4. Six of these nine days having expired, he must recite frequently the Prayer and Confession as will be told him; and on the Seventh Day, the Master being alone, let him enter into a secret place, let him take off his clothes, and bathe himself from head to foot in consecrated and exorcised Water, saying devoutly and humbly the prayer, 'O Lord Adonai,' etc., as it is written in the Second Book, Chapter 2.

The Prayer being finished, let the Master quit the water, and put upon his flesh raiment of white linen clean and unsoiled; and then let him go with his Disciples unto a secret place and command them to strip themselves naked; and they having taken off their clothes, let him take exorcised water and pour it upon their heads so that it flows down to their feet and bathes them completely; and while pouring this water upon them let the Master say:--'Be ye regenerate, renewed, washed, and pure,' etc., as in Book II., Chapter 3.

Which[50] being done, the Disciples must clothe themselves, putting upon their flesh, like their Master, raiment of white linen clean and unsoiled; and the three last days the Master and his Disciples should fast, observing the solemnities and prayers marked in Book II., Chapter 2.

Note that the three last days should be calm weather, without wind, and without clouds rushing hither and thither over the face of the sky. On the last day let the Master go with his Disciples unto a secret fountain of running water, or unto a flowing stream, and there let each of them, taking off his clothes, wash himself with due solemnity, as is rehearsed in Book II. And

---

[49] Sloane MSS. 3091 says, 'before they come to the Circle.'
[50] This paragraph is omitted in Lansdowne MSS. 1202.

when they are clean and pure, let each put upon him garments of white linen, pure, and clean, using the prayers and ceremonies described in Book II. After which let the Master alone say the confession. The which being finished, the Master in sign of penitence will Kiss[51] the Disciples on the forehead, and each of them will Kiss the other. Afterwards let the Master extend his hands over the Disciples, and in sign of absolution absolve and bless them; which being done he will distribute to each of his Disciples the Instruments necessary for Magical Art, which he is to carry into the Circle.

The First Disciple will bear the Censer, the Perfumes and the Spices the Second Disciple will bear the Book, Papers, Pens, Ink, and any stinking or impure materials; the Third will carry the Knife and the Sickle of Magical Art, the Lantern, and the Candles; the Fourth, the Psalms, and the rest of the Instruments; the Fifth, the Crucible or Chafing-dish, and the Charcoal or Fuel; but it is necessary for the Master himself to carry in his hand the Staff, and the Wand or Rod. The things necessary being thus disposed, the Master will go with his Disciples unto the assigned place, where they have proposed to construct the Circle for the Magical Arts and experiments; repeating on the way the prayers and orations which thou wilt find in Book II.

When the Master shall have arrived at the place appointed, together with his Disciples, he having lighted the flame of the fire, and having exorcised it afresh as is laid down in the Second Book, shall light the Candle and place it in the Lantern, which one of the Disciples is to hold ever in his hand to light the Master at his work. Now the Master of the Art, every time that he shall have occasion for some particular purpose to speak with the Spirits, must endeavour to form certain Circles which shall differ somewhat, and shall have some particular reference to the particular experiment under consideration. Now, in order to succeed in forming such a Circle concerning Magical Art, for the greater assurance and efficacy thou shalt construct it in the following manner:--

The Construction of the Circle

Take thou the Knife, the Sickle, or the Sword of Magical Art consecrated after the manner and order which we shall deliver unto thee in the Second Book. With this Knife or with the Sickle of Art thou shalt describe, beyond the inner Circle which thou shalt have already formed, a Second Circle, encompassing the other at the distance of one foot therefrom and having the same centre.[52] Within this space of a foot in breadth between the first and

---

[51] Note the 'holy kiss' in the New Testament. 'Greet ye one another with a holy kiss.'

[52] *i.e.* two Circles enclosed between three circumferential lines.

the second circumferential[53] line, thou shalt trace towards the Four Quarters of the Earth,[54] the Sacred and Venerable Symbols of the holy Letter Tau[55]. And between the first and the second Circle,[56] which thou shalt thyself have drawn with the Instrument of Magical Art, thou shalt make four hexagonal pentacles,[57] and between these thou shalt write four terrible and tremendous Names of God, viz.:--

Between the East and the South the Supreme Name IHVH, Tetragrammaton;--

Between the South and the West the Essential Tetragrammatic Name AHIH, Eheieh;--

Between the West and the North the Name of Power ALIVN, Elion;--

And between the North and the East the Great Name ALH, Eloah;--

Which Names are of supreme importance in the list of the Sephiroth,[58] and their Sovereign Equivalents.

Furthermore, thou shalt circumscribe about these Circles two Squares, the Angles of which shall be turned towards the Four Quarters of the Earth; and the space between the Lines of the Outer and Inner Square shall be half-a-foot. The extreme Angles of the Outer Square shall be made the Centres of four Circles, the measure or diameter of which shall be one foot. All these are to be drawn with the Knife or consecrated Instrument of Art. And within these Four Circles thou must write these four Names of God the Most Holy One, in this order:--

At[59] the East, AL, El;

At the West, IH, Yah;

At the South, AGLA, Agla;

And at the North ADNI, Adonaï.

Between the two Squares the Name Tetragrammaton is to be written in the same way as is shown in the plate. (See Figure 2.)

While constructing the Circle, the Master should recite the following

---

[53] *i.e.* within the first Circle.

[54] *i.e.* the four Cardinal points of the compass.

[55] The letter Tau represents the Cross, and in 10862 Add. MSS. in the drawing of the Circle, the Hebrew letter is replaced by the Cross; in 1307 Sloane MSS. by the T or Tau-Cross.

[56] *i.e.* in the Outer Circle, bounded by the second and third circumferential lines.

[57] 10862 Add. NISS. is the only copy which uses the word hexagonal, but the others show four hexagrams in the drawing; in the drawing, however, 10862 gives the hexagrams formed by various differing interlacements of two triangles, as shown in Figure 2.

[58] The Sephiroth are the ten Qabalistical Emanations of the Deity. The Sovereign Equivalents are the Divine Names referred thereto. See my 'Kabbalah Unveiled.'

[59] The MSS. vary as to the point whereat each Name is to be placed, but I think the above will be found to answer.

Psalms:--Psalm ii.; Psalm liv.; Psalm cxiii.; Psalm lxvii.; Psalm xlvii.; Psalm lxviii.

Or he may as well recite them before tracing the Circle.

The which being finished, and the fumigations being performed, as is described in the chapter on Fumigations in the Second Book, the Master should reassemble his Disciples, encourage them, reassure them, fortify them, and conduct them into the parts of the Circle of Art, where he must place them in the four quarters of the earth, encourage them, and exhort them to fear nothing, and to keep in the places assigned to them. Also, the Disciple who is placed towards the East should have a pen, ink, paper, silk, and white cotton, all clean and suitable for the work. Furthermore, each of the Companions should have a new Sword drawn in his hand (besides the consecrated Magical Sword of Art), and he should keep his hand resting upon the hilt thereof, and he should on no pretext quit the place assigned to him, nor move therefrom.

After this the Master should quit the Circle, light the fuel in the earthen pots, and place upon them the Censers, in the Four Quarters of the Earth; and he should have in his hand the consecrated taper of wax, and he should light it and place it in a hidden and secret place prepared for it. Let him after this re-enter and close the Circle.

The Master should afresh exhort his Disciples, and explain to them all that they have to do and to observe; the which commands they should promise and vow to execute.

Let the Master then repeat this Prayer:--

Prayer

When we enter herein with all humility, let God the Almighty One enter into this Circle, by the entrance of an eternal happiness, of a Divine prosperity, of a perfect joy, of an abundant charity, and of an eternal salutation. Let all the demons fly from this place, especially those who are opposed unto this work, and let the Angels of Peace assist and protect This Circle, from which let discord and strife fly and depart. Magnify and extend upon us, O Lord, Thy most Holy Name, and bless our conversation and our assembly. Sanctify, O Lord our God, our humble entry herein, Thou the Blessed and Holy One of the Eternal Ages! Amen.

After this, let the Master say upon his knees, as follows:--

Prayer

O Lord God, All Powerful and All Merciful, Thou Who desirest not the death of a sinner, but rather that he may turn from his wickedness and live; give and grant unto us Thy grace, by blessing and consecrating this earth and this circle, which is here marked out with the most powerful and holy names of God. And thee, I conjure, O Earth, by the Most Holy Name of ASHER EHEIEH entering within this Circle, composed and made with mine hand. And may God, even ADONAI, bless this place with all the virtues of Heaven, so that no obscene or unclean spirit may have the power to enter into this Circle, or to annoy any person who is therein; through the Lord God ADONAI, Who liveth eternally unto the Ages of the Ages. Amen.

I beseech Thee, O Lord God, the All Powerful and the All Merciful, that Thou wilt deign to bless this Circle, and all this place, and all those who are therein, and that Thou wilt grant unto us, who serve Thee, and rehearse nothing but the wonders of Thy law, a good Angel for our Guardian; remove from us every adverse power; preserve us from evil and from trouble; grant, O Lord, that we may rest in this place in all safety, through Thee, O Lord, Who livest and reignest unto the Ages of the Ages. Amen.

Let the Master now arise and place upon his head a Crown made of paper (or any other appropriate substance), on the which there must be written (with the Colours and other necessary things which we shall describe hereafter), these four Names AGLA, AGLAI, AGLATA, AGLATAI. The which Names are to be placed in the front, behind, and on either side of the head.

Furthermore, the Master ought to have with him in the Circle those Pentacles or Medals which are necessary to his purpose, which are described hereinafter, and which should be constructed according to the rules given in the Chapter on Pentacles. They should be described on virgin paper with a pen; and ink, blood, or colours, prepared according to the manner which we shall hereafter show in the Chapters on these subjects. It win be sufficient to take only those Pentacles which are actually required, they should be sewed to the front of the linen robe, on the chest, with the consecrated needle of the Art, and with a thread which has been woven by a young girl.

After this, let the Master turn himself towards the Eastern Quarter (unless directed to the contrary, or unless he should be wishing to call Spirits which belong to another quarter of the Universe), and pronounce with a loud voice the Conjuration contained in this Chapter. And if the Spirits be disobedient and do not then make their appearance, he must arise and take the exorcised Knife of Art wherewith he hath constructed the Circle, and raise it towards the sky as if he wished to beat or strike the Air, and conjure the Spirits. Let him then lay his right hand and the Knife upon the Pentacles or Medals, constructed of, and described upon virgin paper, which are fastened to or sewn upon his breast, and let him repeat the following Conjuration upon his knees:--

Conjuration

Book One

O Lord, hear my prayer, and let my cry come unto Thee. O Lord God Almighty, Who has reigned before the beginning of the Ages, and Who by Thine Infinite Wisdom hast created the heavens, the earth, and the sea, and all that in them is, all that is visible, and all that is invisible by a single word; I praise Thee, I bless Thee, I adore Thee, I glorify Thee, and I pray Thee now at the present time to be merciful unto me, a miserable sinner, for I am the work of Thine hands. Save me, and direct me by Thy Holy Name, Thou to Whom nothing is difficult, nothing is impossible; and deliver me from the night of mine ignorance, and enable me to go forth therefrom. Enlighten me with a spark of Thine Infinite Wisdom. Take away from my senses the desire of covetousness, and the iniquity of mine idle words. Give unto me, Thy servant, a wise understanding) penetrating and subtle heart, to acquire and comprehend all Sciences and Arts; give unto me capacity to hear, and strength of memory to retain them, so that I may be able to accomplish my desires, and understand and learn all difficult and desirable Sciences; and also that I may be able to comprehend the hidden secrets of the Holy Writings. Give me the virtue to conceive them, so that I may be able to bring forth and pronounce my words with patience and humility, for the instruction of others, as Thou hast ordered me.

O God, the Father, All Powerful and All Merciful, Who hast created all things, Who knowest and conceivest them universally, and to Whom nothing is hidden, nothing is impossible; I entreat Thy Grace for me and for Thy servants, because Thou seest and knowest well that we perform not this work to tempt Thy Strength and Thy Power as if in doubt thereof, but rather that we may know and understand the truth of all hidden things. I beseech Thee to have the kindness to be favourable unto us; by Thy Splendour, Thy Magnificence, and Thy Holiness, and by Thy Holy, Terrible, and Ineffable Name IAH, at which the whole world dothtremble, and by the Fear with which all creatures obey Thee. Grant, O Lord, that we may become responsive unto Thy Grace, so that through it we may have a full confidence in and knowledge of Thee, and that the Spirits may discover themselves here in our presence, and that those which are gentle and peaceable may come unto us, so that they may be obedient unto Thy commands, through Thee, O Most Holy ADONAI, Whose Kingdom is an everlasting Kingdom, and Whose Empire endureth unto the Ages of the Ages. Amen.

After having said all these words devoutly, let the Master arise, and place his hands upon the Pentacles, and let one of the Companions hold the Book open before the Master, who, raising his eyes to heaven, and turning unto the Four Quarters of the Universe, shall say:--

O Lord, be Thou unto me a Tower of Strength against the appearance and assaults of the Evil Spirits.

After this, turning towards the Four Quarters of the Universe, he shall say the following words:--

These be the Symbols and the Names of the Creator, which can bring Terror and Fear unto you. Obey me then, by the power of these Holy Names, and by these Mysterious Symbols of the Secret of Secrets.

The which being said and done, thou shalt see them draw near and approach from all parts. But if they be hindered, detained, or occupied in some way, and so that they cannot come, or if they are unwilling to come, then, the Suffumigations and Censings being performed anew, and (the Disciples) having anew, by especial order, touched their Swords, and the Master having encouraged his Disciples, he shall reform the Circle with the Knife of Art, and, raising the said Knife towards the Sky, he shall as it were strike the air therewith. After this he shall lay his hand upon the Pentacles, and having bent his knees before the Most High, he shall repeat with humility the following Confession; the which his Disciples shall also do, and they shall recite it in a low and humble voice, so that they can scarcely be heard.[60]

---

[60] So as not to interfere with the direction of the Will-currents of the Master.

BOOK ONE

CHAPTER IV

The Confession to be Made by the Exorcist

THE CONFESION

O LORD of Heaven and of Earth, before Thee do I confess my sins, and lament them, cast down and humbled in Thy presence. For I have sinned before Thee by pride, avarice, and boundless desire of honours and riches; by idleness, gluttony, greed, debauchery, and drunkenness; because I have offended Thee by all kinds of sins of the flesh, adulteries, and pollutions, which I have committed myself, and consented that others should commit; by sacrilege, thefts, rapine, violation, and homicide; by the evil use I have made of my possessions, by my prodigality, by the sins which I have committed against Hope and Charity, by my evil advice, flatteries, bribes, and the ill distribution which I have made of the goods of which I have been possessed; by repulsing and maltreating the poor, in the distribution which I have made of the goods committed to my charge, by afflicting those over whom I have been set in authority, by not visiting the prisoners, by depriving the dead of burial, by not receiving the poor, by neither feeding the hungry nor giving drink to the thirsty, by never keeping the Sabbath and the other feasts, by not living chastely and piously on those days, by the easy consent which I have given to those who incited me to evil deeds, by injuring instead of aiding those who demanded help from me, by refusing to give ear unto the cry of the poor, by not respecting the aged, by not keeping my word, by disobedience to my parents, by ingratitude towards those from whom I have received kindness, by indulgence in sensual pleasures, by irreverent behaviour in the Temple of God, by unseemly gestures thereat, by entering therein without reverence, by vain and unprofitable discourse when there, by despising the sacred vessels of the temple, by turning the holy Ceremonies into ridicule, by touching and eating the sacred bread with impure lips and with profane hands, and by the neglect of my prayers and adorations.

I detest also the crimes which I have committed by evil thoughts, vain and impure meditations, false suspicions, and rash judgments; by the evil consent which I have readily given unto the advice of the wicked, by lust of impure and sensual pleasures; by my idle words, my lies, and my deceit; by my false vows in various ways; and by my continual slander and calumny.

I detest also the crimes which I have committed within; the treachery and discord which I have incited; my curiosity, greed, false speaking, violence, malediction, murmurs, blasphemies, vain words, insults, dissimulations; my sins against God by the transgression of the ten commandments, by neglect of my duties and obligations, and by want of love towards God and towards my neighbour.

Furthermore, I hate the sins which I have committed in all my senses, by sight, by hearing, by taste, by smell, and by touch, in every way that human weakness can offend the Creator; by my carnal thoughts, deeds, and meditations.

In which I humbly confess that I have sinned, and recognise myself as being in the sight of God the most criminal of all men.

I accuse myself before Thee, O God, and I adore Thee with all humility. O ye, Holy Angels, and ye, Children of God, in your presence I publish my sins, so that mine Enemy may have no advantage over me, and may not be able to reproach me at the last day; that he may not be able to say that I have concealed my sins, and that 1 be not then accused in the presence of the Lord; but, on the contrary, that on my account there may be joy in Heaven, as over the just who have confessed their sins in thy presence.

O Most Mighty and All Powerful Father, grant through Thine unbounded Mercy that I may both see and know all the Spirits which I invoke, so that by their means I may see my will and desire accomplished, by Thy Sovereign grandeur, and by Thine Ineffable and Eternal Glory, Thou Who art and Who wilt be for ever the Pure and Ineffable Father of All.

The Confession having been finished with great humility, and with the inward feeling of the heart, the Master will recite the following prayer:--

Prayer

O Lord All Powerful, Eternal God and Father of all Creatures, shed upon me the Divine Influence of Thy Mercy, for I am Thy Creature. I beseech Thee to defend me from mine Enemies, and to confirm in me true and steadfast faith.

O Lord, I commit my Body and my Soul unto Thee, seeing I put my trust in none beside Thee; it is on Thee alone that I rely; O Lord my God aid me; O Lord hear me in the day and hour wherein I shall invoke Thee. I pray Thee by Thy Mercy not to put me in oblivion, nor to remove me from Thee. O Lord be Thou my succour, Thou Who art the God of my salvation. O Lord make me a new heart according unto Thy loving Kindness. These, O Lord, are the gifts which I await from Thee, O my God and my Master, Thou Who livest and reignest unto the Ages of the Ages. Amen.

O Lord God the All Powerful One, Who hast formed unto Thyself great and Ineffable Wisdom, and Co-eternal with Thyself before the countless Ages; Thou Who in the Birth of Time hast created the Heavens, and the Earth, the Sea, and things that they contain; Thou Who hast vivified all things by the Breath of Thy Mouth, I praise Thee, I bless Thee, I adore Thee, and I glorify Thee. Be Thou propitious unto me who am but a miserable sinner, and despise me not; save me and succour me) even me the work of Thine hands. I conjure and entreat Thee by Thy Holy Name to banish from my

Spirit the darkness of Ignorance, and to enlighten me with the Fire of Thy Wisdom; take away from me all evil desires, and let not my speech be as that of the foolish. O Thou, God the Living One, Whose Glory, Honour, and Kingdom shall extend unto the Ages of the Ages. Amen.

Chapter V

Prayers and Conjurations

Prayer

O LORD God, Holy Father, Almighty and Merciful One, Who hast created all things, Who knowest all things and can do all things, from Whom nothing is hidden, to Whom nothing is impossible; Thou Who knowest that we perform not these ceremonies to tempt Thy power, but that we may penetrate into the knowledge of hidden things; we pray Thee by Thy Sacred Mercy to cause and to permit that we may arrive at this understanding of secret things, of whatever nature they may be, by Thine aid, O Most Holy ADONAI, Whose Kingdom and Power shall have no end unto the Ages of the Ages. Amen.

The Prayer being finished, let the Exorcist lay his hand upon the Pentacles, while one of the Disciples shall hold open before him the Book wherein are written the prayers and conjurations proper for conquering, subduing, and reproving the Spirits. Then the Master, turning towards each Quarter of the Earth, and raising his eyes to Heaven, shall say:

O Lord, be Thou unto me a strong tower of refuge, from the sight and assaults of the Evil Spirits.

After which let him turn again towards the Four Quarters of the Earth, and towards each let him utter the following words:

Behold the Symbols and Names of the Creator, which give unto ye for ever Terror and Fear. Obey then, by the virtue of these Holy Names, and by these Mysteries of Mysteries.

After this he shall see the Spirits come from every side. But in case they are occupied in some other place, or that they cannot come, or that they are unwilling to come: then let him commence afresh to invoke them after the following manner, and let the Exorcist be assured that even were they bound with chains of iron, and with fire, they could not refrain from coming to accomplish his will.

Book One

The Conjuration[61]

O ye Spirits, ye I conjure by the Power, Wisdom, and Virtue of the Spirit of God, by the uncreate Divine Knowledge, by the vast Mercy of God, by the Strength of God, by the Greatness of God, by the Unity of God; and by the Holy Name of God EHEIEH, which is the root, trunk, source, and origin of all the other Divine Names, whence they all draw their life and their virtue, which Adam having invoked, he acquired the knowledge of all created things.

I conjure ye by the Indivisible Name IOD, which marketh and expresseth the Simplicity and the Unity of the Nature Divine, which Abel having invoked, he deserved[62] to escape from the hands of Cain his brother.

I conjure ye by the Name TETRAGRAMMATON ELOHIM, which expresseth and signifieth the Grandeur of so lofty a Majesty, that Noah having pronounced it, saved himself, and protected himself with his whole household from the Waters of the Deluge.

I conjure ye by the Name of God EL Strong and Wonderful, which denoteth the Mercy and Goodness of His Majesty Divine, which Abraham having invoked, he was found worthy to come forth from the Ur of the Chaldeans.

I conjure ye by the most powerful Name of ELOHIM GIBOR, which showeth forth the Strength of God, of a God All Powerful, Who punisheth the crimes of the wicked, Who seeketh out and chastiseth the iniquities of the fathers upon the children unto the third and fourth generation; which Isaac having invoked, he was found worthy to escape from the Sword of Abraham his father.

I conjure ye and I exorcise ye by the most holy Name of ELOAH VA-DAATH, which Jacob invoked when in great trouble, and was found worthy to bear the Name of Israel, which signifieth Vanquisher of God and he was delivered from the fury of Esau his brother.

I conjure ye by the most potent Name of EL[63] ADONAI TZABAOTH, which is the God of Armies, ruling in the Heavens, which Joseph invoked, and was found worthy to escape from the hands of his Brethren.

---

[61] There is an Invocation bearing the title of 'The Qabalistical Invocation of Solomon,' given by Eliphas Lévi, which differs in many points from the one given above, though resembling it in some particulars. Lévi's is more evidently constructed on the plan indicated in the 'Siphra Dtzenioutha,' C. III.; Annotation §5, sub §8, 9; while the one above more follows that laid down, ibid. §5, sub §3. I see no reason to suppose that Lévi's is unauthentic. It will be noted by the Qabalistical reader, that the above Conjuration rehearses the Divine Names attached to the Ten Sephiroth.

[62] In the French, 'merita d'échapper.'

[63] More usually the Name YETRAGAMMATON TZABAOTR is attributed to the Seventh Sephira.

I conjure ye by the most potent name of ELOHIM TZABAOTH, which expresscth piety, mercy, splendour, and knowledge of God, which Moses invoked, and he was found worthy to deliver the People Israel from Egypt, and from the servitude of Pharaoh.

I conjure ye by the most potent Name of SHADDAI, which signifieth doing good unto all; which Moses invoked, and having struck the Sea, it divided into two parts in the midst, on the right hand and on the left. I conjure ye by the most holy Name of EL[64] CHAT, which is that of the Living God, through the virtue of which alliance with us, and redemption for us have been made; which Moses invoked and all the waters returned to their prior state and enveloped the Egyptians, so that not one of them escaped to carry the news into the Land of Mizraim.

Lastly, I conjure ye all, ye rebellious Spirits, by the most holy Name of God ADONAI MELEKH, which Joshua invoked, and stayed the course of the Sun in his presence, through the virtue of Methratton,[65] its principal Image; and by the troops of Angels who cease not to cry day and night, QADOSCH, QADOSCH, QADOSCH, ADONAI ELOHIM TZABAOTH (that is, Holy, Holy, Holy, Lord God of Hosts, Heaven and Earth are full of Thy Glory); and by the Ten Angels who preside over the Ten Sephiroth, by whom God communicateth and extendeth His influence over lower things, which are KETHER, CHOKMAH, BINAH, GEDULAH, GEBURAH, TIPHERETH, NETZACH, HOD, YESOD, and MALKUTH.

I conjure ye anew, O Spirits, by all the Names of God, and by all His marvellous work; by the heavens; by the earth; by the sea; by the depth of the Abyss, and by that firmament which the very Spirit of God hath moved; by the sun and by the stars; by the waters and by the seas, and all which they contain; by the winds, the whirlwinds, and the tempests; by the virtue of all herbs, plants, and stones; by all which is in the heavens, upon the earth, and in all the Abysses of the Shades.

I conjure ye anew, and I powerfully urge ye, O Demons, in whatsoever part of the world ye may be, so that ye shall be unable to remain in air, fire, water, earth, or in any part of the universe, or in any pleasant place which may attract ye; but that ye come promptly to accomplish our desire, and all things that we demand from your obedience.

I conjure ye anew by the two Tables of the Law, by the five books of Moses, by the Seven Burning Lamps on the Candlestick of Gold before the face of the Throne of the Majesty of God, and by the Holy of Holies wherein the KOHEN HA-GADUL was alone permitted to enter, that is to say, the

---

[64] Both this Name and 'Shaddai' are attributed to the Ninth Sephira, and I have therefore put the two invocations in the same paragraph.

[65] The Archangel, who is called also the Prince of Countenances.

High-Priest.

I conjure ye by Him Who hath made the heavens and the earth, and Who hath measured those heavens in the hollow of His hand, and enclosed the earth with three of His fingers, Who is seated upon the Kerubim and upon the Seraphim; and by the Kerubim, which is called the Kerub, which God constituted and placed to guard the Tree of Life, armed with a flaming sword, after that Man had been driven out of Paradise.

I conjure ye anew, Apostates from God, by Him Who alone hath performed great wonders; by the Heavenly Jerusalem; and by the Most Holy Name of God in Four Letters, and by Him Who enlighteneth all things and shineth upon all things by his Venerable and Ineffable Name, EHEIEH ASHER EHEIEH; that ye come immediately to execute our desire, whatever it may be.

I conjure ye, and I command ye absolutely, O Demons, in whatsoever part of the Universe ye may be, by the virtue of all these Holy Names:--

ADONAI,[66] YAH, HOA, EL, ELOHA, ELOHINU, ELOHIM, EHEIEH, MARON, KAPHU, ESCH, INNON, AVEN, AGLA, HAZOR, EMETH, YAII, ARARITHA, YOVA, HA-KABIR, MESSIACH, IONAH, MAL-KA, EREL, KUZU, MATZPATZ, EL SHADDAI; and by all the Holy Names of God which have been written with blood in the sign of an eternal alliance.

I conjure ye anew by these other Names of God, Most Holy and unknown, by the virtue of which Names ye tremble every day:--BARUC,[67] BACURABON, PATACEL, ALCHEEGHEL, AQUACHAI, HOMORION, EHEIEH, ABBATON, CHEVON, CEBON, OYZROYMAS, CHAI, EHEIEH, ALBAMACHI, ORTAGU, NALE, ABELECH (or HELECH), YEZE (or SECHEZZE); that ye come quickly and without any delay into our presence from every quarter and every climate of the world wherein ye may be, to execute all that we shall command ye in the Great Name of God.

---

[66] I have made these Names as correct as possible; as in all the original MSS. the Hebrew is much mutilated. These names are some of them ordinary titles of God; others Magical and Qabalistical names compounded from the initials of sentences, etc.; and other permutations of other names.

[67] I give these Names as they stand, they do not all appear to be Hebrew; some of them suggest the style of the barbarous names in the Græco-Egyptian Magical Papyri.

Chapter VI

Stronger and More Potent Conjuration

IF they then immediately appear, it is well; if not, let the Master uncover the consecrated Pentacles which he should have made to constrain and command the Spirits, and which he should wear fastened round his neck, holding the Medals (or Pentacles) in his left hand, and the consecrated Knife in his right; and encouraging his Companions, he shall say with a loud voice:--

Address

Here be the Symbols of Secret things, the standards, the ensigns, and the banners, of God the Conqueror; and the arms of the Almighty One, to compel the Aerial Potencies. I command ye absolutely by their power and virtue that ye come near unto us, into our presence, from whatsoever part of the world ye may be in, and that ye delay not to obey us in all things wherein we shall command ye by the virtue of God the Mighty One. Come ye promptly, and delay not to appear, and answer us with humility.

If they appear at this time, show them the Pentacles, and receive them with kindness, gentleness, and courtesy; reason and speak with them, question them, and ask from them all things which thou hast proposed to demand.

But if, on the contrary, they do not yet make their appearance, holding the consecrated Knife in the right hand, and the Pentacles being uncovered by the removal of their consecrated covering, strike and beat the air with the Knife as if wishing to commence a combat, comfort and exhort thy Companions, and then in a loud and stern voice repeat the following Conjuration:--

Conjuration[68]

Here again I conjure ye and most urgently command ye; I force, constrain, and exhort ye to the utmost, by the most mighty and powerful Name of God EL, strong and wonderful, and by God the just and Upright, I exorcise ye and command ye that ye in no way delay, but that ye come immediately and upon the instant hither before us, without noise, deformity, or hideousness, but with all manner of gentleness and mildness.

I exorcise ye anew, and powerfully conjure ye, commanding ye with

---

[68] This Conjuration is almost identical with one given in the 'Lemegeton,' or Lesser Key, a different work, also attributed to Solomon.

strength and violence by Him Who spake and it was done; and by all these names: EL SHADDAI, ELOHIM, ELOHI, TZABAOTH, ELIM, ASHER EHEIEH, YAH, TETRAGRAMMATON, SHADDAI, which signify God the High and Almighty, the God of Israel, through Whom undertaking all our operations we shall prosper in all the works of our hands, seeing that the Lord is now, always, and for ever with us, in our heart and in our lips; and by His Holy Names, and by the virtue of the Sovereign God, we shall accomplish all our work.

Come ye at once without any hideousness or deformity before us, come ye without monstrous appearance, in a gracious form or figure. Come ye, for we exorcise ye with the utmost vehemence by the Name of IAH and ON, which Adam spake and heard; by the Name EL, which Noah heard, and saved himself with all his family from the Deluge; by the Name IOD, which Noah heard, and knew God the Almighty One; by the Name AGLA which Jacob heard, and saw the Ladder which touched Heaven, and the Angels who ascended and descended upon it, whence he called that place the House of God and the Gate of Heaven; and by the Name ELOHIM, and in the Name ELOHIM, which Moses named, invoked, and heard in Horeb the Mount of God, and he was found worthy to hear Him speak from the Burning Bush; and by the Name AIN SOPH, which Aaron heard, and was at once made eloquent, wise, and learned; and by the Name TZABAOTH, which Moses named and invoked, and all the ponds and rivers were covered with blood throughout the land of Egypt;[69] and by the Name IOD, which Moses named and invoked, and striking upon the dust of the earth both men and beasts were struck with disease;[70] and by the Name, and in the Name PRIMEUMATON which Moses named and invoked, and there fell a great and severe hail throughout all the land of Egypt, destroying the vines, the trees, and the woods which were in that country; and by the Name IAPHAR, which Moses heard and invoked, and immediately a great pestilence began to appear through all the land of Egypt, striking and slaying the asses, the oxen, and the sheep of the Egyptians, so that they all died; and by the Name ABADDON which Moses invoked and sprinkled the dust towards heaven, and immediately there fell so great rain upon the men, cattle, and flocks, that they all died throughout the land of Egypt; and by the Name ELION which Moses invoked, and there fell so great hail as had never been seen from the beginning of the world unto that time, so that all men, and herds, and everything that was in the fields perished and died throughout all the land of Egypt. And by the Name ADONAI, which Moses having invoked, there came so great a quantity of locusts which appeared in the land of Egypt, that

---

[69] Some MSS. add, 'et furent purifiés.'
[70] Some MSS. substitute, 'les hommes furent reduits en cendre, comme aussi les bœufs, betail, et troupeaux des Egyptiens.'

they devoured and swallowed up all that the hail had spared; and by the Name of PATHEON,[71] which having invoked, there arose so thick, so awful, and so terrible darkness throughout the land of Egypt, during the space of three days and three nights, that almost all who were left alive died; and by the Name YESOD, and in the Name YESOD, which Moses invoked, and at midnight all the first-born, both of men and of animals, died; and by the Name Of YESHIMON, which Moses named and invoked, and the Red Sea divided itself and separated in two; and by the Name HESION, which Moses invoked, and all the army of Pharaoh was drowned in the waters; and by the Name ANABONA, which Moses having heard upon Mount Sinai, he was found worthy to receive and obtain the tables of stone written with the finger of God the Creator; and by the Name ERYGION, which Joshua having invoked when he fought against the Moabites, he defeated them and gained the victory; and by the Name HOA, and in the Name HOA, which David invoked, and he was delivered from the hand of Goliath; and by the Name YOD, which Solomon having named and invoked, he was found worthy to ask for and to obtain in sleep the Ineffable Wisdom of God; and by the Name YIAI, which Solomon having named and invoked, he was found worthy to have power over all the Demons, Potencies, Powers, and Virtues of the Air.

By these, then, and by all the other Names of God Almighty, Holy, Living, and True, we powerfully command ye, ye who by your own sin have been cast down from the Empyreal Heaven, and from before His Throne; by Him Who hath cast ye down unto the most profound of the Abysses of Hell, we command ye boldly and resolutely; and by that terrible Day of the Sovereign judgment of God, on which all the dry bones in the earth will arise to hear and listen unto the Word of God with their Body, and will present themselves before the face of God Almighty; and by that Last Fire which shall consume all things; by the (Crystal) Sea which is known unto us, which is before the Face of God; by the indicible and ineffable virtue, force, and power of the Creator Himself, by His Almighty power, and by the Light and Flame which emanate from His Countenance, and which are before His Face; by the Angelical Powers which are in the Heavens, and by the most great Wisdom of Almighty God; by the Seal of David, by the Ring and Seal of Solomon, which was revealed unto him by the Most High and Sovereign Creator; and by the Nine Medals or Pentacles, which we have among our Symbols, which proceed and come from Heaven, and are among the Mysteries of Mysteries or Secrets of Secrets, which you can also behold in my hand, consecrated and exorcised with the due and requisite Ceremonies. By these, then, and by all the Secrets which the Almighty encloseth in the Treasures of the Sovereign and Highest Wisdom, by His hand, and by His marvellous power; I conjure,

---

[71] This is often written PATHTUMON in similar Conjurations, but the MSS. before me agree in giving this form.

force, and exorcise ye that ye come without delay to perform in our presence that which we shall command ye.

I conjure ye anew by that most Holy Name which the whole Universe fears, respects, and reveres, which is written by these letters and characters, IOD, HE, VAU, HE; and by the last and terrible judgment; by the Seat of BALDACHIA;[72] and by this Holy Name, YIAI, which Moses invoked, and there followed that great judgment of God, when Dathan and Abiram were swallowed up in the centre of the earth. Otherwise, if ye contravene and resist us by your disobedience unto the virtue and power of this Name YIAI, we curse ye even unto the Depth of the Great Abyss, into the which we shall cast, hurl, and bind ye, if ye show yourselves rebellious against the Secret of Secrets, and against the Mystery of Mysteries. AMEN, AMEN. FIAT, FIAT.

This Conjuration thou shalt say and perform, turning thyself unto the East, and if they appear not, thou shalt repeat it unto the Spirits, turning unto the South, the West, and the North, in succession, when thou wilt have repeated it four times. And if they appear not even then, thou shalt make the Sign of TAU[73] upon the foreheads of thy companions, and thou shalt say:--

Conjuration

Behold anew the Symbol and the Name of a Sovereign and Conquering God, through which all the Universe fears, trembles, and shudders, and through the most mysterious words of the Secret Mysteries and by their Virtue, Strength, and Power.

I conjure ye anew, I constrain and command ye with the utmost vehemence and power, by that most potent and powerful Name of God, EL, strong and wonderful, by Him Who spake and it was done; and by the Name IAH, which Moses heard, and spoke with God; and by the Name AGLA, which Joseph invoked, and was delivered out of the hands of his brethren; and by the Name VAU, which Abraham heard, and knew God the Almighty One; and by the Name of Four Letters, TETRAGRAMMATON, which Joshua named and invoked, and he was rendered worthy and found deserving to lead the Army of Israel into the Promised Land; and by the Name ANABONA, by which God formed Man and the whole Universe; and by the Name ARPHETON,[74] and in the Name ARPHETON, by which the Angels who are destined to that end will summon the Universe, in visible body and form, and will assemble (all people) together by the sound of the

---

[72] Sometimes, but as I think erroneously, written Bas-dathea. I imagine the word to mean 'Lord of Life.'

[73] Or the Cross.

[74] Also written Hipeton; and I believe sometimes replaced by Anapheneton or Anaphaxeton.

Trumpet at that terrible and awful Day of judgment, when the memory of the wicked and ungodly shall perish; and by the Name ADONAI, by which God will judge all human flesh, at Whose voice all men, both good and evil, will rise again, and all men and Angels will assemble in the air before the Lord, Who will judge and condemn the wicked; and by the Name ONEIPHETON,[75] by which God will summon the dead, and raise them up again unto life; and by the Name ELOHIM, and in the Name ELOHIM, by which God will disturb and excite tempests throughout all the seas, so that they will cast out the fish therefrom, and in one day the third part of men about the sea and the rivers shall die; and by the Name ELOHI,[76] and in the Name ELOHI, by which God will dry up the sea and the rivers, so that men can go on foot through their channels; and by the Name ON, and in the Name ON, by which God will restore and replace the sea, the rivers, the streams, and the brooks, in their previous state; and by the Name MESSIACH,[77] and in the Name MESSIACH, by which God will make all animals combat together, so that they shall die in a single day; and by the Name ARIEL, by which God will destroy in a single day all buildings, so that there shall not be left one stone upon another; and by the Name IAHT,[78] by which God will cast one stone upon another, so that all people and nations will fly from the sea-shore, and will say unto them cover us and hide us; and by the Name EMANUEL, by which God will perform wonders, and the winged creatures and birds of the air shall contend with one another; and by the Name ANAEL,[79] and in the Name ANAEL, by which God will cast down the mountains and fill up the valleys, so that the surface of the earth shall be level in all parts; and by the Name ZEDEREZA,[80] and in the Name ZEDEREZA, by which God will cause the Sun and Moon to be darkened, and the Stars of heaven to fall; and by the Name SEPHERIEL,[81] by which God will come to Universal judgment, like a Prince newly crowned entering in triumph into his capital city, girded with a zone of gold, and preceded by Angels, and at His aspect all climes and parts of the Universe shall be troubled

---

[75] This word is given variously in the MSS., as Oneypheon, Onayepheton, and Donecepheron, etc.

[76] Or Elia.

[77] What is said here refers symbolically to the rooting out of the Evil Spirits, and Shells, from the Universe by King Messiach, which is spoken of in the Qabalah. The Qabalah sometimes expresses the Evil Spirits by the words animals, or beasts, and creeping things.

[78] The oldest MSS. gives the above form, in the others it is changed into Iaphat, Taphat, and even Japhet. It is probably a corruption of Achad Unity.

[79] This is also the name of the Angel of Venus.

[80] So written in the oldest MS., the others give it as Zedeesia, Zedeezia, and Zedezias.

[81] Meaning 'emanating from God.' It is corrupted into Sephosiel, etc., in the MSS.

and astonished, and a fire shall go forth before Him, and flames and storms shall surround Him; and by the Name Tau,[82] by which God brought the Deluge, and the waters prevailed above the mountains, and fifteen cubits above their summits; and by the Name RUACHIAH,[83] by which God having purged the Ages, He will make His Holy Spirit to descend upon the Universe, and will cast ye, ye rebellious Spirits, and unclean beings, into the Depths of the Lake of the Abyss, in misery, filth, and mire, and will place ye in impure and foul dungeons bound with eternal chains of fire.

By these Names then, and by all the other Holy Names of God before Whom no man can stand and live, and which Names the armies of the Demons fear, tremble at, and shudder; we conjure ye, we potently exorcise and command ye, conjuring ye in addition by the terrible and tremendous PATHS[84] of GOD and by His Holy habitation wherein He reigneth and commandeth unto the eternal Ages. Amen.

By the virtue of all these aforesaid, we command ye that ye remain not in any place wherein ye are, but to come hither promptly without delay to do that which we shall enjoin ye. But if ye be still contumacious, we, by the Authority of a Sovereign and Potent God, deprive ye of all quality, condition, degree, and place which ye now enjoy, and precipitate ye into and relegate ye unto the Kingdom of Fire and of Sulphur, to be there eternally tormented. Come ye then from all parts of the earth, wheresoever ye may be, and behold the Symbols and Names of that Triumphant Sovereign Whom all creatures obey, otherwise we shall bind ye and conduct ye in spite of yourselves, into our presence bound with chains of fire, because those effects which proceed and issue from our Science and operation, are ardent with a fire which shall consume and burn ye eternally, for by these the whole Universe trembleth, the earth is moved, the stones thereof rush together, all creatures obey, and the rebellious Spirits are tormented by the power of the Sovereign Creator.

Then it is certain that they will come, even if they be bound with chains of fire, unless prevented by affairs of the very greatest importance, but in this latter case they will send ambassadors and messengers by whom thou shalt easily and surely learn what occupies the Spirits and what they are about. But if they appear not yet in answer to the above Conjuration, and are still disobedient, then let the Master of the Art or Exorciser arise and exhort his Companions to be of good cheer and not to despair of the ultimate success of the operation; let him strike the air with the Consecrated Knife towards the Four Quarters of the Universe; and then let him kneel in the midst of the

---

[82] Iaha, in 10862 Add. MSS.
[83] Meaning Spirit of Iah.
[84] That is, the hidden and occult grades and links of emanation in the Sephiroth. The later MSS. have put, by a mistake, voix for voies; the oldest Latin MS. gives Semitis.

Circle, and the Companions also in their several places, and let them say consecutively with him in a low voice, turning in the direction of the East, the following

ADDRESS TO THE ANGELS

I conjure and pray ye, O ye Angels of God, and ye Celestial Spirits, to come unto mine aid; come and behold the Signs of Heaven, and be my witness before the Sovereign Lord, of the disobedience of these evil and fallen Spirits who were at one time your companions.

This being done, let the Master arise, and constrain and force them by a stronger conjuration, in manner following.

Book One

Chapter VII

An Extremely Powerful Conjuration

BEHOLD us again prepared to conjure ye by the Names and Symbols of God, wherewith we are fortified, and by the virtue of the Highest One. We command ye and potently ordain ye by the most strong and powerful Names of God, Who is worthy of all praise, admiration, honour, glory, veneration, and fear, that ye delay not longer, but that ye appear before us without any tumult or disturbance, but, on the contrary, with great respect and courtesy, in a beautiful and human form.

If they then appear, let them see the Pentacles, and say:

Obey ye, Obey ye, behold the Symbols and Names of the Creator; be ye gentle and peaceable, and obey in all things that we shall command ye.

They will then immediately talk with thee, as a friend speaketh unto a friend. Ask of them all that thou desirest, with constancy, firmness, and assurance, and they will obey thee.

But if they appear not yet, let not the Master on that account lose his courage, for there is nothing in the world stronger and of greater force to overawe the Spirits than constancy. Let him, however, re-examine and reform the Circle, and let him take up a little dust of the earth, which he shall cast towards the Four Quarters of the Universe; and having placed his Knife upon the ground, let him say on his knees, turning towards the direction of the North:

In the Name of ADONAI ELOHIM TZABAOTH SHADDAI, Lord God of Armies Almighty, may we successfully perform the works of our hands, and may the Lord be present with us in our heart and in our lips.

These words having been said kneeling upon the earth, let the Master shortly after arise and open his arms wide as if wishing to embrace the air, and say:

Conjuration

By the Holy Names of God written in this Book, and by the other Holy and Ineffable Names which are written in the Book of Life, we conjure ye to come unto us promptly and without any delay, wherefore tarry not, but appear in a beautiful and agreeable form and figure, by these Holy Names: ADONAI, TZABAOTH, EL, ELOHI, ELOHIM, SHADDAI; and by EHEIEH, YOD HE VAU HE, which is the Great Name of God TETRAGRAMMATON written with Four Letters, ANAPHODITON, and Ineffable; by the God of those Virtues and Potencies, Who dwelleth in the Heavens, Who rideth upon the Kerubim, Who moveth upon the Wings of the Wind, He Whose Power is in Heaven and in Earth, Who spake and it was done, Who commanded and the whole Universe was created; and by the Holy Names and in the Holy Names, IAH, IAH, IAH, ADONAI TZABAOTH; and by all the Names of God, the Living, and the True, I reiterate the Conjuration, and I conjure ye afresh ye Evil and rebellious Spirits, abiding in the Abysses of Darkness.

I conjure, I address, and I exorcise ye, that ye may approach unto and come before the Throne of God, the Living and the True, and before the Tribunal of the judgment of His Majesty, and before the Holy Angels of God to hear the sentence of your condemnation.

Come ye then by the Name and in the Name Of SHADDAI, which is that of God Almighty, strong, powerful, admirable, exalted, pure, clean, glorified, virtuous, great, just, terrible, and holy; and by the Name and in the Name of EL, IAH, IAH, IAH, Who hath formed and created the world by the Breath of His Mouth, Who supporteth it by His Power, Who ruleth and governeth it by His Wisdom, and Who hath cast ye for your pride into the Land of Darkness and into the Shadow of Death.

Therefore, by the Name of the Living God, Who hath formed the heavens above, and hath laid the foundations of the earth beneath, we command ye that, immediately and without any delay, ye come unto us from all places, valleys, mountains, hills, fields, seas, rivers, fountains, ponds, brooks, caverns, grottos, cities, towns, villages, markets, fairs, habitations, baths, courtyards, gardens, vineyards, plantations, reservoirs, cisterns, and from every corner of the terrestrial earth where ye may happen to be in your assemblies, so that ye may execute and accomplish our demands with all mildness and courtesy; by that Ineffable Name which Moses heard and invoked, which he received from God from the midst of the Burning Bush, we conjure ye to obey our commands, and to come unto us promptly with all gentleness of manner.

Again we command ye with vehemence, and we exorcise ye with constancy, that ye and all your comrades come unto us in an agreeable and gracious manner like the breeze, to accomplish successively our various commands and desires. Come ye, then, by the virtue of these Names by the which we exorcise ye; ANAI, ÆCHHAD, TRANSIN, EMETH, CHAIA, IONA, PROFA, TITACHE, BEN ANI, BRIAH, THEIT; all which names are written in Heaven in the characters of Malachim,[85] that is to say, the tongue of the Angels.

We then, by the just judgment of God, by the Ineffable and Admirable Virtue of God, just, living, and true, we call ye with power, we force and

---

[85] The Mystic Alphabet known as the 'Writing of Malachim' is formed from the positions of the Stars in the heavens, by drawing imaginary lines from one star to another so as to obtain the shapes of the characters of this Alphabet.

Book One

exorcise ye by and in the admirable Name which was written on the Tables of Stone which God gave upon Mount Sinai; and by and in the wonderful Name which Aaron the High Priest bare written upon his breast, by which also God created the World, the which name is AXINETON; and by the Living God Who is One throughout the Ages, whose dwelling is in the Ineffable Light, Whose Name is Wisdom, and Whose Spirit is Life, before Whom goeth forth Fire and Flame, Who hath from that Fire formed the firmament, the Stars and the Sun; and Who with that Fire will burn ye all for ever, as also all who shall contravene the Words of His Will.

Come ye, then, without delay, without noise, and without rage, before us, without any deformity or hideousness, to execute all our will; come ye from all places wherein ye are, from all mountains, valleys, streams, rivers, brooks, ponds, places, baths, synagogues; for God, strong and powerful, will chase ye and constrain ye, being glorious over all things; He will compel ye, both ye and the Prince of Darkness. Come ye, come ye, Angels of Darkness; come hither before this Circle without fear, terror, or deformity, to execute our commands, and be ye ready both to achieve and to complete all that we shall command ye.

Come ye, then, by the Crown of the Chief of your Emperors, and by the Sceptres of your power, and of SID, the Great Demon, your Master; by the Names and in the Names of the Holy Angels who have been created to be above you, long before the constitution of the world; and by the Names of the two Princes of the Universe, whose Names are IONIEL and SEFONIEL; by the rod of Moses, by the staff of Jacob; by the ring and seal of David, wherein are written the Names of Sovereign God; and by the Names of the Angels by which Solomon has linked and bound ye; and by the sacred bonds by which ANAEL hath environed and hath conquered the Spirit; and by the Name of the Angel who ruleth potently over the rest, and by the praise of all creatures who cry incessantly unto God, Who spake, and immediately all things, even the Ages, were made and formed; and by the Name HA-QADOSCH BERAKHA, which signifieth the Holy and Blessed One; and by the Ten Choirs of the Holy Angels, CHAIOTH HA-QADESH, AUPHANIM, ARALIM, CHASHMALIM, SERAPHIM, MALACHIM, ELOHIM, BENI ELOHIM, KERUBIM, and ISHIM; and by and in the Sacred name of Twelve Letters of which each Letter is the Name of an Angel, and the letters of the Name are ALEPH,[86] BETH, BETH, NUN, VAU,

---

[86] Which Letters I have, with much care, corrected, for in the MSS. the letters are jumbled together in hopeless confusion, Seym is written for Shin, Res for Beth, etc. The Name is Ab, Ben, Ve Ruach Ha-Qadesch, Father, Son, and Holy Spirit, There are two other Names of Twelve Letters frequently employed, HQDVSh BRVK HVA, Holy and Blessed be He; and ADNI HMLK NAMN, The Lord, the faithful King; besides other forms.

RESH, VAU, CHETH, HE, QOPH, DALETH, SHIN.

By these Names therefore, and by all the other Holy Names, we conjure ye and we exorcise ye by the Angel ZECHIEL; by the Angel DUCHIEL; by the Angel DONACHIEL and by the Great Angel METATRON, Who is the Prince of the Angels, and introduceth the Souls before the Face of God; and by the Angel SANGARIEL, by whom the portals of Heaven are guarded; and by the Angel KERUB, who was made the Guardian of the Terrestrial Paradise, with a Sword of Flame, after the expulsion of Adam our forefather; and by the Angel MICHAEL by whom ye were hurled down from the Height of the THRONE into the Depth of the Lake and of the Abyss, the same Name meaning, 'Who is like God upon Earth'; and by the Angel ANIEL; and by the Angel OPHIEL; and by the Angel BEDALIEL; wherefore, by these and by all the other Holy Names of the Angels, we powerfully conjure and exorcise ye, that ye come from all parts of the world immediately, and without any delay, to perform our will and demands, obeying us quickly and courteously, and that ye come by the Name and in the Name of ALEPH, DALETH, NUN, IOD, for we exorcise ye anew by the application of these Letters, by whose power burning fire is quenched, and the whole Universe trembleth.

We constrain ye yet again by the Seal of the Sun which is the Word of God; and by the Seal of the Moon and of the Stars we bind ye; and by the other Animals and Creatures which are in Heaven, by whose wings Heaven cleanseth itself, we force and attract ye imperiously to execute our will without failure. And we conjure, oblige, and terribly exorcise ye, that ye draw near unto us without delay and without fear, as far as is possible unto ye, here before this Circle, as supplicants gently and with discretion, to accomplish our will in all and through all. If ye come promptly and voluntarily, ye shall inhale our perfumes, and our suffumigations of pleasant odour, which will be both agreeable and delightful unto ye. Furthermore ye will see the Symbol of your Creator, and the Names of his Holy Angels, and we shall afterwards dismiss ye, and send ye hence with thanks. But if, on the contrary, ye come not quickly, and ye show yourselves self-opinionated, rebellious, and contumacious, we shall conjure ye again, and exorcise ye ceaselessly, and will repeat all the aforesaid words and Holy Names of God and of the Holy Angels; by the which Names we shall harass you, and if that be not sufficient we will add thereunto yet greater and more powerful ones, and we will thereunto again add other Names which ye have not yet heard from us, which are those of an Almighty God, and which will make ye tremble and quake with fear, both ye and your princes; by the which Names we conjure both you and them also, and we shall not desist from our work until the accomplishment of our will. But if perchance ye yet shall harden yourselves, and show yourselves self-opinionated, disobedient, rebellious, refractory, and contumacious, and if ye yet resist our powerful conjurations, we shall pronounce against you this warrant of arrest in the Name of God Almighty, and this definite sentence that ye shall fall into dangerous disease and leprosy; and that in sign of the Divine Vengeance ye shall all perish by a terrifying and horrible death, and that a fire shall consume and devour you on every side, and utterly crush you; and that by the Power of God, a flame shall go forth from His Mouth which shall burn ye up and reduce ye unto nothing in Hell. Wherefore delay ye not to come, for we shall not cease from these powerful conjurations until ye shall be- obliged to appear against your will.

Thus then, therefore, we anew conjure and exorcise ye by and in the Holy Name Of ON, which is interpreted and called God; by the Name and in the Name of EHEIEH, which is the true Name of God, 'I am He Who is'; by and in the Ineffable Name of Four Letters YOD HE VAU HE, the Knowledge and understanding of which is hidden even from the Angels; by the Name and in the Name of EL, which signifieth and denoteth the powerful and consuming fire which issueth from His Countenance, and which shall be your ruin and destruction; and by the Light of the Angels which is kindled and taken ineffably from that flame of Divine ardour.

By these then, and by other Most Holy Names which we pronounce against you from the bottom of our hearts, do we force and constrain ye, if ye be yet rebellious and disobedient. We conjure ye powerfully and strongly exorcise ye, that ye come unto us with joy and quickness, without fraud or deceit, in truth and not in error.

Come ye then, come ye, behold the Signs and the Names of your Creator, behold the Holy Pentacles by the virtue of which the Earth is moved, the trees thereof and the Abysses tremble. Come ye; come ye; come ye.

These things being thus done and performed, ye shall see the Spirits come from all sides in great haste with their Princes and Superiors; the Spirits of the First Order, like Soldiers, armed with spears, shields, and corslets; those of the Second Order like Barons, Princes, Dukes, Captains, and Generals of Armies. For the Third and last Order their King will appear, before whom go many players on instruments of music, accompanied by beautiful and melodious voices which sing in chorus.

Then the Exorcist, or Master of the Art, at the arrival of the King, whom he shall see crowned with a Diadem, should uncover the Holy Pentacles and Medals which he weareth upon his breast covered with a cloth of silk or of fine twined linen, and show them unto him, saying:--

Behold the Signs and Holy Names by and before whose power every knee should bow, of all that is in Heaven, upon Earth, or in Hell. Humble ye yourselves, therefore, under the Mighty hand of God.

Then will the King bow the knee before thee, and will say, 'What dost thou wish, and wherefore hast thou caused us to come hither from the Infernal Abodes?'

Then shall the Exorcist, or Master of Magical Art, with an assured air and a grave and imperious voice, order and command him to be tranquil, to keep the rest of his attendants peaceable, and to impose silence upon them.

Let him, also, renew his fumigations, and offer large quantities of Incense, which he should at once place upon the fire, in order to appease the Spirits as he hath promised them. He should then cover the Pentacles, and he will see wonderful things, which it is impossible to relate, touching worldly matters and all sciences.

This being finished, let the Master uncover the Pentacles, and demand all that he shall wish from the King of the Spirits, and if there are one or two Spirits only, it will be the same; and having obtained all his desire, he shall thus license them to depart:--

THE LICENSE TO DEPART

In the Name of ADONAI, the Eternal and Everlasting One, let each of you return unto his place; be there peace between us and you, and be ye ready to come when ye are called.

After this he should recite the first chapter of Genesis, 'Berashith Bara Elohim, In the beginning, etc.'

This being done, let them all in order quit the Circle, one after the other, the Master first. Furthermore let them bathe their faces with the exorcised water, as will be hereafter told, and then let them take their ordinary raiment and go about their business.

Take notice and observe carefully that this last conjuration is of so great importance and efficacy, that even if the Spirits were bound with chains of iron and fire, or shut up in some strong place, or retained by an oath, they could not even then delay to come. But supposing that they were being conjured in some other place or part of the Universe by some other Exorcist or Master of the Art, by the same conjuration; the Master should add to his conjuration that they should at least send him some Messengers, or some individual to declare unto him where they are, how employed, and the reason why they cannot come and obey him.

But if (which is almost impossible) they be even yet self-opinionated and disobedient, and unwilling to obey; in this case their names should be written on virgin paper, which he should soil and fill with mud, dust, or clay. Then he shall kindle a fire with dry rue, upon which he shall put powdered assafœtida, and other things of evil odour; after which let him put the aforesaid names, written on parchment or-virgin paper, upon the fire, saying:-

BOOK ONE

The Conjuration of Fire

I conjure thee, O Creature of Fire, by Him who removeth the Earth, and maketh it tremble, that thou burn and torment these Spirits, so that they may feel it intensely, and that they may be burned eternally by thee.

This being said, thou shalt cast the aforesaid paper into the fire, saying:--

The Curse

Be ye accursed, damned, and eternally reproved; and be ye tormented with perpetual pain, so that ye may find no repose by night nor by day, nor for a single moment of time, if ye obey not immediately the command of Him Who maketh the Universe to tremble; by these Names, and in virtue of these Names, the which being named and invoked all creatures obey and tremble with fear and terror, these Names which can turn aside lightning and thunder; and which will utterly make you to perish, destroy, and banish you. These Names then are Aleph, Beth, Gimel, Daleth, He, Vau, Zayin, Cheth, Teth, Yod, Kaph, Lamed, Mem, Nun, Samekh, Ayin, Pe, Tzaddi, Qoph, Resh, Shin, Tau.[87]

By these secret Names, therefore, and by these signs which are full of Mysteries, we curse ye, and in virtue of the power of the Three Principles, Aleph,[88] Mem, Shin, we deprive ye of all office and dignity which ye may have enjoyed up till now; and by their virtue and power we relegate you into a lake of sulphur and of flame, and unto the deepest depths of the Abyss, that ye may burn therein eternally for ever.

Then will they assuredly come without any delay, and in great haste, crying: ' O Our Lord and Prince, deliver us out of this suffering.'

All this time thou shouldest have near thee ready an exorcised pen, paper, and ink, as will be described hereinafter. Write their Names afresh, and kindle fresh fire, whereon thou shalt put gum benjamin, olybdanum, and storax to make therewith a fumigation; with these odours thou shalt afresh perfume the aforesaid paper with the Names; but thou shouldest have these names ready prepared beforehand. Then show them the Holy Pentacles, and ask of them what thou wilt, and thou shalt obtain it; and having gained thy purpose, send away the Spirits, saying:--

---

[87] Which are the Names of the Letters of the Hebrew Alphabet, to each of which a special mystic meaning and power is attached, besides its ordinary application.
[88] The Literal Symbols of Air, Water, and Fire; which are called by the Sepher Yetzirah the Three Mother Letters.

The License to Depart

By the virtue of these Pentacles, and because ye have been obedient, and have obeyed the commandments of the Creator, feel and inhale this grateful odour, and afterwards depart ye unto your abodes and retreats; be there peace between us and you; be ye ever ready to come when ye shall be cited and called; and may the blessing of God, as far as ye are capable of receiving it, be upon you, provided ye be obedient and prompt to come unto us without solemn rites and observances on our part.

Thou shouldest further make a Book of virgin paper, and therein write the foregoing conjurations, and constrain the Demons to swear upon the same Book that they will come whenever they be called, and present themselves before thee, whenever thou shalt wish to consult them. Afterwards thou canst cover this Book with sacred Sigils on a plate of silver, and therein write or engrave the Holy Pentacles. Thou mayest open this Book either on Sundays or on Thursdays, rather at night than by day, and the Spirits will come.

Regarding the expression 'night,' understand the night following, and not the night preceding the aforesaid days. And remember that by day (the Demons) are ashamed, for they are Animals of Darkness.

BOOK ONE

CHAPTER VIII

Concerning the Medals or Pentacles, and the Manner of Constructing Them

As we have already made mention of the Pentacles, it is necessary that thou shouldest understand that the whole Science and understanding of our Key dependeth upon the operation, Knowledge, and use of Pentacles.

He then who shall wish to perform any operation by the means of the Medals, or Pentacles, and therein to render himself expert, must observe what hath been hereinbefore ordained. Let him then, O my Son Roboam, know and understand that in the aforesaid Pentacles he shall find those Ineffable and Most Holy Names which were written by the finger of God in the Tablets of Moses; and which I, Solomon, have received through the Ministry of an Angel by Divine Revelation. These then have I collected together, arranged, consecrated, and kept, for the benefit of the human race, and the preservation of Body and of Soul.

The Pentacles should then be made in the days and hours of Mercury, when the Moon is in an aerial[89] or terrestrial sign; she should also be in her increase, and in equal number of days with the Sun.

It is necessary to have a Chamber or Cabinet specially set apart and newly cleaned, wherein thou canst remain without interruption, the which having entered with thy Companions, thou shalt incense and perfume it with the odours and perfumes of the Art. The sky should be clear and serene. It is necessary that thou shouldest have one or more pieces of virgin paper prepared and arranged ready, as we shall tell you more fully later on, in its place.

Thou shalt commence the writing or construction of the Pentacles in the hour aforesaid. Among other things, thou shalt chiefly use these colours: Gold, Cinnabar or Vermilion Red, and celestial or brilliant Azure Blue. Furthermore, thou shalt make these Medals or Pentacles with exorcised pen and colours, as we shall hereafter show thee. Whensoever thou constructest them, if thou canst complete them in the hour wherein thou didst begin them, it is better. However, if it be absolutely necessary to interrupt the work, thou shouldest await the proper day and hour before re-commencing it.

The Pentacles being finished and completed, take a cloth of very fine silk, as we shall hereafter ordain thee, in the which thou shalt wrap the Pentacles. After which thou shalt take a large Vessel of Earth filled with Charcoal, upon the which there must be put frankincense, mastic, and aloes, all having been previously conjured and exorcised as shall hereafter be told thee. Thou must also be thyself pure, clean, and washed, as thou shalt find given in the proper place. Furthermore, thou shouldest have the Sickle or Knife of Magical Art,

---

[89] *i.e.* in Gemini, Libra, Aquarius, Taurus, Virgo, or Capricorn.

with the which thou shalt make a Circle, and trace within it an inner circle, and in the space between the two thou shalt write the Names of God,[90] which thou shalt think fit and proper. It is necessary after this that thou shouldest have within the Circle a vessel of earth with burning coals and odoriferous perfumes thereon; with the which thou shalt fumigate the aforesaid Pentacles; and, having turned thy face towards the East, thou shalt hold the said Pentacles over the smoke of the Incense, and shalt repeat devoutly the following Psalms of David my Father: Psalms viii., xxi., xxvii., xxix., xxxii., li., lxxii., cxxxiv.[91]

(For a convenient form of Circle which may be used for preparing Instruments and other things of the same kind, as well as for consecrating the Pentacles, see Figure 3.)

After this thou shalt repeat the following Oration:--

The Oration

O ADONAI most powerful, EL most strong, AGLA most holy, ON Most righteous, the ALEPH[92] and the TAU, the Beginning and the End; Thou Who hast established all things in Thy Wisdom; Thou Who has chosen Abraham Thy faithful servant, and hast promised that in his seed shall all nations of the earth be blessed, which seed Thou hast multiplied as the Stars of Heaven; Thou Who hast appeared unto Thy servant Moses in flame in the midst of the Burning Bush, and hast made him walk with dry feet through the Red Sea; Thou Who gavest the Law to him upon Mount Sinai; Thou Who hast granted unto Solomon Thy Servant these Pentacles by Thy great Mercy, for the preservation of Soul and of Body; we most humbly implore and supplicate Thy Holy Majesty, that these Pentacles may be consecrated by Thy power, and prepared in such manner that they may obtain virtue and strength against all Spirits, through Thee, O Most Holy ADONAI, Whose Kingdom, Empire, and principality remaineth and endureth without end.

These words being said, thou shalt perfume the Pentacles with the same sweet scents and perfumes, and afterwards having wrapped them in a piece of prepared silk cloth, thou shalt put them in a place fit and clean, which thou mayest open whenever it shall please thee, and close it again, at thy pleasure and according unto thy will. We will hereafter show thee the method and manner of preparing the aforesaid place, of perfuming it with scents and sweet odours, and of sprinkling it with the Water and Water-Sprinkler of Magical Art; for all these things contain many good properties, and

---

[90] Preferably those having some reference to the work in hand.
[91] I have given the numbers of the Psalms according to the English, not the Hebrew numbers.
[92] The Qabalistic word AZOTH may be substituted for 'the Aleph and the Tau.'

innumerable virtues, as experience will easily teach thee.

We have already said sufficient regarding the Solemn Conjuration of Spirits.

We have also spoken enough in our present Key, regarding the manner in which it is necessary to attract the Spirits so as to make them speak. Now, by Divine aid, I will teach thee how to perform certain experiments with success.

Know,[93] O my Son Roboam, that all the Divine Sigils, Characters, and Names (which are the most precious and excellent things in Nature, whether Terrestrial or Celestial), should be written by thee each separately, when thou art in a state of grace and purity, upon virgin parchment, with ordinary ink, in the beginning of the month[94] of August before sunrise, raising thine eyes unto heaven, and turning towards the east. Thou shalt preserve them to suspend from thy neck, whichever thou wilt, on the day and hour wherein thou wast born, after which thou shalt take heed to name every day ten times, the Name which is hung from thy neck, turning towards the East, and thou mayest be assured that no enchantment or any other danger shall have power to harm thee.

Furthermore thou shalt vanquish all adversities, and shalt be cherished and loved by the Angels and Spirits, provided that thou hast made their characters and that thou hast them upon thee; I assure thee that this is the true way to succeed with ease in all thine operations, for being fortified with a Divine Name, and the Letters, Characters, and Sigils, applicable unto the operation, thou shalt discover with what supernatural exactitude and very great promptitude, both Terrestrial and Celestial things will be obedient unto thee. But all this will only be true, when accompanied by the Pentacles which hereinafter follow, seeing that the Seals, Characters, and Divine Names, serve only to fortify the work, to preserve from unforeseen accidents, and to attract the familiarity of the Angels and Spirits which is one reason, my Son, that before making any experiment, I order thee to read and re-read my Testament, not once only but many times, so that being perfectly instructed In the several Ceremonies thou mayest in no way fail, and that thus what shall have previously appeared to thee difficult and lengthy, may become in process of time easy and of very great use.

I am about to endow thee with many secrets, which I charge thee never to employ for an evil purpose, for ACCURSED BE HE WHO TAKETH THE NAME OF ALMIGHTY GOD IN VAIN; but thou mayest without any other ceremonies make use of them, provided that, as I have already said, thou hast only the Glory of Eternal God for thine object. Thus, after having taught thee all the Ceremonies which concern the manner of performing the

---

[93] From here to the end of the Chapter is only given in Lansdowne MSS. 1203.
[94] *i.e.* When the Sun is in the Sign Leo.

Operations, I am at length determined to make thee a partaker in the secrets of which I have particular knowledge, unknown to this day unto the generality of men; but, nevertheless, only on the condition that thou attemptest not the ruin and destruction of thy neighbour, for his blood will cry for vengeance unto God, and in the end thou and thine shall feel the just wrath of an offended Deity. However, God not having forbidden honest and lawful pleasures, thou mayest perform boldly the Operations which follow, it being always especially necessary to distinguish between the good and the evil, so as to choose the former and avoid the latter, which is why I command thee to be attentive to all that is contained in this my Testament.

BOOK ONE

Chapter IX

Of the Experiment Concerning Things Stolen, and How it Should be Preformed

My beloved Son, if thou findest any Theft, thou shalt do as is hereinafter ordained, and with the help of God thou shalt find that which hath been taken away.

If the hours and days be not otherwise ordained in this operation, thou must refer to what hath already been said. But before commencing any operation whatsoever for the recovery of things stolen, after having made all necessary preparations, thou shalt say the following Oration:--

The Oration

Ateh [95] Adonai Elohim Asher Ha-Shamain Ve-Ha-Aretz, etc.

Thou, O Lord, Who hast made both Heaven and Earth, and hast measured them in the hollow of Thy hand; Thou Who art seated upon the Kerubim and the Seraphim, in the high places, whereunto human understanding cannot penetrate; Thou Who hast created all things by Thine agency, in Whose Presence are the Living Creatures, of which four are marvellously volatile, which have six wings, and who incessantly cry aloud: 'QADOSCH, QADOSCH, QADOSCH, ADONAI ELOHIM TZABAOTH, Heaven and Earth are full of Thy glory'; O Lord God, Thou Who hast expelled Adam from the Terrestrial Paradise, and Who hast placed the Kerubim to guard the Tree of Life, Thou art the Lord Who alone doest wonders; show forth I pray Thee Thy Great Mercy, by the Holy City of Jerusalem, by Thy wonderful Name of four letters which are YOD, HE, VAU, HE, and by Thy Holy and Admirable Name, give unto me the power and virtue to enable me to accomplish this experiment, and to come unto the desired end of this operation; through Thee Who art Life, and unto Whom Life belongeth unto the eternal ages. Amen.

After this perfume and cense the place with good scents and sweet odours. This aforesaid place should be pure, clean, safe from interruption or disturbance, and proper to the work, as we shall hereafter show. Then sprinkle the aforesaid place with consecrated Water, as is laid down in the Chapter concerning Circles.

The Operation being in such wise prepared, thou shalt rehearse the Conjuration necessary for this experiment, at the end of which Thou shalt say as follows:--

O Almighty Father and Lord, Who regardest the Heavens, the Earth, and

---

[95] This is simply the Hebrew of the prayer which follows; but in the MS. Codices it is so mutilated as to be worthless.

the Abyss, mercifully grant unto me by Thy Holy Name written with four letters, YOD, HE, VAU, HE, that by this exorcism I may obtain virtue, Thou Who art IAH, IAH, IAH, grant that by Thy power these Spirits may discover that which we require and which we hope to find, and may they show and declare unto us the persons who have committed the theft, and where they are to be found.

I conjure ye anew, ye Spirits above named, by all the aforesaid Names, through which all things created tremble, that ye show openly unto me (or unto this child here present with us[96]) those things which we seek.

These things being accomplished they will make thee to see plainly that which thou seekest. Take note that the Exorcist, or Master of the Art, should be such as is ordained in the Chapter concerning the Exorcist and his Companions; and if in this experiment it should be necessary to write down characters or Names, thou shalt do that which it is necessary to observe regarding the pen, ink, and paper, as is duly prescribed in the Chapters concerning them.

For if thou dost not regard these things, thou wilt neither accomplish that which thou desirest, nor arrive at thy desired end.

How to Know Who Has Committed a Theft[97]

Take a Sieve and suspend it by a piece of cord wherewith a man has been hung, which should be fastened round the circumference of the rim. Within the rim write with blood in the four divisions thereof the characters given in Figure 4. After this take a basin of brass perfectly clean which thou shalt fill with water from a fountain, and having pronounced these words: DIES MIES YES-CHET BENE DONE FET DONNIMA METEMAUZ, make the sieve spin round with thy left hand, and at the same time turn with thy right hand the water in the basin in a contrary direction, by stirring it with a twig of green laurel. When the water becometh still and the sieve no longer whirls, gaze fixedly into the water, and thou shalt see the form of him who hath committed the theft; and in order that thou mayest the more easily recognise him, thou shalt mark him in some part of his face with the Magical Sword of Art; for that sign which thou shalt have cut therewith in the water, shall be really found thereafter upon his own person.

---

[96] A child employed as a clairvoyant in the operation; as is still the custom in some places in the East.
[97] The rest of this Chapter is from 1203 Lansdowne MSS.

Book One

The Manner of Causing the Sieve to Turn, That Thow Mayest Know Who Committed the Theft[98]

Take a Sieve and stick into the outside of the rim the open points of a pair of scissors, and having rested the rings of the said opened scissors on the thumb-nails of two persons, let one of them say the following Prayer:--

Prayer

DIES MIES YES-CHET BENE DONE FET DONNIMA METEMAUZ; O Lord, Who liberatedst the holy Susanna from a false accusation of crime; O Lord, Who liberatedst the holy Thekla; O Lord, Who rescuedst the holy Daniel from the den of lions, and the Three Children from the burning fiery furnace, free the innocent and reveal the guilty.

After this let him or her pronounce aloud the names and surnames of all the persons living in the house where the theft hast been committed, who may be suspected of having stolen the things in question, saying:--

'By Saint Peter and Saint Paul, such a person hath not done this thing.'

And let the other reply

'By Saint Peter and Saint Paul, he (or she) hath not done it.'

Let this be repeated thrice for each person named and suspected, and it is certain that on naming the person who hath committed the theft or done the crime, the sieve will turn of itself without its being able to stop it, and by this thou shalt know the evil doer.

---

[98] This is the ancient divination by the sieve and shears, and from St. Peter and St. Paul being mentioned in it, has evidently undergone a mediaeval reconstruction.

Chapter X

Of the Experiment of Invisibility and How it Should Be Preformed

IF thou wishest to perform the Experiment of Invisibility, thou shalt follow the instructions for the same. If it be necessary to observe the day and the hour, thou shalt do as is said in their Chapters. But if thou needest not observe the day and the hour as marked in the Chapter thereon, thou shalt do as taught in the Chapter which precedeth it. If in the course of the experiment it be necessary to write anything, it should be done as is described in the Chapters pertaining thereto, with the proper pen, paper, and ink, or blood. But if the matter is to be accomplished by invocation, before thy conjurations, thou shalt say devoutly in thine heart:--

SCEABOLES, ARBARON, ELOHI, ELIMIGITH, HERENOBULCULE, METHE, BALUTH, TIMAYAL, VILLAQUIEL, TEVENI, YEVIE, FERETE, BACUHABA, GUVARIN; through Him by Whom ye have empire and power over men, ye must accomplish this work so that I may go and remain invisible.

And if it be necessary in this operation to trace a Circle, thou shalt do as is ordained in the Chapter concerning Circles; and if it be necessary to write characters, etc., thou shalt follow the instructions given in the respective Chapters.

This operation being thus prepared, if there be an especial Conjuration to perform, thou shalt repeat it in the proper manner; if not, thou shalt say the general Conjuration, at the end of which thou shalt add the following words:--

O thou ALMIRAS, Master of Invisibility, with thy Ministers CHEROG, MAITOR, TANGEDEM, TRANSIDIM, SUVANTOS, ABELAIOS, BORED, BELAMITH, CASTUMI, DABUEL; I conjure ye by Him Who maketh Earth and Heaven to tremble, Who is seated upon the Throne of His Majesty, that this operation may be perfectly accomplished according to my will, so that at whatsoever time it may please me, I may be able to be invisible.

I conjure thee anew, O ALMIRAS, Chief of Invisibility, both thee and thy Ministers, by Him through Whom all things have their being, and by SATURIEL, HARCHIEL, DANIEL, BENIEL, ASSIMONEM, that thou immediately comest hither with all thy Ministers, and achievest this operation, as thou knowest it ought to be accomplished, and that by the same operation thou render me invisible, so that none may be able to see me.

In order then to accomplish this aforesaid operation, thou must prepare all things necessary with requisite care and diligence, and put them in practice with all the general and particular ceremonies laid down for these experiments; and with all the conditions contained in our first and second Books. Thou shalt also in the same operations duly repeat the appropriate

Conjurations, with all the solcmnitie5 marked in the respective Chapters. Thus shalt thou accomplish the experiment surely and without hindrance, and thus shalt thou find it true.

But, on the contrary, if thou lettest any of these things escape thee, or if thou despiseth them, never shalt thou be able to arrive at thy proposed end; as, for example, we enter not easily into a fenced city over its walls but through its gates.

How[99] to Render Oneself Invisible

Make a small image of yellow wax, in the form of a man, in the month January and in the day and hour of Saturn, and at that time write with a needle above the crown of its head and upon its skull which thou shalt have adroitly raised, the character following. (See Figure 5.) After which thou shalt replace the skull in proper position. Thou shalt then write upon a small strip of the skin of a frog or toad which thou shalt have killed, the following words and characters. (See Figure 6.) Thou shalt then go and suspend the said figure by one of thy hairs from the vault of a cavern at the hour of midnight, and perfuming it with the proper incense thou shalt say:--

METATRON, MELEKH, BEROTH, NOTH, VENIBBETH, MACH, and all ye, I conjure thee, O Figure of wax, by the Living God, that by the virtue of these Characters and words, thou render me invisible, wherever I may bear thee with me. Amen.

And after having censed it anew, thou shalt bury it in the same place in a small deal box, and every time that thou wishest to pass or enter into any place without being seen, thou shalt say these words, bearing the aforesaid figure in thy left pocket:--

Come unto me and never quit me whithersoever I shall go.

Afterwards thou shalt take it carefully back unto the before-mentioned place and cover it with earth until thou shalt need it again.

---

[99] The rest of this Chapter is from 1203 Lansdowne MSS.

Chapter XI

To Hinder a Sportsman from Killing Any Game[100]

TAKE a stick of green elder, from the two ends of which thou shalt clean out the pith. In each end place a strip of parchment of hare-skin, having written thereon with the blood of a black hen the following character and word. (See Figure 7.) Having made two of these slips, place one in each end of the stick and close the apertures up with pith, afterwards on a Friday in the month of February thou shalt fumigate the aforesaid stick with suitable incense thrice in the air, and having taken it thence thou shalt bury it in the earth under an elder-tree. Afterwards thou shalt expose it in the pathway by which the sportsman will pass, and once he has passed by it, he need not hope to kill any game during that day. If thou shalt wish a second time to lay a spell upon him in like manner, thou needest but to expose the stick again in his path; but take care to bury it again in the earth under an elder-tree, so as to be able to take it from thence each time that thou shalt have need of it; and to take it up each time as soon as the sportsman shall have passed.

---

[100] This Chapter is taken from 1203 Lansdowne MSS.

CHAPTER XII

How[101] to Make the Magic Garters

TAKE enough of the skin of a stag to make two hollow tubular Garters, but before stitching them up thou shalt write on the side of the skin which was next the flesh the words and characters shown in Figure 8, with the blood of a hare killed on the 25th of June, and having filled the said Garters with green mugwort gathered also on the 25th of June before sunrise, thou shalt put in the two ends of each the eye of the fish called barbel; and when thou shalt wish to use them thou shalt get up before sunrise and wash them in a brook of running water, and place them one on each leg above the knee. After this thou shalt take a short rod of holm-oak cut on the same 25th of June, turn in the direction thou wishest to go, write upon the ground the name of the place, and commencing thy journey thou wilt find it accomplished in a few days and without fatigue. When thou wishest to stop thou hast only to say AMECH and beat the air with the aforesaid wand, and incontinently thou shalt be on firm ground.

---

[101] This Chapter is also taken from 1203 Lansdowne MSS.

Chapter XIII[102]

How to Make the Magic Carpet Proper for Interrogating the Intelligences, So as to Obtain an Answer Regarding Whatsoever Matter One May Wish to Learn

MAKE a Carpet of white and new wool, and when the Moon shall be at her full, in the Sign of Capricorn and in the hour of the Sun, thou shalt go into the country away from any habitation of man, in a place free from all impurity, and shalt spread out thy Carpet so that one of its points shall be towards the east, and another towards the west, and having made a Circle without it and enclosing it, thou shalt remain within upon the point towards the east, and holding thy wand in the air for every operation, thou shalt call upon MICHAEL,[103] towards the north upon RAPHAEL, towards the west upon GABRIEL, and towards the south upon MURIEL. After this thou shalt return unto the point of the East and devoutly invoke the Great Name AGLA, and take this point of the Carpet in thy left hand; turning then towards the North thou shalt do the same, and so continuing to the other points of the Carpet, thou shalt raise them so that they touch not the ground, and holding them up thus, and turning anew towards the East thou shalt say with great veneration the following Prayer:--

Prayer

AGLA, AGLA, AGLA, AGLA; O God Almighty Who art the Life of the Universe and Who rulest over the four divisions of its vast form by the strength and virtue of the Four Letters of Thy Holy Name Tetragrammaton, YOD, HE, VAU, HE, bless in Thy Name this covering which I hold as Thou hast blessed the Mantle of Elijah in the hands of Elisha, so that being covered by Thy Wings, nothing may be able to injure me, even as it is said:--'He shall hide thee under His Wings and beneath His feathers shall thou trust, His truth shall be thy shield and buckler.'

After this thou shalt fold it up, saying these words following:-- RECABUSTIRA, CABUSTIRA, BUSTIRA, TIRA, RA, A; and shall keep it carefully to serve thee at need.

When thou shalt be desirous to make thine interrogations, choose the night of full or of new moon, and from midnight until daybreak. Thou shalt transport thyself unto the appointed spot if it be for the purpose of discovering a treasure; if not, any place will serve provided it be clean and

---

[102] This Chapter is also taken from 1203 Lansdowne MSS.
[103] I have usually found Michael attributed to the South; Raphael to the East; Gabriel to the West; and Auriel to the North. Likewise I think the operator should turn following the course of the Sun, and not contrariwise as in the text.

pure. Having had the precaution on the preceding evening to write upon a slip of virgin parchment coloured azure-blue, with a pen made from the feather of a dove, this Character and Name (see Figure 9); taking thy carpet, thou shalt cover thy head and body therewith, and taking the censer, with new fire therein, thou shalt place it in or upon the proper place, and cast thereon some incense. Then shalt thou prostrate thyself upon the ground, with thy face towards the earth, before the incense beginneth to fume, keeping the fire of the same beneath the carpet, holding thy wand upright, against which to rest thy chin; thou shalt hold with thy right hand the aforesaid strip of parchment against thy forehead, and thou shalt say the following words:--

VEGALE, HAMICATA, UMSA, TERATA, YEH, DAH, MA, BAXASOXA, UN, HORAH, HIMESERE;[104] O God the Vast One send unto me the Inspiration of Thy Light, make me to discover the secret thing which I ask of Thee, whatsoever such or such a thing may be, make me to search it out by the aid of Thy holy ministers RAZIEL, TZAPHNIEL, MATMONIEL; Lo, Thou hast desired truth in the young, and in the hidden thing shalt Thou make me know wisdom. RECABUSTIRA, CABUSTIRA, BUSTIRA, TIRA, RA, A, KARKAHITA, KAHITA, HITA, TA.

And thou shalt hear distinctly the answer which thou shalt have sought.

---

[104] These are probably corrupted Hebrew words derived from the prayer itself.

Chapter XIV[105]

How to Render Thyself Master of a Treasure Possessed by the Spirits

THE Earth being inhabited, as I have before said unto thee, by a great number of Celestial Beings and Spirits, who by their subtilty and prevision know the places wherein treasures are hidden, and seeing that it often happeneth that those men who undertake a search for these said treasures are molested and sometimes put to death by the aforesaid Spirits, which are called Gnomes; which, however, is not done through the Avarice of these said Gnomes, a Spirit being incapable of possessing anything, having no material senses wherewith to bring it into use, but because these Spirits, who are enemies of the passions, are equally so of Avarice, unto which men are so much inclined; and foreseeing the evil ends for which these treasures will be employed have some interest and aim in maintaining the earth in its condition of price and value, seeing that they are its inhabitants, and when they slightly disturb the workers in such kind of treasures, it is a warning which they give them to cease from the work, and if it happen that the greedy importunity of the aforesaid workers oblige them to continue, notwithstanding the aforesaid warnings, the Spirits, irritated by their despising the same, frequently put the workmen to death. But know, O my Son, that from the time that thou shalt have the good fortune to be familiar with such kinds of Spirits, and that thou shalt be able by means of what I have taught thee to make them submit unto thine orders, they will be happy to give thee, and to make thee partaker in that which they uselessly possess, provided that thine object and end shall be to make a good use thereof.

The Master of Performing the Operation

On a Sunday before sunrise, between the 10th of July and the 20th of August, when the moon is in the Sign of the Lion, thou shalt go unto the place where thou shalt know either by interrogation of the Intelligences, or otherwise, that there is a treasure; there thou shalt describe a Circle of sufficient size with the Sword of Magical Art wherein to open up the earth, as the nature of the ground will allow; thrice during the day shalt thou cense it with the incense proper for the day, after which being clothed in the raiment proper for the Operation thou shalt suspend in some way by a machine immediately above the opening a lamp, whose oil should be mingled with the fat of a man who has died in the month of July, and the wick being made from the cloth wherein he has been buried. Having kindled this with fresh fire, thou shalt fortify the workmen with a girdle of the skin of a goat

---

[105] This is also taken from 1203 Lansdowne MSS.

newly slain, whereon shall be written with the blood of the dead man from whom thou shalt have taken the fat these words and characters (see Figure 10); and thou shalt set them to work in safety, warning them not to be at all disturbed at the Spectres which they will see, but to work away boldly. In case they cannot finish the work in a single day, every time they shall have to leave it thou shalt cause them to put a covering of wood over the opening, and above the covering about six inches of earth; and thus shalt thou continue unto the end, being all the time present in the raiment of the Art, and with the Magic Sword, during the operation. After which thou shalt repeat this prayer

Prayer

ADONAI, ELOHIM, EL, EHEIEH ASHER EHEIEH, Prince of Princes, Existence of Existences, have mercy upon me, and cast Thine eyes upon Thy Servant (N.), who invokes Thee most devoutly, and supplicates Thee by Thy Holy and tremendous Name Tetragrammaton to be propitious, and to order Thine Angels and Spirits to come and take up their abode in this place; O ye Angels and Spirits of the Stars, O all ye Angels and Elementary Spirits, O all ye Spirits present before the Face of God, I the Minister and faithful Servant of the Most High conjure ye, let God Himself, the Existence of Existences, conjure ye to come and be present at this Operation, I, the Servant of God, most humbly entreat ye. Amen.

Having then caused the workmen to fill in the hole, thou shalt license the Spirits to depart, thanking them for the favour they have shown unto thee, and saying:--

The Licesnse to Depart

O ye good and happy Spirits, we thank ye for the benefits which we have just received from your liberal bounty; depart ye in peace to govern the Element which God hath destined for your habitation. Amen.

Chapter XV

Of the Experiment of Seeking Favour and Love[106]

IF thou wishest to perform the Experiment of seeking favour and love, observe in what manner the Experiment is to be carried out, and if it be dependent upon the day and the hour, perform it in the day and the hour required, as thou wilt find it in the Chapter concerning the hours; and if the Experiment be one that requireth writing, thou shalt write as it is said in the Chapter concerning the same; and if it be with penal bonds, pacts, and fumigations, then thou shalt cense with a fit perfume as is said in the Chapter concerning suffumigations; and if it be necessary to sprinkle it with water and hyssop, then let it be as in the Chapter concerning the same; similarly if such Experiment require characters, names, or the like, let such names be written as the Chapter concerning the writing of characters, and place the same in a clean place as hath been said. Then thou shalt repeat over it the following Oration:--

The Oration

O ADONAI, most Holy, Most Righteous, and most Mighty God, Who hast made all things through Thy Mercy and Righteousness wherewith Thou art filled, grant unto us that we may be found worthy that this Experiment may be found consecrated and perfect, so that the Light may issue from Thy Most Holy Seat, O ADONAI, which may obtain for us favour and love. Amen.

This being said, thou shalt place it in clean silk, and bury it for a day and a night at the junction of four cross-roads; and whensoever thou wishest to obtain any grace or favour from any, take it, having first properly consecrated it according to the rule, and place it in thy right hand, and seek thou what thou wilt it shall not be denied thee. But if thou doest not the Experiment carefully and rightly, assuredly thou shalt not succeed in any manner. For obtaining grace and love write down the following words

SATOR,[107] AREPO, TENET, OPERA, ROTAS, IAH, IAH, IAH, ENAM, IAH, IAH, IAH, KETHER, CHOKMAH, BINAH, GEDULAH, GEBURAH, TIPHERETH, NETZACH, HOD, YESOD, MALKUTH, ABRAHAM, ISAAC, JACOB, SHADRACH, MESHACH, ABEDNEGO, be ye all present in my aid and for whatsoever I shall desire to obtain.

Which words being properly written as above, thou shalt also find thy desire brought to pass.

---

[106] This Chapter is taken from 10862 Add. MSS.
[107] This Incantation is also given in 1307 Sloane MSS., page 76.

BOOK ONE

CHAPTER XVI[108]

How Operations of Mockery, Invisibility, and Deceit Should be Prepared

EXPERIMENTS relating to tricks, mockeries, and deceits, may be performed in many ways. When thou shalt wish to practise these experiments with regard to any person, thou shalt observe the day and the hour as we have already said. Should it be necessary to write Characters or Words, it should be done upon virgin paper, as we shall show farther on. As for the ink, if it be not specially ordained in this operation, it is advisable to use the blood of a bat with the pen and the needle of art. But before describing or writing the Characters or Names, all the necessary rules should be observed as given in the proper Chapters, and having carefully followed out all these, thou shalt pronounce with a loud voice the following words :--

ABAC, ALDAL, IAT, HUDAC, GUTHAC, GUTHOR, GOMEH, TISTATOR, DERISOR, DESTATUR, come hither all ye who love the times and places wherein all kinds of mockeries and deceits are practised. And ye who make things disappear and who render them invisible, come hither to deceive all those who regard these things, so that they may be deceived, and that they may seem to see that which they see not and hear that which they hear not, so that their senses may be deceived, and that they may behold that which is not true.

Come ye then hither and remain, and consecrate this enchantment, seeing that God the Almighty Lord hath destined ye for such.

When this Experiment is completed in this manner in the hour and time which we have shown and taught, also the foregoing words ABAC, ALDAL, etc., should be written with the pen as hereinafter ordained; but if the Experiment be performed in a different way, yet shalt thou always say the aforesaid words, and they should be repeated as before given.

If thou practisest these things in this manner correctly, thou shalt arrive at the effect of thine operations and experiments, by the which thou mayest easily deceive the senses.

---

[108] This Chapter is given in 10862 Add. MSS., 3981 Harleian MSS., 288 King's MSS., 3091 Sloane MSS., and 1307 Sloane MSS., but is wanting in 1202 Lansdowne MSS., as are all the Chapters of the First Book after Chap. 8.

Chapter XVII

How Extraordinary Experiments and Operations Should be Prepared

WE have spoken in the preceding Chapters of common experiments and operations, which it is more usual to practise and put in operation, and therein thou mayest easily see that we have told thee sufficient for their perfection. In this Chapter we treat of extraordinary and unusual experiments, which can also be done in many ways.

None the less should those who wish to put in practice the like experiments and operations observe the days and hours as is laid down in the proper Chapters, and should be provided with virgin paper and other necessary things. Having prepared a similar experiment thou shalt say

Prayer

O God Who hast created all things, and hast given unto us discernment to understand the good and the evil; through Thy Holy Name, and through these Holy Names:--IOD, IAH, VAU, DALETH, VAU, TZABAOTH, ZIO, AMATOR, CREATOR, do Thou, O Lord, grant that this experiment may become true and veritable in my hands through Thy Holy Seal, O ADONAI, Whose reign and empire remaineth eternally and unto the Ages of the Ages. Amen.

This being done, thou shalt perform the experiment, observing its hour, and thou shalt perfume and incense as is laid down in the proper Chapter; sprinkling with exorcised water, and performing all the ceremonies and solemnities as we shall instruct thee in the Second Book of our Key.

Chapter XVIII

Concerning the Holy Pentacles or Medals

THE Medals or Pentacles, which we make for the purpose of striking terror into the Spirits and reducing them to obedience, have besides this wonderful and excellent virtue. If thou invokest the Spirits by virtue of these Pentacles, they will obey thee without repugnance, and having considered them they will be struck with astonishment, and will fear them, and thou shalt see them so surprised by fear and terror, that none of them will be sufficiently bold to wish to oppose thy will. They are also of great virtue and efficacy against all perils of Earth, of Air, of Water, and of Fire, against poison which hath been drunk, against all kinds of infirmities and necessities, against binding, sortilege, and sorcery, against all terror and fear, and wheresoever thou shalt find thyself, if armed with them, thou shalt be in safety all the days of thy life.

Through them do we acquire grace and good-will from man and woman, fire is extinguished, water is stayed, and all Creatures fear at the sight of the Names which are therein, and obey through that fear.

These Pentacles are usually made of the metal the most suitable to the nature of the Planet; and then there is no occasion to observe the rule of particular colours. They should be engraved with the instrument of Art in the days and hours proper to the Planet.

Saturn ruleth over Lead; Jupiter over Tin; Mars over Iron; the Sun over Gold; Venus over Copper; Mercury over the mixture of Metals; and the Moon over Silver.

They may also be made with exorcised virgin paper, writing thereon with the colours adopted for each Planet, referring to the rules already laid down in the proper Chapters, and according to the Planet with which the Pentacle is in sympathy.

Wherefore unto Saturn the colour of Black is appropriated; Jupiter ruleth over Celestial Blue; Mars over Red; the Sun over Gold, or the colour of Yellow or Citron; Venus over Green; Mercury over Mixed Colours; the Moon over Silver, or the colour of Argentine Earth.

The Matter of which the Pentacle is constructed should be Virgin, never having been used for any other purpose; or if it be metal it should be purified by fire.

As regards the size of the Pentacles it is arbitrary, so long as they are made according to the rules, and with the requisite solemnities, as hath been ordained.

The[109] virtues of the Holy Pentacles are no less advantageous unto thee

---

[109] This and the four following paragraphs are from 1203 Lansdowne MSS.

than the knowledge of the secrets which I have already given unto thee; and thou shouldest take particular care if thou makest them upon virgin parchment to use the proper colours; and if thou engravest them upon metal, to do so in the manner taught thee; and so shalt thou have the satisfaction of seeing them produce the promised effect. But seeing that this Science is not a Science of argument and open reasoning, but that, on the contrary, it is entirely mysterious and occult, we should not argue and deliberate over these matters, and it is sufficient to believe firmly to enable us to bring into operation that which hath already been taught.

When thou shalt construct these Pentacles and Characters, it is necessary never to forget the Incense, nor to employ anything beyond that of which mention is made.

It is necessary, above all things, to be attentive to the operation, and never to forget or omit those things which contribute to the success which the Pentacles and Experiments promise, having ever in thy mind no other intention than the Glory of God, the accomplishment of thy desires, and loving-kindness towards thy neighbour.

Furthermore, my beloved Son, I order thee not to bury this Science, but to make thy friends partakers in the same, subject however to the strict command never to profane the things which are Divine, for if thou doest this, far from rendering thee a friend of the Spirits, it will but be the means of bringing thee unto destruction.

But never must thou lavish these things among the ignorant, for that would be as blameable as to cast precious gems before swine; on the contrary, from one Sage the secret knowledge should pass unto another Sage, for in this manner shall the Treasure of Treasures never descend into oblivion.

Adore[110] and revere the Most Holy Names of God which are found in these Pentacles and Characters, for without this never shalt thou be able to come to the end of any enterprise, nor to accomplish the Mystery of Mysteries.

Above all things, remember that to perform any of these operations thou must be pure in body and in mind, and without blemish, and on not any of the preparations.

This Key, full of Mysteries, hath been revealed unto me by an Angel.

Accursed be he who undertaketh our Art without having the qualities requisite to thoroughly understand our Key, accursed be he who invoke the Name of God in vain, for such an one prepareth for himself the punishments which await the unbelievers, for God shall abandon them a relegate them unto the depths of Hell amongst the impure Spirits.

For God is great and Immutable, He hath been for ever, and He shall remain even unto the end of the Ages.

---

[110] The rest of the Chapter is from 1202 Lansdowne MSS., except the last sentence.

ACCURSED BE HE WHO TAKETH THE NAME OF GOD IN VAIN! ACCURSED BE HE WHO USETH THIS KNOWLEDGE UNTO AN EVIL END, BE HE ACCURSED IN THIS WORLD AND IN THE WORLD TO COME. AMEN. BE HE ACCURSED THE NAME WHICH HE HATH BLASPHEMED!

THE END OF THE FIRST BOO

The Plates

Book One

The Order of the Pentacles

Here Follow the Holy Pentacles, Expressed in their Proper Figures and Characters, Together with their Especial Virtues; for the Use of the Master of Art

(1.) Seven Pentacles consecrated to Saturn Black.

(2.) Seven Pentacles consecrated to Jupiter Blue.

(3.) Seven Pentacles consecrated to Mars = Red.

(4.) Seven Pentacles consecrated to the Sun = Yellow.

(5.) Five Pentacles consecrated to Venus = Green.

(6.) Five Pentacles consecrated to Mercury = Mixed Colours.

(7.) Six Pentacles consecrated to the Moon = Silver.

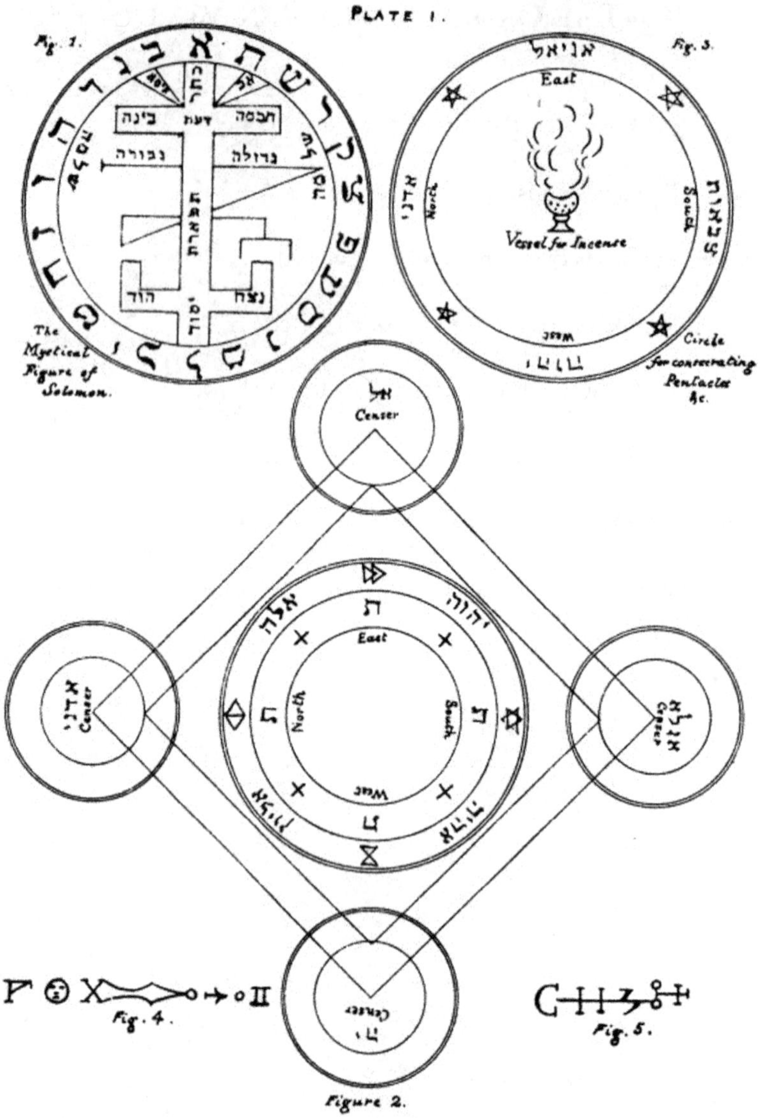
PLATE I.
Fig. 1.
חכמה
דעת
בינה
גדולה
גבורה
נצח
הוד
יסוד
The Mystical Figure of Solomon.
Fig. 3.
East
Vessel for Incense
North
South
West
Circle for consecrating Pentacles &c.
אל
Censer
East
North
South
West
Censer
Censer
Censer
Fig. 4.
Fig. 5.
Figure 2.

BOOK ONE

PLATE II.

Fig. 6.
hels, hels, hels, ✶ ❖ ✝ A ⊏⊐

Fig. 7.
ABIMEGH ○⇉⇉○

Fig. 8.
Du ROSA ○ E ❊ ○─○ ○ ○ M 3 ∧ 3

Fig. 9.
RAZIEL רזיאל

Fig. 10.
NOPA ⇐▭▭⇐○ PADOUS

Fig. 11.

Fig. 12.

Fig. 13.

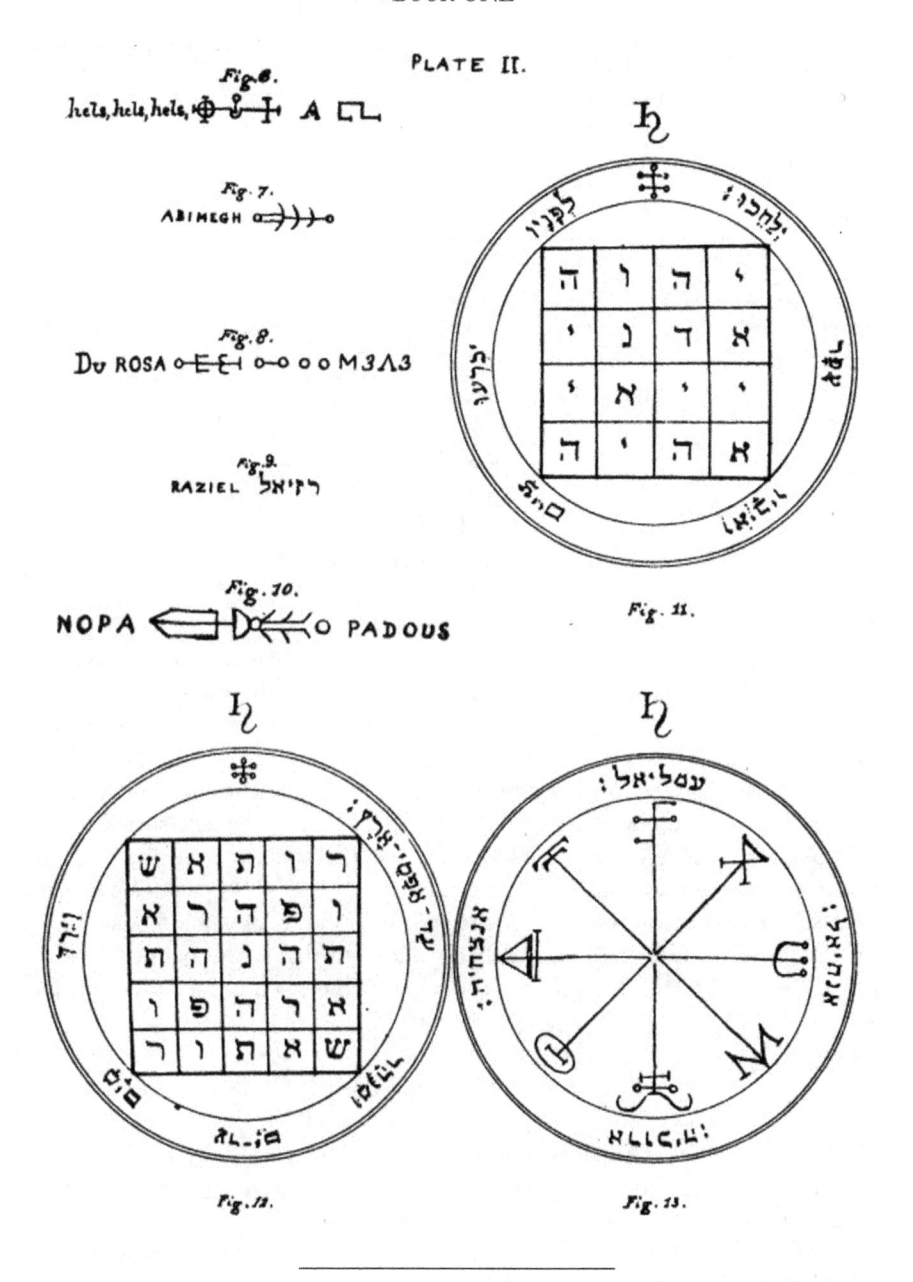

Figure 11.--The First Pentacle of Saturn.--This Pentacle is of great value and utility for striking terror into the Spirits. Wherefore, upon its being shown to them they submit, and kneeling upon the earth before it, they obey.

Editor's Note.--The Hebrew letters within the square are the four great Names of God which are written with four letters:--IHVH, Yod, He, Vau,

181

He; ADNI, Adonai; IIAI, Yiai (this Name has the same numerical value in Hebrew as the Name EL); and AHIH, Eheieh. The Hebrew versicle which surrounds it is from Psalm lxxii. 9: 'The Ethiopians shall kneel before Him, His enemies shall lick the dust.'

Figure 12.--The Second Pentacle of Saturn.--This Pentacle is of great value against adversities; and of especial use in repressing the pride of the Spirits.

Editor's Note.--This is the celebrated

> SATOR
> AREPO
> TENET
> OPERA
> ROTAS,

the most perfect existing form of double acrostic, as far as the arrangement of the letters is concerned; it is repeatedly mentioned in the records of mediæval Magic; and, save to very few, its derivation from the present Pentacle has been unknown. It will be seen at a glance that it is a square of five, giving twenty-five letters, which, added to the unity, gives twenty six, the numerical value of IHVH. The Hebrew versicle surrounding it is taken from Psalm lxxii. 8, 'His dominion shall be also from the one sea to the other, and from the flood unto the world's end.' This passage consists also of exactly twenty-five letters, and its total numerical value (considering the final letters with increased numbers), added to that of the Name Elohim, is exactly equal to the total numerical value of the twenty-five letters in the Square.

Figure 13.--The Third Pentacle of Saturn.--This should be made within the Magical Circle, and it is good for use at night when thou invokest the Spirits of the nature of Saturn.

Editor's Note.--The characters at the ends of the rays of the Mystic Wheel are Magical Characters of Saturn. Surrounding it are the Names of the Angels:--Omeliel, Anachiel, Arauchiah, and Anazachia, written in Hebrew.

BOOK ONE

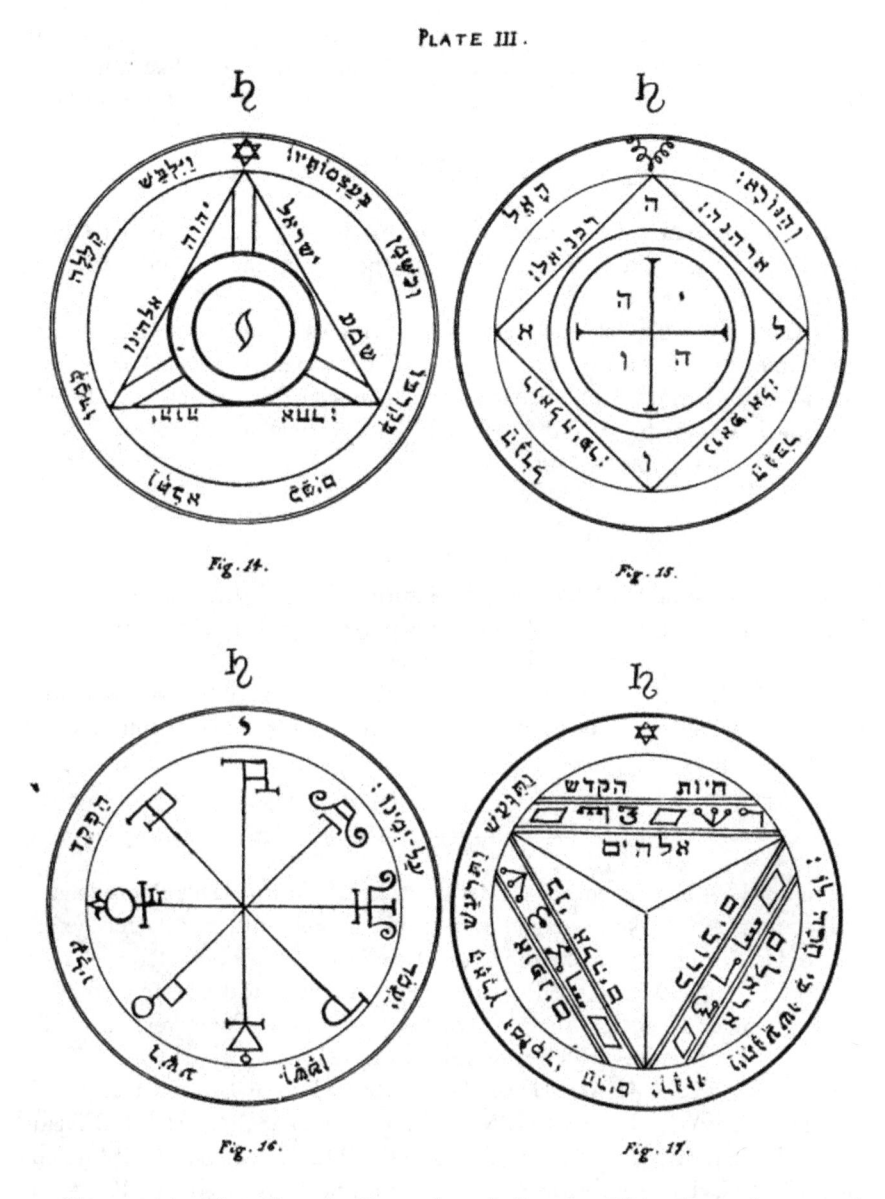

PLATE III.

Fig. 14.

Fig. 15.

Fig. 16.

Fig. 17.

Figure 14.--The Fourth Pentacle of Saturn.--This Pentacle serveth principally for executing all the experiments and operations of ruin, destruction, and death. And when it is made in full perfection, it serveth also for those Spirits which bring news, when thou invokest them from the side of the South.

Editor's Note.--The Hebrew words around the sides of the triangle are from Deut. Vi. 4:--'Hear, O Israel, IHVH ALHINV is IHVH AChD.' The surrounding versicle is from Psalm cix. 18:--'As he clothed himself with cursing like as with a garment, so let it come into his bowels like water, and like oil into his bones.' In the centre of the Pentacle is the mystic letter Yod.

Figure 15.--The Fifth Pentacle of Saturn.--This Pentacle defendeth those who invoke the Spirits of Saturn during the night; and chaseth away the Spirits which guard treasures.

Editor's Note.--The Hebrew letters in the angles of the Cross are those of the Name IHVH. Those in the angles of the Square form ALVH, Eloah. Round the four sides of the Square are the Names of the Angels:--Arehanah, Rakhaniel, Roelhaiphar, and Noaphiel. The versicle is:--'A Great God, a Mighty, and a Terrible.'--Deut. x. 17.

Figure 16.--The Sixth Pentacle of Saturn.--Around this Pentacle is each Name symbolised as it should be. The person against whom thou shalt pronounce it shall be obsessed by Demons.

Editor's Note.--It is formed from Mystical Characters of Saturn. Around it is written in Hebrew: 'Set thou a wicked one to be ruler over him, and let Satan stand at his right hand.'

Figure 17.--The Seventh and Last Pentacle of Saturn.--This Pentacle is fit for exciting earthquakes, seeing that the power of each order of Angels herein invoked is sufficient to make the whole Universe tremble.

Editor's Note.--Within the Pentacle are the Names of the Nine Orders of Angels, those of six of them in ordinary Hebrew Characters, and the remainder in the letters which are known as 'The Passing of the River.' These Nine Orders are:--1. CHAIOTH HA-QADESCH, Holy Living Creatures; 2. AUPHANIM, Wheels; 3. ARALIM, Thrones; 4. CHASCHMALIM, Brilliant Ones; 5. SERAPHIM, Fiery Ones; 6. MELAKIM, Kings; 7. ELOHIM, Gods; 8. BENI ELOHIM, Sons of the Elohim; 9. KERUBIM, Kerubim. The versicle is from Psalm xviii. 7:--'Then the earth shook and trembled, the foundations of the hills also moved and were shaken, because He was wroth.'

Plate IV.

Fig. 18.

Fig. 19.

Fig. 20.

Fig. 21.

JUPITER

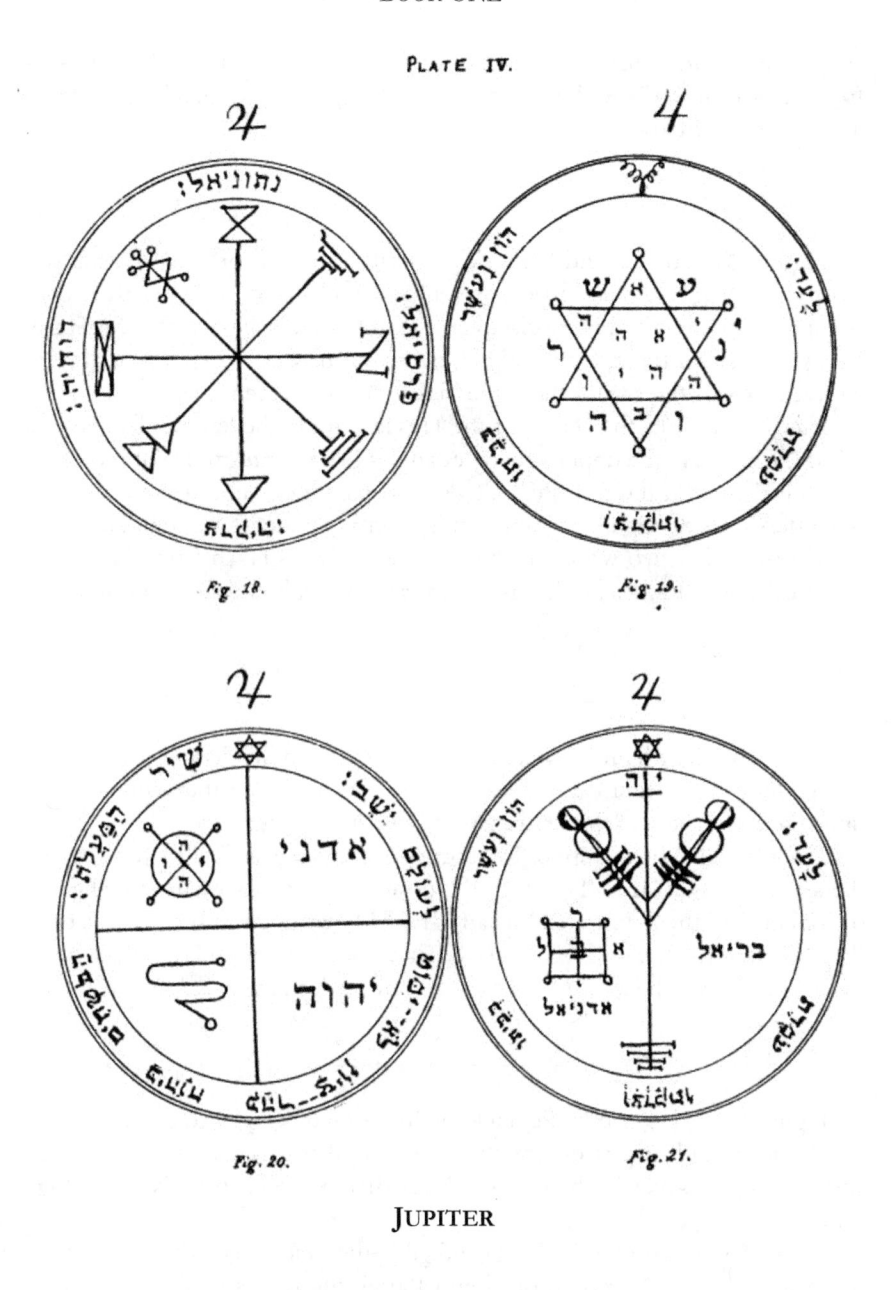

Figure 18.--The First Pentacle of Jupiter.--This serveth to invoke the Spirits of Jupiter, and especially those whose Names are written around the Pentacle, among whom Parasiel is the Lord and Master of Treasures, and teacheth how to become possessor of places wherein they are.

Editor's Note.--This Pentacle is composed of Mystical Characters of Jupiter. Around it are the Names of the Angels:--Netoniel, Devachiah, Tzedeqiah, and Parasiel, written in Hebrew.

Figure 19.--The Second Pentacle of Jupiter.--This is proper for acquiring glory, honours, dignities, riches, and all kinds of good, together with great tranquillity of mind; also to discover Treasures and chase away the Spirits who preside over them. It should be written upon virgin paper or parchment, with the pen of the swallow and the blood of the screech-owl.

Editor's Note.--In the centre of the Hexagram are the letters of the Name AHIH, Eheieh; in the upper and lower angles of the same, those of the Name AB, the Father; in the remaining angles those of the Name IHVH. I believe the letters outside the Hexagram in the re-entering angles to be intended for those of the first two words of the versicle, which is taken from Psalm cxii. 3:--'Wealth and Riches are in his house, and his righteousness endureth for ever.'

Figure 20.--The Third Pentacle of Jupiter.--This defendeth and protecteth those who invoke and cause the Spirits to come. When they appear show unto them this Pentacle, and immediately they will obey.

Editor's Note.--In the upper left corner is the Magical Seal of Jupiter with the letters of the Name IHVH. In the others are the Seal of the Intelligence of Jupiter, and the Names Adonai and IHVH.--Around it is the versicle from Psalm cxxv. 1:--'A Song of degrees. They that trust in IHVH shall be as Mount Zion, which cannot be removed, but abideth for ever.'

Figure 21.--The Fourth Pentacle of Jupiter.--It serveth to acquire riches and honour, and to possess much wealth. Its Angel is Bariel. It should be engraved upon silver in the day and hour of Jupiter when he is in the Sign Cancer.

Editor's Note.--Above the Magical Sigil is the Name IH, Iah. Below it are the Names of the Angels Adoniel and Bariel, the letters of the latter being arranged about a square of four compartments. Around is the versicle from Psalm cxii. 3:--'Wealth and Riches are in his house, and his righteousness endureth for ever.'

BOOK ONE

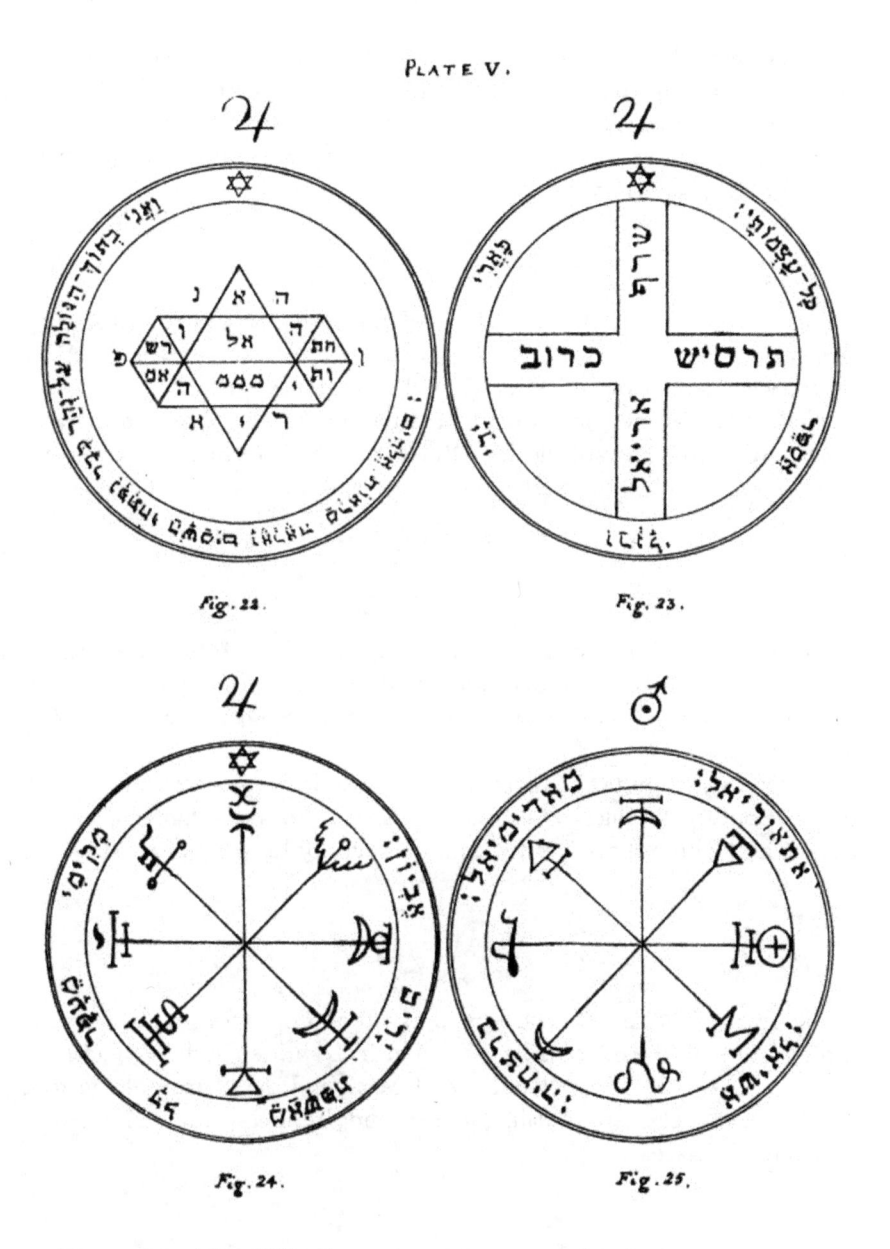

PLATE V.

Fig. 22.

Fig. 23.

Fig. 24.

Fig. 25.

Figure 22.--The Fifth Pentacle of Jupiter.--This hath great power. It serveth for assured visions. Jacob being armed with this Pentacle beheld the ladder which reached unto heaven.

Editor's Note.--The Hebrew letters within the Pentacle are taken from the five last words of the versicle which surrounds it, each of which contains five letters. These are, then, recombined so as to form certain Mystical Names.

The versicle is taken from Ezekiel i. 1:--' As I was among the captives by the river of Chebar, the heavens were opened, and I saw visions of Elohim.' In my opinion the versicle should only consist of the five last words thereof, when the anachronism of Jacob using a Pentacle with a sentence from Ezekiel will no longer exist.

Figure 23.--The Sixth Pentacle of Jupiter.--It serveth for protection against all earthly dangers, by regarding it each day devoutedly, and repeating the versicle which surroundeth it. Thus shalt thou never perish.

Editor's Note.--The four Names in the Arms of the Cross are Seraph, Kerub, Ariel, and Tharsis; the four Rulers of the Elements. The versicle is from Psalm xxii. 16, 17:-' They pierced my hands and my feet, I may tell all my bones.'

Figure 24.--The Seventh and last Pentacle of Jupiter.--It hath great power against poverty, if thou considerest it with devotion, repeating the versicle. It serveth furthermore to drive away those Spirits who guard treasures, and to discover the same.

Editor's Note.--Mystical Characters of Jupiter with the verse:--'Lifting up the poor out of the mire, and raising the needy from the dunghill, that he may set him with princes, even with the princes of his people.'--Psalm cxiii, 7.

MARS

Figure 25.--The first Pentacle of Mars.--It is proper for invoking Spirits of the Nature of Mars, especially those which are written in the Pentacle.

Editor's Note.--Mystical Characters of Mars, and the Names of the four Angels:--Madimiel, Bartzachiah, Eschiel, and Ithuriel written in Hebrew around the Pentacle.

PLATE VI.

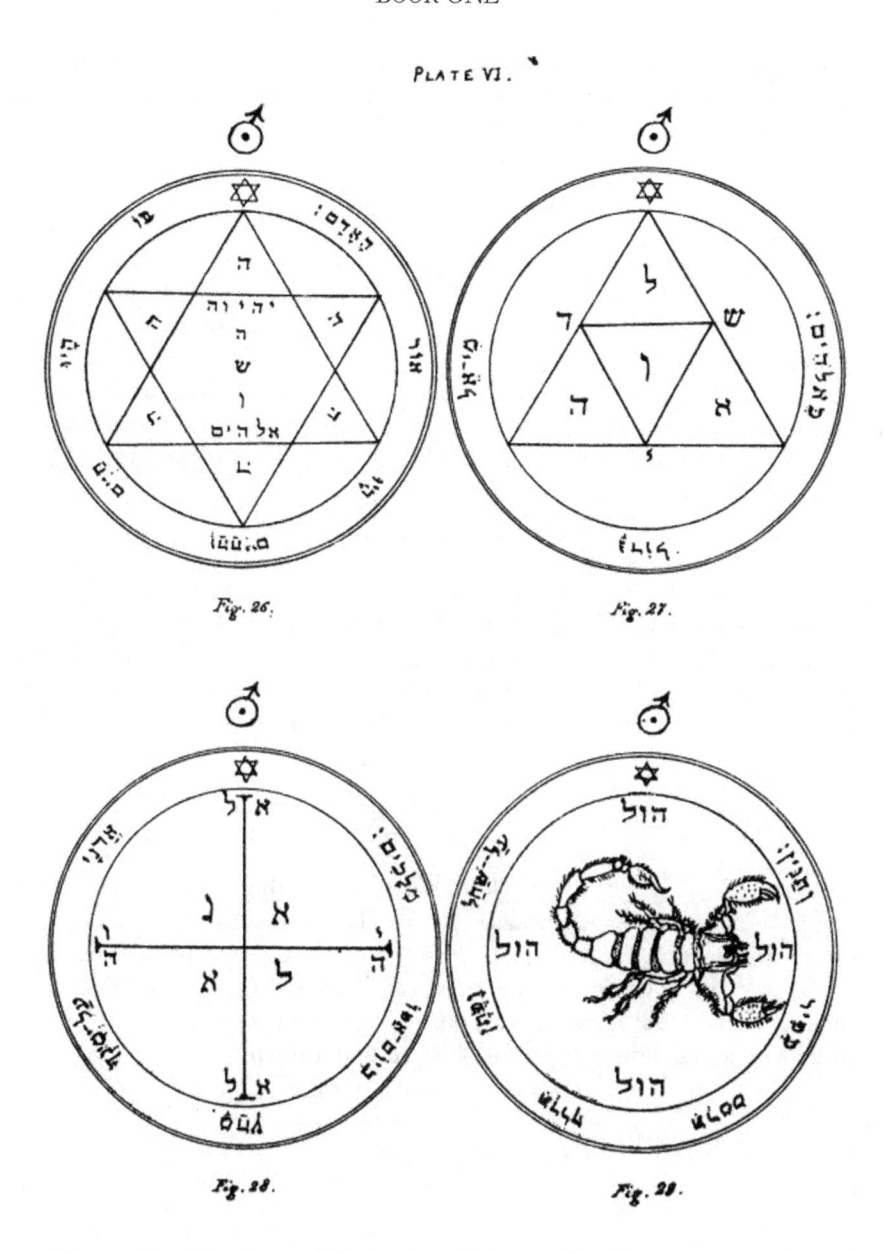

Fig. 26.

Fig. 27.

Fig. 28.

Fig. 29.

Figure 26.--The Second Pentacle of Mars.--This Pentacle serveth with great success against all kinds of diseases, if it be applied unto the afflicted part.

Editor's Note.--The letter Hé, in the angles of the Hexagram. Within the same the Names IHVH, IHSHVH Yeheshuah (the mystic Hebrew Name for Joshua or Jesus, formed of the ordinary IHVH with the letter SH placed therein as emblematical of the Spirit), and Elohim. Around it is the sentence,

John i. 4:--'In Him was life, and the life was the light of man.' This may be adduced as an argument of the greater antiquity of the first few mystical verses of the Gospel of St. John.

Figure 27.--The Third Pentacle of Mars.--It is of great value for exciting war, wrath, discord, and hostility; also for resisting enemies, and striking terror into rebellious Spirits; the Names of God the All Powerful are therein expressly marked.

Editor's Note.--The Letters of the Names Eloah and Shaddai. In the Centre is the great letter Vau, the signature of the Qabalistic Microprosopus. Around is the versicle from Psalm lxxvii. 13:--'Who is so great a God as our Elohim?'

Figure 28.--The Fourth Pentacle of Mars.--It is of great virtue and power in war, wherefore without doubt it will give thee victory.

Editor's Note.--In the Centre is the great Name Agla; right and left, the letters of the Name IHVH; above and below, El. Round it is the versicle from Psalm cx. 5:--'The Lord at thy right hand shall wound even Kings in the day of His Wrath.'

Figure 29.--The Fifth Pentacle of Mars.--Write thou this Pentacle upon virgin parchment or paper, because it is terrible unto the Demons, and at its sight and aspect they will obey thee, for they cannot resist its presence.

Editor's Note.--Around the figure of the Scorpion is the word HVL. The versicle is from Psalm xci. 13:--'Thou shalt go upon the lion and adder, the young lion and the dragon shalt thou tread under thy feet.'

PLATE VII.

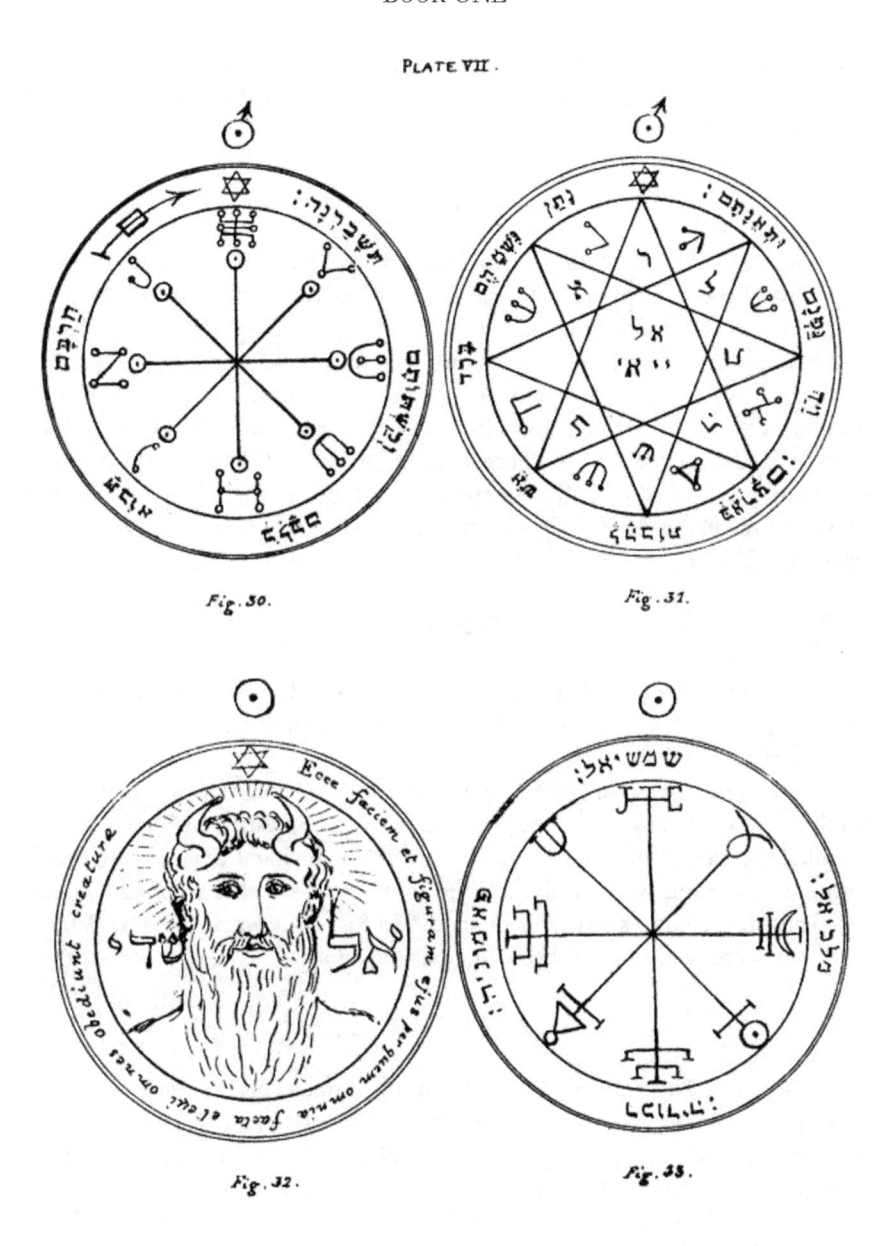

Fig. 30.

Fig. 31.

Fig. 32.

Fig. 33.

Figure 30.--The Sixth Pentacle of Mars.--It hath so great virtue that being armed therewith, if thou art attacked by any one, thou shalt neither be injured nor wounded when thou fightest with him, and his own weapons shall turn against him.

Editor's Note.--Around the eight points of the radii of the Pentacle are the words 'Elohim qeber, Elohim hath covered (or protected),' written in the

THE KEY OF SOLOMON THE KING

Secret Alphabet of Malachim, or the writing of the Angels. The versicle is from Psalm xxxvii. 15:--'Their sword shall enter into their own heart, and their bow shall be broken.'

Figure 31.--The Seventh and last Pentacle of Mars.--Write thou this upon virgin parchment or paper with the blood of a bat, in the day and hour of Mars; and uncover it within the Circle, invoking the Demons whose Names are therein written; and thou shalt immediately see hail and tempest.

Editor's Note.--In the centre of the Pentacle are the Divine Names, El and Yiai, which have the same numerical value when written in Hebrew. The Letters in Hebrew, and in the Secret Alphabet called the Celestial, compose the Names of Spirits. Round the Pentacle is:--'He gave them hail for rain, and flaming fire in their land. He smote their vines also, and their fig-trees.'--Psalm cv. 32, 33.

THE SUN

Figure 32.--The First Pentacle of the Sun.--The Countenance of Shaddaï the Almighty, at Whose aspect all creatures obey, and the Angelic Spirits do reverence on bended knees.

Editor's Note.--This singular Pentacle contains the head of the great Angel Methtraton or Metatron, the vice-gerent and representative of Shaddaï, who is called the Prince of Countenances, and the right-hand masculine Cherub of the Ark, as Sandalphon is the left and feminine. On either side is the Name 'El Shaddaï.' Around is written in Latin:'Behold His face and form by Whom all things were made, and Whom all creatures obey.'

Figure 33.--The Second Pentacle of the Sun.--This Pentacle, and the preceding and following, belong to the nature of the Sun. They serve to repress the pride and arrogance of the Solar Spirits, which are altogether proud and arrogant by their nature.

Editor's Note.--Mystical characters of the Sun and the Names of the Angels:--Shemeshiel, Paimoniah, Rekhodiah, and Malkhiel.

BOOK ONE

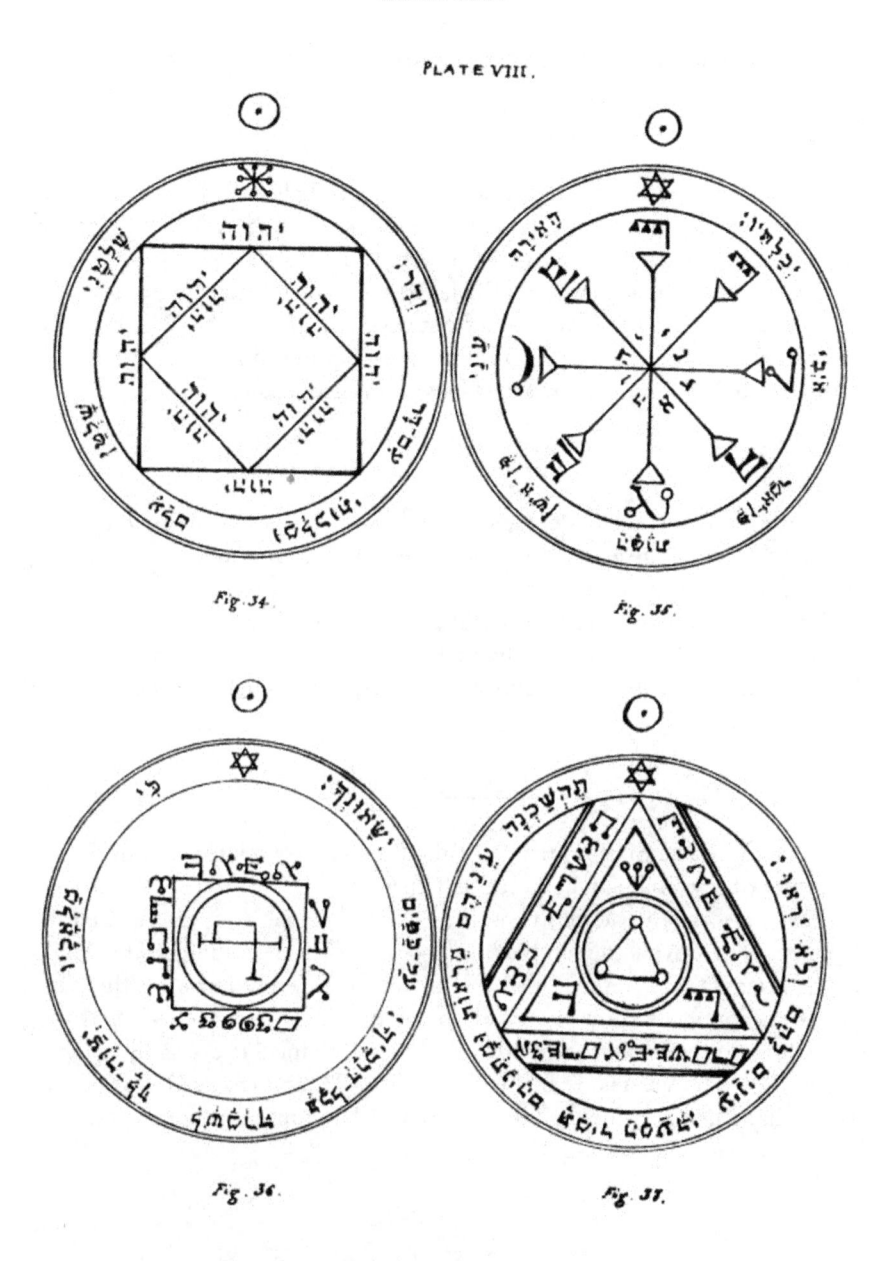

PLATE VIII.

Fig. 34.

Fig. 35.

Fig. 36.

Fig. 37.

Figure 34.--The Third Pentacle of the Sun.--This serveth in addition (to the effects of the two preceding) to acquire Kingdom and Empire, to inflict loss, and to acquire renown and glory, especially through the Name of God, Tetragrammaton, which therein is twelve times contained.

Editor's Note.--The Name IHVH, twelve times repeated; and a versicle somewhat similar to Daniel iv. 34:--'My Kingdom is an everlasting Kingdom, and my dominion endureth from age unto age.'

Figure 35.--The Fourth Pentacle of the Sun.--This serveth to enable thee to see the Spirits when they appear invisible unto those who invoke them; because, when thou hast uncovered it, they will immediately appear visible.

Editor's Note.--The Names IHVH, Adonai, are written in the centre in Hebrew; and round the radii in the mystical characters of the 'Passing of the River.' The versicle is from Psalm xiii. 3, 4:--'Lighten mine eyes that I sleep not in death, lest mine enemy say, I have prevailed against him.'

Figure 36.--The Fifth Pentacle of the Sun.--It serveth to invoke those Spirits who can transport thee from one place unto another, over a long distance and in short time.

Editor's Note.--Characters in the 'Passing of the River' Alphabet, forming Spirits' Names. The versicle is from Psalm xci. 11, 12:--'He shall give His Angels charge over thee, to keep thee in all thy ways. They shall bear thee up in their hands.'

Figure 37.--The Sixth Pentacle of the Sun.--It serveth excellently for the operation of invisibility, when correctly made.

Editor's Note.--In the centre is the Mystical letter Yod, in the Celestial Alphabet. The three letters in the 'Passing of the River' writing, in the Angles of the triangle, form the great Name Shaddaï. The words in the same characters round its three sides are, in my opinion, from Genesis 1. 1:--'In the beginning the Elohim created,' etc.; but the characters are sadly mangled in the MSS. The versicle is from Psalms lxix. 23, and cxxxv. 16:--'Let their eyes be darkened that they see not and make their loins continually to shake. They have eyes and see not.'

Book One

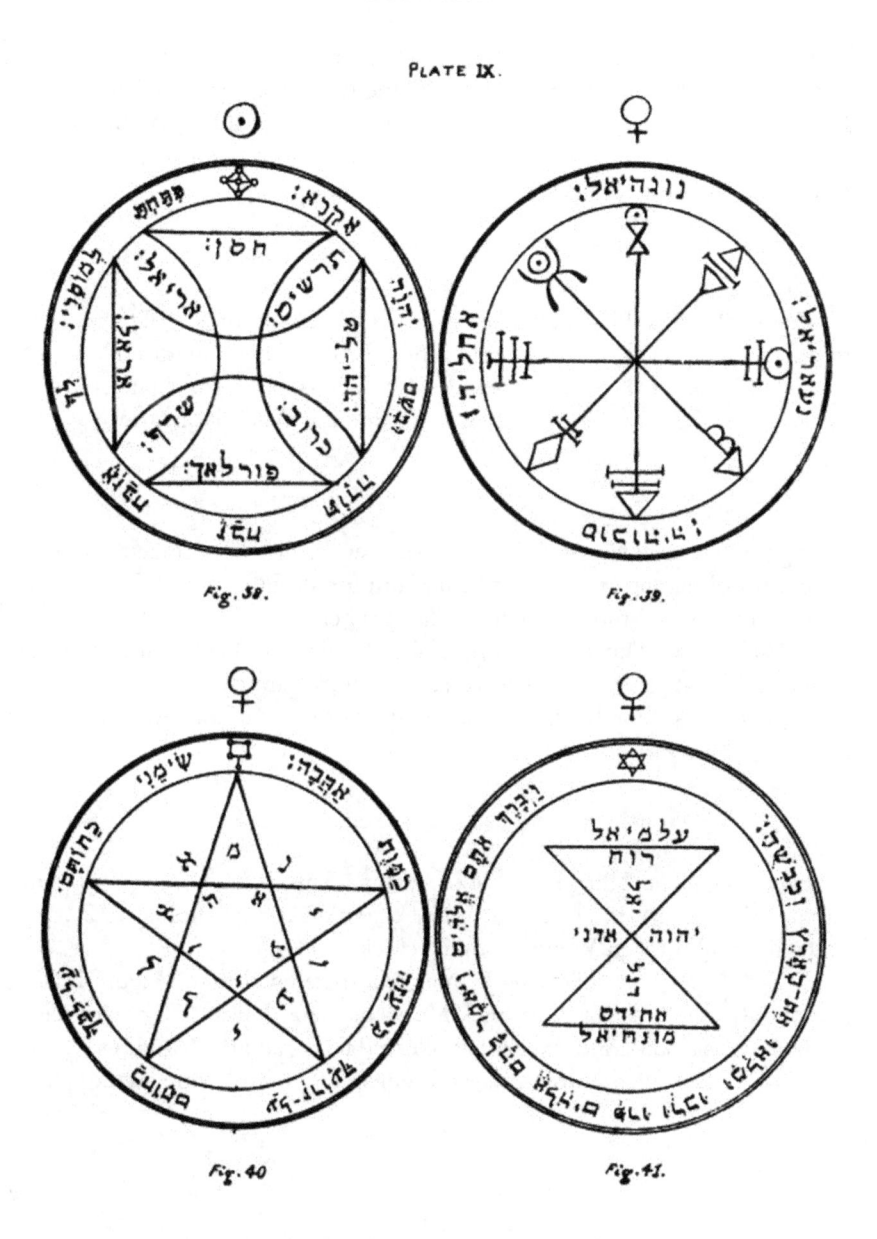

Plate IX.

Fig. 38.

Fig. 39.

Fig. 40.

Fig. 41.

Figure 38.--The Seventh and last Pentacle of the Sun.--If any be by chance imprisoned or detained in fetters of iron, at the presence of this Pentacle, which should be engraved in Gold on the day and hour of the Sun, he will be immediately delivered and set at liberty.

Editor's Note.--On the Arms of the Cross are written the Names of Chasan, Angel of Air; Arel, Angel of Fire; Phorlakh, Angel of Earth; and

Taliahad, Angel of Water. Between the four Arms of the Cross are written the names of the four Rulers of the Elements: Ariel, Seraph, Tharshis, and Cherub. The versicle is from Psalm cxvi. 16, 17:--'Thou hast broken my bonds in sunder. I will offer unto thee the sacrifice of thanksgiving, and will call upon the Name of IHVH.'

VENUS

Figure 39.--The First Pentacle of Venus.--This and those following serve to control the Spirits of Venus, and especially those herein written.
Editor's Note.--Mystical Characters of Venus, and the Names of the Angels: Nogahiel, Acheliah, Socodiah (or Socohiah) and Nangariel.

Figure 40.--The Second Pentacle of Venus.--These Pentacles are also proper for obtaining grace and honour, and for all things which belong unto Venus, and for accomplishing all thy desires herein.
Editor's Note.--The letters round and within the Pentagram form the Names of Spirits of Venus. The versicle is from Canticles viii. 6:--'Place me as a signet upon thine heart, as a signet upon thine arm, for love is strong as death.'

Figure 41.--The Third Pentacle of Venus.--This, if it be only shown unto any person, serveth to attract love. Its Angel Monachiel should be invoked in the day and hour of Venus, at one o'clock or at eight.
Editor's Note.--The following Names are written within the Figure IHVH, Adonai, Ruach, Achides, Ægalmiel, Monachiel, and Degaliel. The versicle is from Genesis i. 28:--'And the Elohim blessed them, and the Elohim said unto them, Be ye fruitful, and multiply, and replenish the earth, and subdue it.'

PLATE X.

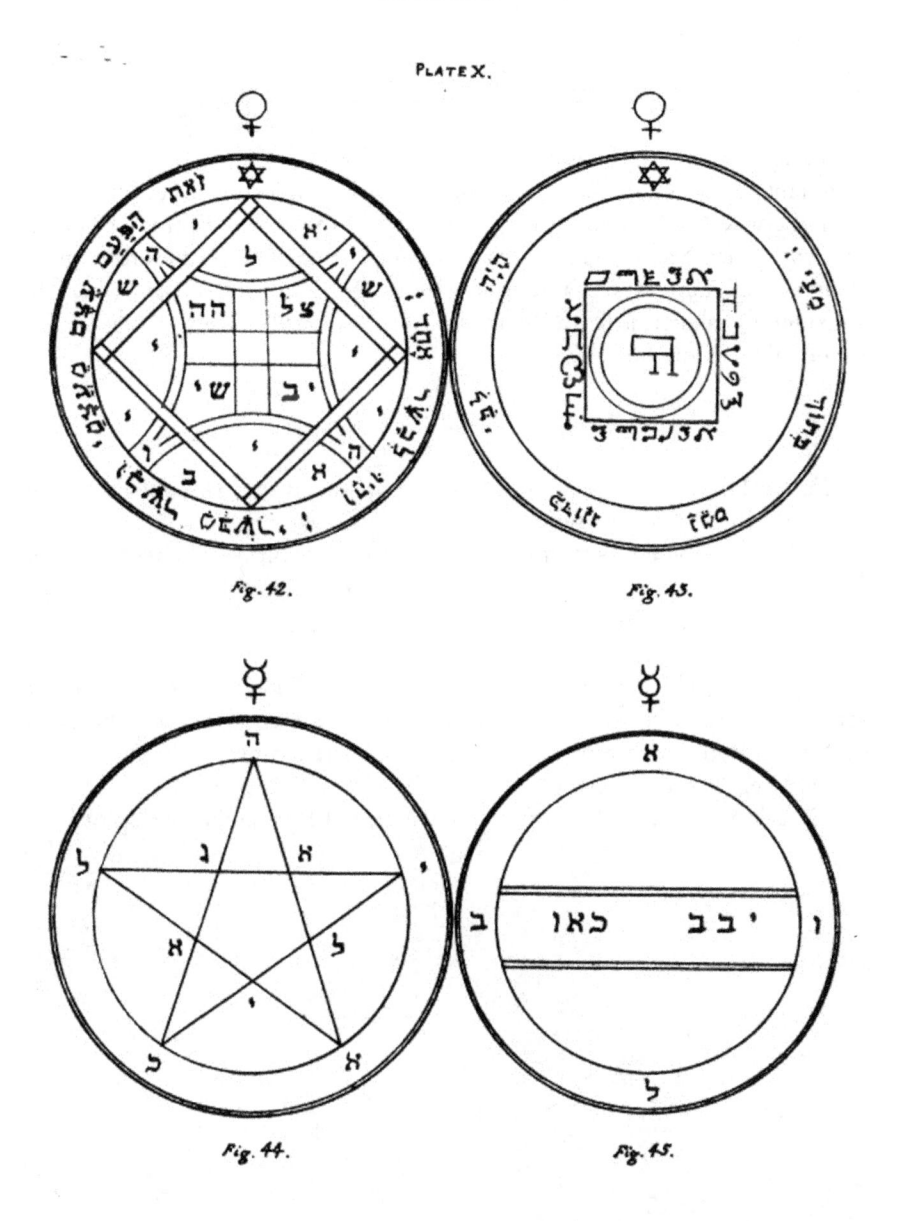

Fig. 42.

Fig. 43.

Fig. 44.

Fig. 45.

Figure 42.--The Fourth Pentacle of Venus.--It is of great power, since it compels the Spirits of Venus to obey, and to force on the instant any person thou wishest to come unto thee.

Editor's Note.--At the four Angles of the Figure are the four letters of the Name IHVH. The other letters form the Names of Spirits of Venus, e.g.:-- Schii, Eli, Ayib, etc. The versicle is from Genesis ii. 23, 24:--'This is bone of my bones, and flesh of my flesh. And they two were one flesh.'

The Key of Solomon the King

Figure 43.--The Fifth and last Pentacle of Venus.--When it is only showed unto any person soever, it inciteth and exciteth wonderfully unto love.

Editor's Note.--Around the central Square are the Names Elohim, El Gebil, and two other Names which I cannot decipher, and have, therefore, given them as they stand. The characters are those of the 'Passing of the River.' The surrounding versicle is from Psalm xxii. 14:--'My heart is like wax, it is melted in the midst of my bowels.'

MERCURY

Figure 44.--The First Pentacle of Mercury.--It serveth to invoke the Spirits who are under the Firmament.

Editor's Note.--Letters forming the Names of the Spirits Yekahel and Agiel.

Figure 45.--The Second Pentacle of Mercury.--The Spirits herein written serve to bring to effect and to grant things which are contrary unto the order of Nature; and which are not contained under any other head. They easily give answer, but they can with difficulty be seen.

Editor's Note.--The Letters form the Names of Böel and other Spirits.

PLATE XI.

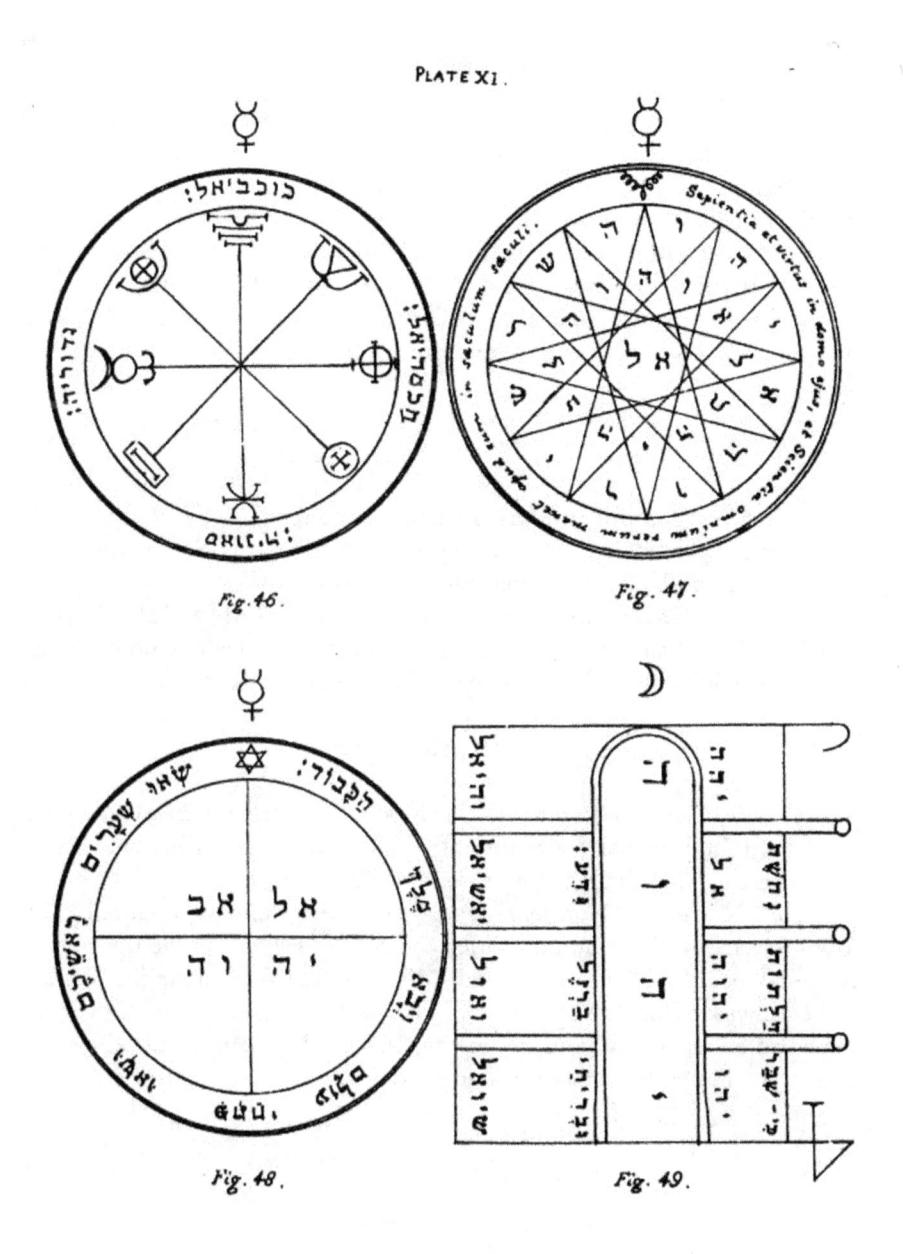

Fig. 46.

Fig. 47.

Fig. 48.

Fig. 49.

Figure 46.--The Third Pentacle of Mercury.--This and the following serve to invoke the Spirits subject unto Mercury; and especially those who are written in this Pentacle.

Editor's Note.--Mystical Characters of Mercury, and the Names of the Angels: Kokaviel, Ghedoriah, Savaniah, and Chokmahiel.

Figure 47.--The Fourth Pentacle of Mercury.--This is further proper to acquire the understanding and Knowledge of all things created, and to seek out and penetrate into hidden things; and to command those Spirits which are called Allatori to perform embassies. They obey very readily.

Editor's Note.--In the centre is the Name of God, El. The Hebrew letters inscribed about the dodecagram make the sentence, 'IHVH, fix Thou the Volatile, and let there be unto the void restriction.' The versicle is:--'Wisdom and virtue are in his house, and the Knowledge of all things remaineth with him for ever.'

Figure 48.--The Fifth and Last Pentacle of Mercury.--This commandeth the Spirits of Mercury, and serveth to open doors in whatever way they may be closed, and nothing it may encounter can resist it.

Editor's Note.--Within the Pentacle are the Names El Ab, and IHVH. The versicle is from Psalm xxiv. 7:--'Lift up your heads, O ye gates, and be ye lift up ye everlasting doors, and the King of Glory shall come in.'

THE MOON

Figure 49.--The First Pentacle of the Moon.--This and the following serve to call forth and invoke the Spirits of the Moon; and it further serveth to open doors, in whatever way they may be fastened.

Editor's Note.--The Pentacle is a species of hieroglyphic representation of a door or gate. In the centre is written the Name IHVH. On the right hand are the Names IHV, IHVH, AL, and IHH. On the left hand are the Names of the Angels: Schioel, Vaol, Yashiel, and Vehiel. The versicle above the Names on either side is from Psalm cvii. 16:--'He hath broken the Gates of brass, and- smitten the bars of iron in sunder.'

PLATE XII.

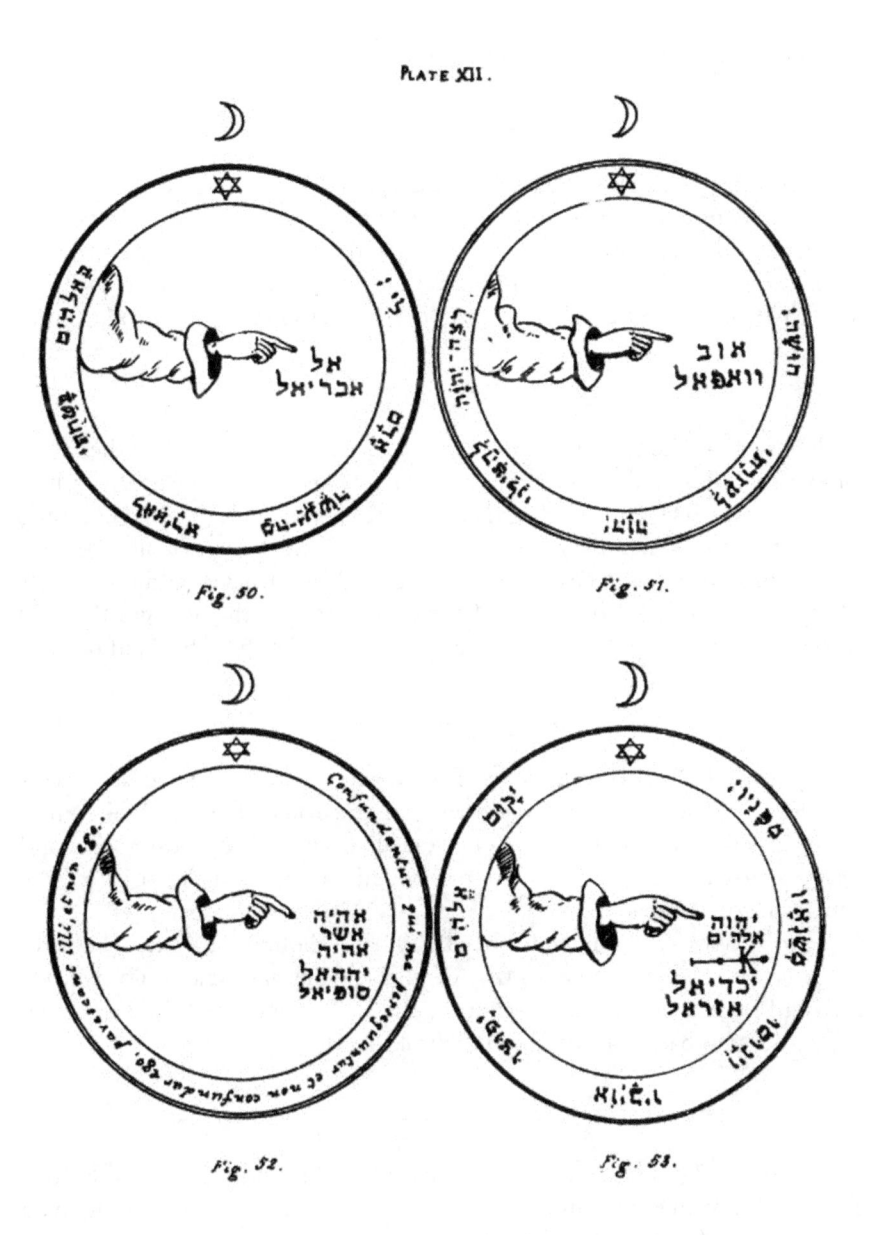

Fig. 50.

Fig. 51.

Fig. 52.

Fig. 53.

Figure 50.--The Second Pentacle of the Moon.--This serveth against all perils and dangers by water, and if it should chance that the Spirits of the Moon should excite and cause great rain and exceeding tempests about the Circle, in order to astonish and terrify thee; on showing unto them this Pentacle, it will all speedily cease.

Editor's Note.--A hand pointing to the Name El, and to that of the Angel Abariel. The versicle is from Psalm lvi. ii:--'In Elohim have I put my trust, I will not fear, what can man do unto me

---

Figure 51.--The Third Pentacle of the Moon.--This being duly borne with thee when upon a journey, if it be properly made, serveth against all attacks by night, and against every kind of danger and peril by Water.

Editor's Note.--The Names Aub and Vevaphel. The versicle is from Psalm xl. 13:--'Be pleased O IHVH to deliver me, O IHVH make haste to help me.'

Figure 52.--The Fourth Pentacle of the Moon.--This defendeth thee from all evil sorceries, and from all injury unto soul or body. Its Angel, Sophiel, giveth the knowledge of the virtue of all herbs and stones; and unto whomsoever shall name him, he will procure the knowledge of all.

Editor's Note.--The Divine Name Eheieh Asher Eheieh, and the Names of the Angels Yahel and Sophiel. The versicle is:--'Let them be confounded who persecute me, and let me not be confounded; let them fear,and not I.'

Figure 53.--The Fifth Pentacle of the Moon.--It serveth to have answers in sleep. Its Angel Iachadiel serveth unto destruction and loss, as well as unto the destruction of enemies. Thou mayest also call upon him by Abdon and Dalé against all Phantoms of the night, and to summon the souls of the departed from Hades.

Editor's Note.--The Divine Names IHVH and Elohim, a mystical character of the Moon, and the Names of the Angels Iachadiel and Azarel. The versicle is from Psalm lxviii. 1:--'Let God arise, and let His enemies be scattered; let them also who hate Him flee before Him.'

Figure 54--The Sixth and Last Pentacle of the Moon.--This is wonderfully good, and serveth excellently to excite and cause heavy rains, if it be engraved upon a plate of silver; and if it be placed under water, as long as it remaineth there, there will be rain. It should be engraved, drawn, or written in the day and hour of the Moon.

Editor's Note.--The Pentacle is composed of mystical characters of the Moon, surrounded by a versicle from Genesis vii. 11, 12:--'All the fountains of the great deep were broken up . . . and the rain was upon the earth.'

This is the end of the Holy Pentacles, in all which I have, to the best of my power, restored the Hebrew letters and mystical characters correctly. I have further given nearly every versicle in pointed Hebrew, instead of in the Latin; so that the Occult student might not be inconvenienced by having to search out the same in a Hebrew Bible. The restoration of the Hebrew letters in the body of the Pentacles has been a work of immense difficulty, and has extended over several years.

The Key of Solomon the King

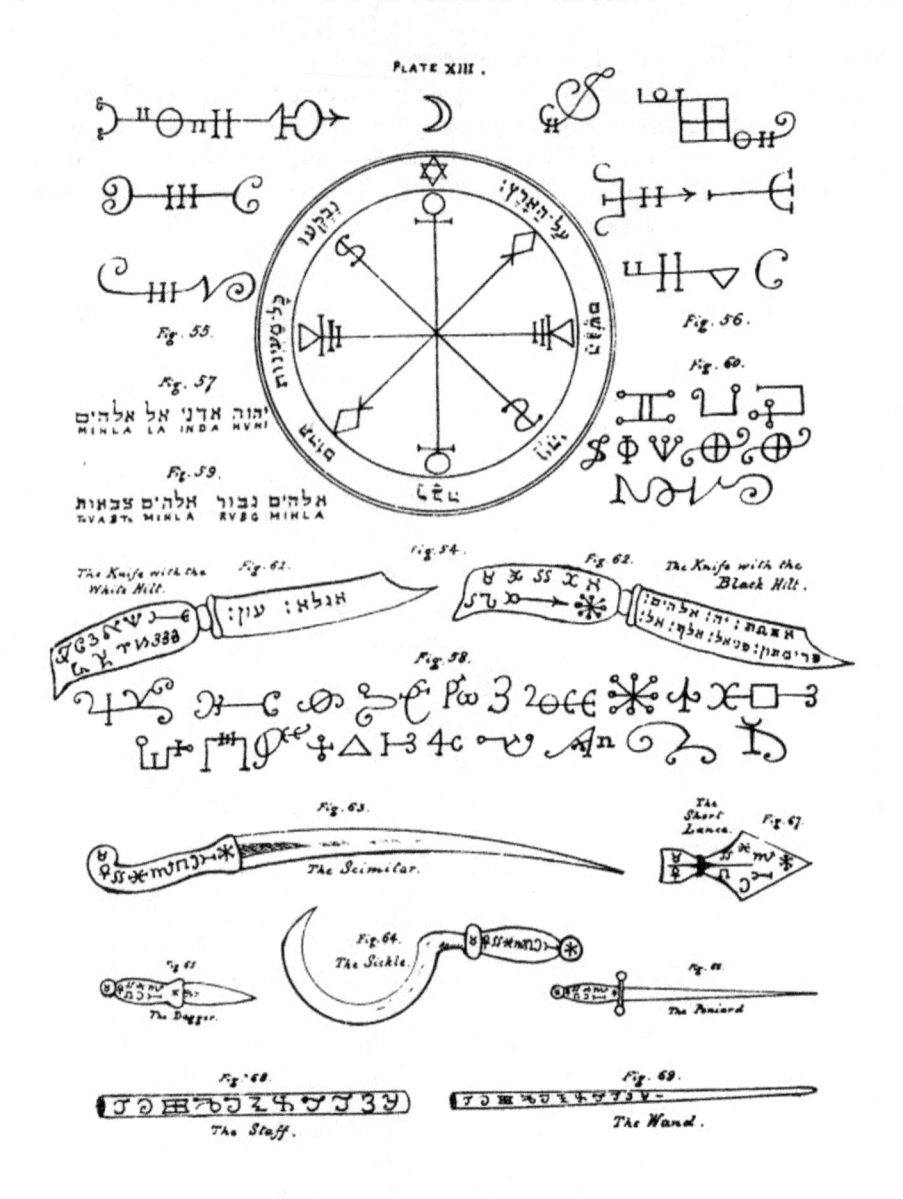

PLATE XIII.

Fig. 55.   Fig. 56.

Fig. 57.
יהוה אדני אל אלהים
MINLA LA INDA HVHI

Fig. 60.

Fig. 59.
אלהים גבור אלה׳ים צבאות
TVABT MINLA RVBG MINLA

Fig. 61. The Knife with the White Hilt.   Fig. 54.   Fig. 62. The Knife with the Black Hilt.

Fig. 58.

Fig. 63. The Scimitar.

Fig. 67. The Short Lance.

Fig. 65. The Dagger.   Fig. 64. The Sickle.   Fig. 66. The Poniard.

Fig. 68. The Staff.   Fig. 69. The Wand.

BOOK ONE

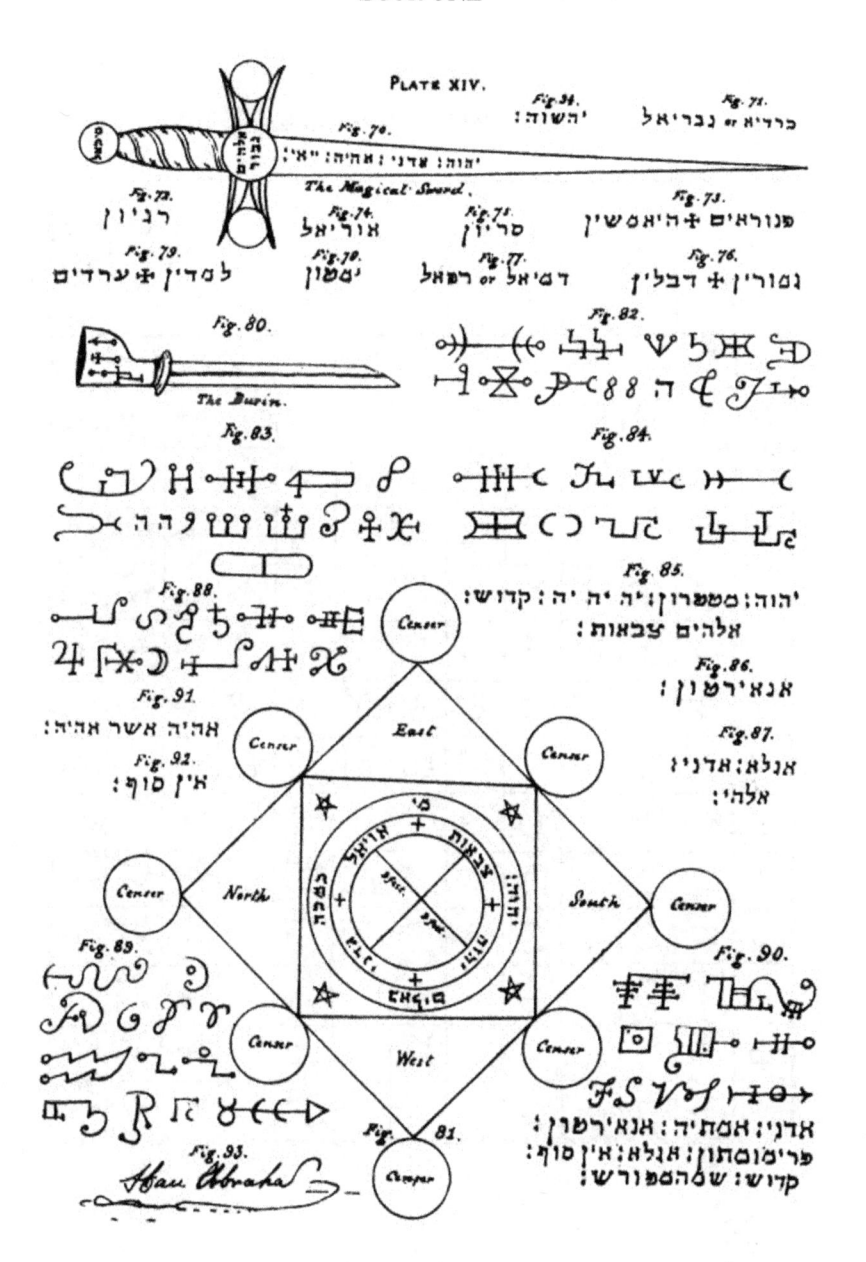

PLATE XIV.

THE KEY OF SOLOMON THE KING

PLATE XV.

The Mystical Alphabets.

Hebrew Alphabet.	Alphabet of the Magi.	The Characters of Celestial Writing.	Malachim or the Writing of the Angels.	The Writing called "Passing the River."	Names of the Letters.	The Powers of the Letters.
א					Aleph	Samekh	a'	s
ב					Beth	Ayin	a,h,v	da,ng
ג					Gimel	Pé	g,gh	p,ph
ד					Daleth	Tzaddi	d,dh	tz
ה					Hé	Qoph	h'	q,qh
ו					Vau	Resh	v,u,o	r
ז					Zain	Schin	z	s,sh
ח					Cheth	Tau	ch,gut.	t,th
ט	Finals				Teth		t	
י					Yod	Final Kaph	i,y	k
כ					Kaph	Final Mem	k,kh	m
ל					Lamed	Final Nun	l	n
מ					Mem	Final Pé	m	p
נ					Nun	Final Tzaddi	n	tz

THE KEY OF SOLOMON THE KING

BOOK TWO

THE KEY OF SOLOMON THE KING

PREFATORY NOTE[111]

THIS Work of Solomon is divided into two books. In the first thou mayest see and know how to avoid errors in Experiments, Operations, and in the Spirits themselves. In the second thou art taught in what manner Magical Arts may be reduced to the proposed object and end.

It is for this reason that thou shouldest take great heed and care that this Key of Secrets fall not into the hands of the foolish, the stupid, and the ignorant. For he who is the possessor hereof, and who availeth himself hereof according to the ordinances herein contained, will not only be able to reduce the Magical Arts herein unto their proposed end, but will, even if he findeth certain errors herein, be able to correct them.

Any Art or Operation of this kind will not be able to attain its end, unless the Master of the Art, or Exorcist, shall have this Work completely in his power, that is to say, unless he thoroughly understand it, for without this he will never attain the effect of any operation.

For this reason I earnestly pray and conjure the person into whose hands this Key of Secrets may fall, neither to communicate it, nor to make any one a partaker in this knowledge, if he be not faithful, nor capable of keeping a secret, nor expert in the Arts. And I most humbly entreat the possessor of this, by the Ineffable Name of God in four Letters, YOD, HE, VAU, HE, and by the Name ADONAI, and by all the other Most High and Holy Names of God, that he values this work as dearly as his own soul, and that he makes no foolish or ignorant man a partaker therein.

---

[111] This Prefatory Note is only found in 3991 Harleian MSS., 3091 Sloane MSS., and 288 King's MSS.

BOOK TWO

Chapter I

At What Hour After the Preparation of All Things Necessary, We Should Bring the Exercise of the Art to Perfection

THE Days and Hours have already been treated of, in general, in the First Book. It is now necessary to notice in particular at what hour accomplishment and perfection should be given to the Arts, all things necessary having been previously prepared.

Should it then happen that thou hast undertaken any secret operation for conversing with or conjuring Spirits, in which the day and the hour are not marked, thou shalt put it in execution on the days and hours of Mercury, at the sixteenth or twenty-third hour, but it will be still better at the eighth, which is the third [112] of the same night, which is called and means before the morning, for then thou shalt be able to put in practice all the Arts and Operations which should be performed, according as it shall please thee by day or by night, provided that they have been prepared at the hours suitable to them, as hath been already said. But when neither hour nor time of operation or invocation is specified, it is then much better to perform these experiments at night, seeing that it is more easy to the Spirits to appear in the peaceful silence of night than during the day. And thou shouldest inviolably observe, that wishing to invoke the Spirits, either by day or by night, it is necessary that it should be done in a place hidden, removed, secret, convenient, and proper for such Art, where no man frequenteth or inhabiteth, as we shall relate more fully in its place.

If then thou shouldest operate touching anything which hath been stolen, in whatever way it be performed and whatever way it may have been prepared, it is necessary to practise it on the days and hours of the Moon, being if possible in her increase, and from the first unto the eighth hour of the day.

But if it be by night, then it should be at the fifth or at the third hour; but it is better by day than by the night, for the light justifieth them, and maketh them much more fit for publication.

But if the Operations be regarding Invisibility, they should be put in practice at the first, second, and third hour of Mars by day. But if by night, until the third hour.

If they be Operations of seeking love, grace, or favour, they should be performed until the eighth hour of the same day, commencing with the first hour of the Sun; and from the first hour of Venus unto the first hour of the same day of Venus.

As for Operations of destruction and desolation, we should practise and

---

[112] In 10862 Add. MSS. it says 'the second.'

put them into execution on the day of Saturn at the first hour, or rather at the eighth or fifteenth of the day; and from the first until the eighth hour of the night.

Experiments of games, raillery, deceit, illusion, and invisibility, ought to be done at the first hour of Venus, and at the eighth hour of the day but by night at the third and at the seventh.

At all times of practising and putting into execution Magical Arts, the Moon should be increasing in light, and in an equal number of degrees with the Sun; and it is much better from the first quarter to the Opposition, and the Moon should be in a fiery Sign, and notably in that of the Ram or of the Lion.

Therefore, to execute these Experiments in any manner whatsoever, it should be done when the Moon is clear, and when she is increasing in light.

In order to put in execution those of Invisibility after everything is properly prepared, the Moon should be in the Sign of the Fishes, in the hours proper and fitting, and she should be increasing in light.

For experiments of seeking love and favour, in whatever way it may be desired, they will succeed, provided that they have been prepared at the proper hours, and that the Moon be increasing in light and in the Sign of the Twins.

So exact a preparation of days and hours is not necessary for those who are adepts in the Art, but it is extremely necessary for apprentices and beginners, seeing that those who have been little or not at all instructed herein, and who only begin to apply themselves to this Art, do not have as much faith in the experiments as those who are adepts therein, and who have practised them. But as regards beginners, they should always have the days and hours well disposed and appropriate unto the Art. And the Wise should only observe the precepts of the Art which are necessary, and in observing the other solemnities necessary they will operate with a perfect assurance.

It is, nevertheless, necessary to take care that when thou shalt have prepared any experiment thyself for the days and hours ordained, that it should be performed in clear, serene, mild, and pleasant weather, without any great tempest or agitation of the air, which should not be troubled by winds. For when thou shalt have conjured any Spirits in any art or experiment, they will not come when the air is troubled or agitated by winds, seeing that Spirits have neither flesh nor bones, and are created of different substances.

Some are created from Water.

Others from Wind, unto which they are like.

Some from Earth.

Some from Clouds.

Others from Solar Vapours.

Others from the keenness and strength of Fire; and when they are invoked or summoned, they come always with great noise, and with the terrible nature of fire.

When the Spirits which are created of Water are invoked, they come with great rains, thunder, hail, lightning, thunder-bolts, and the like.

When the Spirits which are created of Clouds are invoked, they come with great deformity, in a horrible form, to strike fear into the Invocator, and with an exceeding great noise.

Others[113] which are formed from Wind appear like thereunto and with exceeding swift motion, and whensoever those which are created from Beauty[114] appear, they will show themselves in a fair and agreeable form; moreover, whensoever thou shalt call the Spirits created from Air, they will come with a kind of gentle breeze.

When the Spirits which are created from the Vapours of the Sun are invoked, they come under a very beautiful and excellent form, but filled with pride, vanity, and conceit. They are clever, whence it comes that these last are all specified by Solomon in his book of ornament, or of beauty. They show great ostentation and vainglory in their dress, and they rejoice in many ornaments; they boast of possessing mundane beauty, and all sorts of ornaments and decorations. Thou shalt only invoke them in serene, mild, and pleasant weather.

The Spirits[115] which are created of Fire reside in the east, those created of Wind in the south.

Note then that it will be much better to perform the experiments or operations in the direction of the east, putting everything necessary in practice towards that point.

But for all other operations or extraordinary experiments, and for those of love, they will be much more efficacious directed towards the north.

Take heed further, that every time that thou performest any experiment, to reduce it unto perfection with the requisite solemnities, thou shalt recommence the former experiment if interrupted therein, without the preparation of hours or other solemnities:

If by chance it should happen that having performed an experiment with due observance of days, hours, and requisite solemnities, thou shalt find it unsuccessful, it must be in some manner false, ill-arranged and defective, and thou must assuredly have failed in some matter; for if thou doest ill in one single point, these experiments or these Arts will not be verified.

Thus upon this Chapter dependeth this whole Key of Arts, Experiments, and Operations, and although every solemnity be rightly observed, no experiment will be verified, unless thou canst penetrate the meaning of this

---

[113] This paragraph is only found in 10862 Add. MSS.
[114] The Name of the Sixth Qabalistical Sephira or Emanation from the Deity, which is called Tiphereth, or Beauty.
[115] I have usually found it said exactly vice versâ.

Chapter.

BOOK TWO

CHAPTER II

In What Manner the Master of the Art Should Keep, Rule, and Govern Himself

HE who wisheth to apply himself unto so great and so difficult a Science should have his mind free from all business, and from all extraneous ideas of whatever nature they may be.

He should then thoroughly examine the Art or Operation which he should undertake, and write it regularly out on paper, particularly set aside for that purpose, with the appropriate conjurations and exorcisms. If there be anything to mark or write down, it should be performed in the manner specified regarding the paper, ink, and pen. He should also observe at what day and at what hour this Experiment should be undertaken, and what things are necessary to prepare for it, what should be added, and what can be dispensed with.

The which matters being prepared, it is necessary for thee to search out and arrange some fitting place wherein the Magical Art and its Experiments can be put in practice. All these things being thus arranged and disposed, let the Master of the Art go into a proper and fitting place, or into his Cabinet or Secret Chamber if it be convenient for the purpose, and he can there dispose and set in order the whole operation; or he can use any other convenient secret place for the purpose, provided that no one knoweth where it is, and that no man can see him when there.

After this he must strip himself entirely naked, and let him have a bath ready prepared, wherein is water exorcised, after the manner which we shall describe, so that he may bathe and purify himself therein from the crown of his head unto the sole of his foot, saying:--

O Lord ADONAI, Who hast formed me Thine unworthy servant in Thine Image and resemblance of vile and of abject earth; deign to bless and to sanctify this Water, so that it may be for the health and purification of my sotd, and of my body, so that no foolishness or deceitfulness may therein in any way have place.

O Most Powerful and Ineffable God, Who madest Thy people pass dryshod through the Red Sea when they came up out of the Land of Egypt, grant unto me grace that I may be purified and regenerated from all my past sins by this Water, that so no uncleanness may appear upon me in Thy Presence.

After this thou shalt entirely immerse thyself in the Water, and thou shalt dry thyself with a towel of clean white linen, and then thou shalt put upon thy flesh the garments of pure white linen whereof we shall speak hereafter.

Hereafter, for three days at least, thou shalt abstain from all idle, vain, and impure reasonings, and from every kind of impurity and sin, as will be shown in the Chapter of fast and of vigil. Each day shalt thou recite the following prayer, at least once in the morning, twice about noon, thrice in the afternoon, four times in the evening, and five times before lying down to sleep; this shalt thou do on the three ensuing days:--

Prayer

HERACHIO, ASAC, ASACRO, BEDRIMULAEL, TILATH, ARABONAS, IERAHLEM, IDEODOC, ARCHARZEL, ZOPHIEL, BLAUTEL, BARACATA, EDONIEL, ELOHIM, EMAGRO, ABRAGATEH, SAMOEL, GEBURAHEL, CADATO, ERA, ELOHI, ACHSAH, EBMISHA, IMACHEDEL, DANIEL, DAMA, ELAMOS, IZACHEL, BAEL, SEGON, GEMON, DEMAS.

O Lord God, Who art seated upon the Heavens, and Who regardest the Abysses beneath, grant unto me Thy Grace I beseech Thee, so that what I conceive in my mind I may accomplish in my work, through Thee, O God, the Sovereign Ruler of all, Who livest and reignest unto the Ages of the Ages. Amen.

These three days having passed, thou must have all things in readiness, as hath been said, and after this a day appointed and set apart. It will be necessary for thee to wait for the hour in which thou shouldest commence the Operation; but when once it shall be commenced at this hour, thou shalt be able to continue it unto the end, seeing that it deriveth its force and virtue from its beginning, which extendeth to and spreadeth over the succeeding hours, so that the Master of the Art will be enabled to complete his work so as to arrive at the desired result.

Chapter III

How the Companions of the Master of the Art Ought to Regulate and Govern Themselves

WHEN the Master of the Art wisheth to put in practice any Operation or Experiment, especially one of importance, he should first consider of what Companions he should avail himself. This is the reason why in every Operation whose Experience should be carried out in the Circle, it is well to have three Companions. And if he cannot have Companions, he should at least have with him a faithful and attached dog. But if it be absolutely necessary for him to have Companions, these Companions should be obligated and bound by oath to do all that the Master shall order and prescribe them, and they should study, observe, and carefully retain, and be attentive unto all which they shall hear. For those who shall act otherwise shall suffer and endure many pains and labours, and run into many dangers, which the Spirits will cause and procure for them, and for this cause sometimes they shall even die.

The Disciples then, being well and thoroughly instructed, and fortified with a wise and understanding heart, the Master shall take exorcised water, and he shall enter with his Disciples into a secret place purified and clean, where he must strip them entirely naked; after this, let him pour exorcised water upon their heads, which he should cause to flow from the crown of their head unto the sole of their feet, so as to bathe them entirely therewith; and while bathing them thus, he should say:--

Be ye regenerate, cleansed, and purified, in the Name of the Ineffable, Great, and Eternal God, from all your iniquities, and may the virtue of the Most High descend upon you and abide with you always, so that ye may have the power and strength to accomplish the desires of your heart. Amen.

After this let the Disciples robe themselves as the Master hath done, and fast like him for three days, repeating the same prayer; let them act like him, and in the work let them implicitly follow and obey him in all things.

But if the Master of the Art wisheth to have a dog for his Companion, he must bathe him thoroughly with the exorcised water in the same manner as the Disciples, and let him perfume him with the odours and incense of Art, and let him repeat the following Conjuration over him:--

I conjure thee, O thou Creature, being a Dog, by Him Who hath created thee, I bathe and I perfume thee in the Name of the Most High, Most Powerful, and Eternal God, so that thou mayest be my true Companion in this operation, and that thou mayest be also my faithful friend in whatsoever operation I may hereafter perform.

But if he wisheth to have for his companion a little boy or girl, which will be still better, he must ordain them as he hath ordained the dog; and he must pare and cut the nails of their hands and of their feet, saying:--

I conjure thee, O thou Creature, being a young girl (or boy), by the Most High God, the Father of all Creatures, by the Father ADONAI ELOHIM, and by the Father ELION, that thou shalt have neither will nor power to hide from me anything, nor yet to keep back from me the truth in all which I shall demand of thee, and that thou be obedient and faithful unto me. Amen.

Let him purify, cleanse, and wash this young child anew, with the Water of Art, saying:--

Be thou regenerate, cleansed, and purified, so that the Spirits may neither harm thee nor abide in thee. Amen.

Then perfume the child with odours as above.

When the Companions shall be thus ordained and disposed, the Master shall be able to operate in surety together with them, every time that it shall please him; and he shall perform his operation happily, and shall attain his end.

But for the safety both of soul and of body, the Master and the Companions should have the Pentacles before their breasts, consecrated, and covered with a silken veil, and perfumed with the proper fumigations. By the which being assured and encouraged, they may enter into the matter without fear or terror, and they shall be exempt and free from all perils and dangers, provided that they obey the commands of the Master and do all that he ordain them. If they shall act thus, all things shall go according unto their desires.

All being thus arranged, the Master should take heed that His Disciples are perfectly instructed in those things which they have to perform.

These Companions or Disciples should be three in number, without including the Master. They may also be of the number of five, of seven, or of nine; but so that they ever implicitly obey the orders of their Master; for thus only shall all things come to a successful issue.

BOOK TWO

CHAPTER IV

Concerning the Fasting, Care and Things to be Observed

WHEN the Master of the Art shall wish to perform his operations, having previously arranged all things which it is necessary to observe and practise; from the first day of the Experiment, it is absolutely necessary to ordain and to prescribe care and observation, to abstain from all things unlawful, and from every kind of impiety, impurity, wickedness, or immodesty, as well of body as of soul; as, for example, eating and drinking superabundantly, and all sorts of vain words, buffooneries, slanders, calumnies, and other useless discourse; but instead to do good deeds, speak honestly, keep a strict decency in all things, never lose sight of modesty in walking, in conversation, in eating and drinking, and in all things; the which should be principally done and observed for nine days, before the commencement of the Operation. The Disciples should do the same, and should equally put in practice all things necessary to be observed, if they wish to make use of all these operations and experiments.

But before the commencement of the work, it is absolutely necessary that the Master with his Disciples repeat the following Conjuration once in the morning, and twice in the evening:--

THE CONJURATION

O Lord God Almighty, be propitious unto me a miserable sinner, for I am not worthy to raise mine eyes unto heaven, because of the iniquity of my sins and the multitude of my faults. O pitying and merciful Father, who wouldest not the death of a sinner but rather that he should turn from his wickedness and live, O God have mercy upon me and pardon all my sins; for I unworthy entreat Thee, O Father of all Creatures, Thou Who art full of mercy and of compassion, by Thy great goodness, that Thou deign to grant unto me power to see and know these Spirits which I desire to behold and to invoke to appear before me and to accomplish my will. Through Thee Who art Conqueror, and Who art Blessed unto the Ages of the Ages. Amen.

O Lord God the Father Eternal, Who art seated upon the Kerubim and the Seraphim, Who lookest upon Earth and upon Sea; unto Thee do I raise my hands and implore Thine aid alone, Thou Who alone art the accomplishment of good works, Thou Who givest rest unto those who labour, Who humblest the proud, Who art the Author of Life and the Destroyer of Death; Thou art our rest, Thou art the Protector of those who invoke Thee; protect, guard, and defend me in this matter, and in this enterprise which I propose to carry out, O Thou Who livest, reignest, and abidest unto the Eternal Ages. Amen.

During the three last days before the commencement of this action, thou shalt content thyself with only eating fasting diet, and that only once in the day; and it will be better still if thou only partakest of bread and water. Thou shalt also abstain from every impure thing; reciting the prayer above written. And on the last day, when thou shalt wish to commence the Operation, thou shalt remain all day without eating, and later on thou shalt go into a secret place, where thou shalt confess all thy sins unto God with a contrite heart. The Disciples also, together with the Master, shall recite the same confession with a low but distinct voice, as hath been already said in the First Book.

This having been done thrice with a devout, pure, and contrite heart, in a place withdrawn from men, cleansed, and pure, where thou canst not be seen, taking the water and the hyssop, thou shalt say:--

Purify me, O Lord, with hyssop, and I shall be pure; wash me, and I shall be whiter than snow.

After this, bathe thyself with the exorcised water, and clothe thyself again with the consecrated garment which thou hast taken off; cerise thyself, and surround thyself with odours, as will be told farther on, when we speak of perfumes and suffumigations.

The which being done, thou shalt go unto the ordained place with thy Companions, and all things being prepared, thou shalt make the Circle, as hath been already said, with all other necessary ceremonies; then shalt thou commence to invoke the Spirits by the Exorcisms; thou shalt also repeat anew the foregoing Confession as hath been already said in the First Book. After which, in sign of amendment and of repentance, each shall mutually kiss the other.

Mark well, that up to this point, the Disciples should do the same things as the Master.

Let the Master now give his commands unto his Disciples, and pursue the course of the Experiment, and work with all diligence to bring it unto perfection.

Chapter V

Concerning the Baths and How They Are to Be Arranged

THE Bath is necessary for all Magical and Necromantic Arts; wherefore, if thou wishest to perform any experiment or operation, having arranged all things necessary thereunto according to the proper days and hours, thou shalt go unto a river or running stream, or thou shalt have warm water ready in some large vessel or tub in thy secret cabinet, and while disrobing thyself of thy raiment thou shalt repeat the following Psalms:--Psalms xiv. or liii.; xxvii.; liv.; lxxxi.; cv.

And when the Master shall be entirely disrobed let him enter into the water or into the Bath, and let him say:--

The Exorcism of the Water

I exorcise thee, O Creature of Water, by Him Who hath created thee and gathered thee together into one place so that the dry land appeared, that thou uncover all the deceits of the Enemy, and that thou cast out from thee all the impurities and uncleannesses of the Spirits of the World of Phantasm, so they may harm me not, through the virtue of God Almighty Who liveth and reigneth unto the Ages of the Ages. Amen.

Then shalt thou begin to wash thyself thoroughly in the Bath, saying:--

MERTALIA, MUSALIA, DOPHALIA, ONEMALIA, ZITANSEIA, GOLDAPHAIRA, DEDULSAIRA, GHEVIALAIRA, GHEMINAIRA, GEGROPHEIRA, CEDAHI, GILTHAR, GODIEB, EZOIIL, MUSIL, GRASSIL, TAMEN, PUERI, GODU, HUZNOTH, ASTACHOTH, TZABAOTH, ADONAI, AGLA, ON, EL, TETRAGRAMMATON, SHEMA, ARESION, ANAPHAXETON, SEGILATON, PRIMEUMATON.

All the which Names thou shalt repeat twice or thrice, until thou art completely washed and clean, and when thou are perfectly pure thou shalt quit the Bath, and sprinkle thyself with exorcised water, in the manner described later on, and thou shalt say:--

Purge me, O Lord, with hyssop, and I shall be clean; wash me, and I shall be whiter than snow.

Whilst again clothing thyself, thou shalt recite the following Psalms: Psalms cii.; li.; iv.; xxx.; cxix., Mem, v. 97; cxiv.; cxxvi.; cxxxix.

After which thou shalt recite the following Prayer:--

The Key of Solomon the King

Prayer

EL Strong and Wonderful, I bless Thee, I adore Thee, I glorify Thee, I invoke Thee, I render Thee thanks from this Bath, so that this Water may be able to cast from me all impurity and concupiscence of heart, through Thee, O Holy ADONAI; and may I accomplish all things through Thee Who livest and reignest unto the Ages of the Ages. Amen.

After this take the Salt and bless it in this manner:--

The Benediction of the Salt

The Blessing of the Father Almighty be upon this Creature of Salt, and let all malignity and hindrance be cast forth hence from, and let all good enter herein, for without Thee man cannot live, wherefore I bless thee and invoke thee, that thou mayest aid me.

Then thou shalt recite over the Salt Psalm ciii.

Then taking the grains of the exorcised Salt thou shalt cast them into the aforesaid Bath; and thou shalt again disrobe thyself, pronouncing the following words:--

IMANEL, ARNAMON, IMATO, MEMEON, RECTACON, MUOBOII, PALTELLON, DECAION, YAMENTON, YARON, TATONON, VAPHORON, GARDON, EXISTON, ZAGVERON, MOMERTON, ZARMESITON, TILEION, TIXMION.

After this thou shalt enter a second time into the Bath and recite Psalms civ. and lxxxi.

Then thou shalt quit the Bath and clothe thyself as before in linen garments clean and white, and over them thou shalt put the garments, of which we shall speak in the proper Chapter, and thus clothed thou shalt go to finish thy work.

The Disciples should wash themselves in like manner, and with like solemnities.

BOOK TWO

CHAPTER VI

Of the Garments and Shoes of the Art

THE exterior habiliments which the Master of the Art should wear ought to be of linen, as well as those which he weareth beneath them; and if he hath the means they should be of Silk. If they be of linen the thread of which they are made should have been spun by a young maiden.

The characters shown in Figure 55 should be embroidered on the breast with the needle of Art in red silk.

The shoes should also be White, upon the which the characters in Figure 56 should be traced in the same way.

The shoes or boots should be made of white leather, on the which should be marked the Signs and Characters of Art. These shoes should be made during the days of fast and abstinence, namely, during the nine days set apart before the beginning of the Operation, during which the necessary instruments also should be prepared, polished, brightened, and cleaned.

Besides this, the Master of the Art should have a Crown made of virgin paper, upon the which should be written these four Names: YOD, HE, VAU, HE, in front; ADONAI behind; EL on the right; and ELOHIM on the left. (See Figure 57.) These Names should be written with the ink and pen of the Art, whereof we shall speak in the proper Chapter. The Disciples should also each have a Crown of virgin paper whereon these Divine symbols should be marked in scarlet. (See Figure 58.)

Take heed also that in clothing thyself with these aforesaid habiliments, that thou recite these Psalms:--Psalms xv.; cxxxi.; cxxxvii.; cxvii.; lxvii.; lxviii.; and cxxvii.

After this perfume the vestments with the perfumes and suffumigations of the Art, and sprinkle them with the water and hyssop of the Art.

But when the Master and His Disciples shall commence to robe themselves after the first Psalm, and before continuing with the others, he should pronounce these words:--

AMOR, AMATOR, AMIDES, IDECIDANIACH, PAMOR, PLAIOR, ANITOR; through the merits of these holy Angels will I robe and indue myself with the Vestments of Power, through which may I conduct unto the desired end those things which I ardently wish, through Thee, O Most Holy ADONAI, Whose Kingdom and Empire endureth for ever. Amen.

Take notice that if the linen garments were vestments of the Levites or of the Priests, and had been used for holy things, that they would be all the better.

Chapter VII

Of Places Wherein We May Conveniently Execute the Experiments and Operations of the Art

THE places best fitted for exercising and accomplishing Magical Arts and Operations are those which are concealed, removed, and separated from the habitations of men. Wherefore desolate and uninhabited regions are most appropriate, such as the borders of lakes, forests, dark and obscure places, old and deserted houses, whither rarely and scarce ever men do come, mountains, caves, caverns, grottos, gardens, orchards; but best. of all are cross-roads, and where four roads meet, during the depth and silence of night. But if thou canst not conveniently go unto any of these places, thy house, and even thine own chamber, or, indeed, any place, provided it hath been purified and consecrated with the necessary ceremonies, will be found fit and convenient for the convocation and assembling of the Spirits.

These Arts or Operations should be carried out at the prescribed time, but if there be no time specially appointed it will be always better to perform them at night, which is the most fit and proper time for the Operations of Necromancy; this is also a symbol that it is just and right to hide them from the sight of the foolish, the ignorant, and the profane.

But when thou shalt have selected a place fitting, thou mayest perform thine experiments by day or by night. It should be spacious, clear, and bounded on all sides by hedges, shrubs, trees, or walls. Thou shalt thyself cleanse it thoroughly and render it neat and pure, and while doing this thou shalt recite Psalms ii.; lxvii.; and liv.

After this thou shalt perfume it with the odours and suffumigations of the Art, and shalt sprinkle it with the water and the hyssop; and after this thou mayest in this place make all the necessary preparations for an operation.

But when, later on, thou shalt go unto th4 place, to complete and accomplish the operation, thou shalt repeat on the way thither the following Prayer in a low and distinct voice:--

The Prayer

ZAZAII, ZAMAII, PUIDAMON Most Powerful, SEDON Most Strong, EL, YOD HE VAU HE, IAH, AGLA, assist me an unworthy sinner who have had the boldness to pronounce these Holy Names which no man should name and invoke save in very great danger. Therefore have I recourse unto these Most Holy Names, being in great peril both of soul and of body. Pardon me if I have sinned in any manner, for I trust in Thy protection alone, especially on this journey.

Let the Master as he goeth sprinkle the path with the water and hyssop of the Art, while each of his Disciples shall repeat in a low voice the Prayer which we have enjoined for the days of fasting and preparation.

Furthermore, let the Master appoint his Disciples to carry the things necessary for the Art.

The first shall bear the Censer, the Fire, and the Incense.

The Second; the Book, the Paper, the Pens, the Ink, and the various Perfumes.

The Third; the Knife, and the Sickle.

The Master; the Staff, and the Wand.

But if there be more Disciples present, the Master shall distribute the things for each to carry, according to their number.

When they shall have arrived at the place, and all things being disposed in their proper order, the Master shall take the Knife or other convenient consecrated Magical implement of Steel, wherewith to form the Circle of Art which he intends to construct. This being done, he must perfume it, and sprinkle it with water; and having warned and exhorted his Disciples, he shall work thus:--

First let him have a trumpet made of new wood, on the one side of which shall be written in Hebrew with the pen and ink of the Art these Names of God, ELOHIM GIBOR, ELOHIM TZABAOTH (see Figure 59); and on the other side these characters (see Figure 60).

Having entered into the Circle to perform the Experiment, he should sound this Trumpet towards the four quarters of the Universe, first towards the East, then towards the South, then towards the West, and lastly towards the North. Then let him say:--

Hear ye, and be ye ready, in whatever part of the Universe ye may be, to obey the Voice of God the Mighty One, and the Names of the Creator. We let you know by this signal and sound that ye will be convoked hither, wherefore hold ye yourselves in readiness to obey our commands.

This being done let the Master complete his work, renew the Circle, and make the incensements and fumigations.

Chapter VIII

Of the Knife, Sword, Sickle, Poniard, Dagger, Lance, Wand, Staff, and Other Instruments of Magical Art

IN order to properly carry out the greatest and most important Operations of the Art, various Instruments are necessary, as a Knife with a white hilt, another with a black hilt, a short Lance, wherewith to trace Circles, Characters, and other things.

The Knife with the white hilt (see Figure 61) should be made in the day and hour of Mercury, when Mars is in the Sign of the Ram or of the Scorpion. It should be dipped in the blood of a gosling and in the juice of the pimpernel, the Moon being at her full or increasing in light. Dip therein also the white hilt, upon the which thou shalt have engraved the Characters shown. Afterwards perfume it with the perfumes of the Art.

With this Knife thou mayest perform all the necessary Operations of the Art, except the Circles. But if it seemeth unto thee too troublesome to make a similar Knife, have one made in the same fashion; and thou shalt place it thrice in the fire until it becometh red-hot, and each time thou shalt immerse it in the aforesaid blood and juice, fasten thereunto the white hilt having engraved thereon the aforesaid characters, and upon the hilt thou shalt write with the pen of Art, commencing from the point and going towards the hilt, these Names Agla, On, as shown in Figure 61. Afterwards thou shalt perfume and sprinkle it, and shalt wrap it in a piece of silken cloth.

But as for the Knife with the black hilt (see Figure 62) for making the Circle, wherewith to strike terror and fear into the Spirits, it should be made in the same manner, except that it should be done in the day and hour of Saturn, and dipped in the blood of a black cat and in the juice of hemlock, the Characters and Names shown in Figure 62 being written thereon, from the point towards the hilt. Which being completed, thou shalt wrap it in a black silk cloth.

The Scimitar (Figure 63), and the Sickle (Figure 64), are made in the same way, as also the Dagger (Figure 65), the Poniard (Figure 66), and the short Lance (Figure 67), in the day and hour of Mercury, and they should be dipped in the blood of a magpie and the juice of the herb Mercury. Thou must make for them handles of white boxwood cut at a single stroke from the tree, at the rising of the Sun, with a new knife, or with any other convenient instrument. -The characters shown should be traced thereon. Thou shalt perfume them according to the rules of Art; and wrap them in silk cloth like the others.

The Staff (Figure 68) should be of elderwood, or cane, or rosewood; and the Wand (Figure 69) of hazel or nut tree, in all cases the wood being virgin, that is of one year's growth only. They should each be cut from the tree at a

Book Two

single stroke, on the day of Mercury, at sunrise. The characters shown should be written or engraved thereon in the day and hour of Mercury.

This being done, thou shalt say:--

ADONAI, Most Holy, deign to bless and to consecrate this Wand, and this Staff, that they may obtain the necessary virtue, through Thee, O Most Holy ADONAI, Whose kingdom endureth unto the Ages of the Ages. Amen.

After having perfumed and consecrated them, put them aside in a pure and clean place for use when required.

Swords are also frequently necessary for use in Magical Arts. Thou shalt therefore take a new Sword which thou shalt clean and polish on the day of Mercury, and at the first or the fifteenth hour, and after this thou shalt write on one side these Divine Names in Hebrew, YODHE VAU HE, ADONAI, EHEIEH, YAYAI; and on the other side ELOHIM GIBOR (Figure 70); sprinkle and cense it and repeat over it the following conjuration:--

THE CONJURATION OF THE SWORD

I conjure thee, O Sword, by these Names, ABRAHACH, ABRACH, ABRACADABRA, YODHE VAU HE, that thou serve me for a strength and defence in all Magical Operations, against all mine Enemies, visible and invisible.

I conjure thee anew by the Holy and Indivisible Name of EL strong and wonderful; by the Name SHADDAI Almighty; and by these Names QADOSCH, QADOSCH, QADOSCH, ADONAI ELOHIM TZABAOTH, EMANUEL, the First and the Last, Wisdom, Way, Life, Truth, Chief, Speech, Word, Splendour, Light, Sun, Fountain, Glory, the Stone of the Wise, Virtue, Shepherd, Priest, Messiach Immortal; by these Names then, and by the other Names, I conjure thee, O Sword, that thou servest me for a Protection in all adversities. Amen.

This being finished thou shalt wrap it also in silk like all the other Instruments, being duly purified and consecrated by the Ceremonies requisite for the perfection of all Magical Arts and Operations.

Three[116] other Swords should be made for the use of the Disciples.

The first one should have on the pommel the Name CARDIEL or GABRIEL (Figure 71); on the Lamen of the Guard, REGION (Figure 72); on the Blade, PANORAIM HEAMESIN (Figure 73).

The Second should have on the pommel the Name AURIEL (Figure 74); on the Lamen of the Guard, SARION (Figure 75); on the Blade, GAMORINDEBALIN (Figure 76).

---

[116] The description of these three Swords for the Disciples is only given in 1307 Sloane MSS.

The third should have on the pommel the Name DAMIEL or RAPHAEL (Figure 77); on the Lamen of the Guard, YEMETON (Figure 78); on the Blade, LAMEDIN ERADIM (Figure 79).

The Burin[117] (Figure 80) or Graver is useful for engraving or incising characters. In the day and hour either of Mars or of Venus thou shalt engrave thereon the characters shown, and having sprinkled and censed it thou shalt repeat over it the following Prayer:--

Prayer

ASOPHIEL, ASOPHIEL, ASOPHIEL, PENTAGRAMMATON, ATHANATOS, EHEIEH ASHER EHEIEH, QADOSCH, QADOSCH, QADOSCH; O God Eternal, and my Father, bless this Instrument prepared in Thine honour, so that it may only serve for a good use and end, for Thy Glory. Amen.

Having again perfumed, thou shalt put it aside for use. The Needle may be consecrated in the same way.

---

[117] From here to the end of the Chapter is from 1203 Lansdowne MSS.

BOOK TWO

CHAPTER IX

Of[118] the Formation of the Circle

HAVING chosen a place for preparing and constructing the Circle, and all things necessary being prepared for the perfection of the Operations, take thou the Sickle or Scimitar of Art and stick it into the centre of the place where the Circle is to be made; then take a cord of nine feet in length, fasten one end thereof unto the Sickle and with the other end trace out the circumference of the Circle, which may be marked either with the Sword or with the Knife with the Black hilt. Then within the Circle mark out four regions, namely, towards the East, West, South, and North, wherein place Symbols; and beyond the limits of this Circle describe with the Consecrated Knife or Sword another Circle, but leaving an open space therein towards the North whereby thou mayest enter and depart beyond the Circle of Art. Beyond this again thou shalt describe another Circle at a foot distance with the aforesaid Instrument, yet ever leaving therein an open space for entrance and egress corresponding to the open space already left in the other. Beyond this again make another Circle at another foot distance, and beyond these two Circles, which are beyond the Circle of Art yet upon the same Centre, thou shalt describe Pentagrams with the Symbols and Names of the Creator therein so that they may surround the Circle already described. Without these Circles shalt thou circumscribe a Square, and beyond that another Square, so that the Angles of the former may touch the centres of the sides of the latter, and that the Angles of the latter may stretch towards the four quarters of the Universe, East, West, North, and South; and at the four Angles of each square, and touching them, thou shalt describe lesser Circles wherein let there be placed standing censers with lighted charcoal and sweet odours.

These things being done, let the Magus of Art[119] assemble his Disciples, exhort, confirm, and cheer them; lead them into the Circle of Art and station them therein towards the Four Quarters of the Universe, exhort them to fear nothing, and to abide in their assigned places. Furthermore, let each of the Companions have a Sword besides the Sword of the Art, which he must hold naked in his hand. Then let the Magus quit the Circle, and Kindle the Censers, and place thereon exorcised Incense, as is said in the Chapter of Fumigations; and let him have the Censer in his hand and kindle it, and then place it in the part prepared. Let him now enter within the Circle and carefully close the openings left in the same, and let him again warn his Disciples, and take the Trumpet of Art prepared as is said in the Chapter concerning the same, and let him incense the Circle towards the Four Quarters of the Universe.

---

[118] This Chapter is only given in 10862 Add. MSS.
[119] 'Maghus' in MS., not 'Magister.'

After this let the Magus commence his Incantations, having placed the Sickle, Sword, or other Implement of Art upright in the ground at his feet. Having sounded the trumpet as before taught let him invoke the Spirits, and if need be conjure them, as is said in the First Book, and having attained his desired effect, let him license them to depart.

Here followeth the Form of the Circle (see Figure 81), wherein whosoever entereth he shall be at safety as within a fortified Castle, and nothing shall be able to harm him.

BOOK TWO

CHAPTER X

Concerning Incense, Suffumigations, Perfumes, Odors, and Similar Things Which Are Used in Magical Arts

THERE are many kinds of Incense, Suffumigations, and Perfumes, which are made for and offered unto the Spirits; those which are of sweet odour are for the good, those which are of evil savour are for the evil.

For perfumes of good odour, take thou incense, aloes, nutmeg, gum benjamin, musk, and other fragrant spices, over the which thou shalt say:--

THE EXORCISM OF THE INCENSE

O God of Abraham, God of Isaac, God of Jacob, deign to bless these odoriferous spices so that they may receive strength, virtue, and power to attract the Good Spirits, and to banish and cause to retire all hostile Phantoms. Through Thee, O Most Holy ADONAI, Who livest and reignest unto the Ages of the Ages. Amen.

I exorcise thee, O Spirit impure and unclean, thou who art a hostile Phantom, in the Name of God, that thou quit this Perfume, thou and all thy deceits, that it may be consecrated and sanctified in the name of God Almighty. May the Holy Spirit of God grant protection and virtue unto those who use these Perfumes; and may the hostile and evil Spirit and Phantom never be able to enter therein, through the Ineffable Name of God Almighty. Amen.

O Lord, deign to bless and to sanctify this Creature of Perfume so that it may be a remedy unto mankind for the health of body and of soul, through the Invocation of Thy Holy Name. May all Creatures who receive the odour of this incense and of these spices receive health of body and of soul, through Him Who hath formed the Ages. Amen.

After this thou shalt sprinkle the various Spices with the Water of the Art, and thou shalt place them aside in a piece of silk as in other cases, or in a box destined for the purpose, so that thou mayest have them ready prepared for use when necessary.

When thou wishest to use the incense, thou shalt kindle a fire of fresh charcoal, in earthen vessels newly glazed within and without, and thou shalt kindle fire fresh with flint and steel, and the fire being lighted thou shalt say over it as follows, before putting the Spices thereon.

The Exorcism of the Fire

I exorcise thee, O Creature of Fire, by Him through Whom all things have been made, so that every kind of Phantasm may retire from thee, and be unable to harm or deceive in any way, through the Invocation of the Most High Creator of all. Amen.

Bless, O Lord All Powerful, and All Merciful, this Creature of Fire, so that being blessed by Thee, it may be for the honour and glory of Thy Most Holy Name, so that it may work no hindrance or evil unto those who use it. Through Thee, O Eternal and Almighty Lord, and through Thy Most Holy Name. Amen.

This being done, thou shalt put the Spices upon the Fire, and make what perfumes and suffumigations thou requirest.

Over Fumigations of evil odour thou shalt say:--

ADONAI, LAZAI, DALMAI, AIMA, ELOHI, O Holy Father, grant unto us succour, favour, and grace, by the Invocation of thy Holy Name, so that these things may serve us for aid in all that we wish to perform therewith, that all deceit may quit them, and that they may be blessed and sanctified through Thy Name. Amen.

Chapter XI

Of Water, and Of the Hyssop

IF it be necessary to sprinkle with water anything required in the Art it should be clone with a Sprinkler.

Prepare a Censer in the day and hour of Mercury, with the odoriferous Spices of the Art. After this thou shalt take a vessel of brass, of lead varnished within and without, or of earth, which thou shalt fill with most clear spring water, and thou shalt have salt, and say these words over the salt:--

TZABAOTHI MESSIACH, EMANUEL, ELOHIM GIBOR, YOD HE VAU HE; O God, Who art the Truth and the Life, deign to bless and sanctify this Creature of Salt, to serve unto us for help, protection, and assistance in this Art, experiment, and operation, and may it be a succour unto us.

After this cast the salt into the vessel wherein is the Water, and say the following Psalms: cii.; liv.; vi.; lxvii.

Thou shalt then make unto thyself a Sprinkler of vervain, fennel, lavender, sage, valerian, mint, garden-basil, rosemary, and hyssop, gathered in the day and hour of Mercury, the moon being in her increase. Bind together these herbs with a thread spun by a young maiden, and engrave upon the handle on the one side the characters shown in Figure 82, and on the other side those given in Figure 83.

After this thou wayest use the Water, using the Sprinkler whenever it is necessary; and know that wheresoever thou shalt sprinkle this Water, it will chase away all Phantoms, and they shall be unable to hinder or annoy any. With this same Water thou shalt make all the preparations of the Art.

Chapter XII

Of Light, and Of the Fire

IT hath been ever the custom among all nations to use fire and light in sacred things. For this reason the Master of the Art should also employ them in sacred rites, and besides those for reading the Conjurations by, and for the incense, in all operations Lights are necessary in the Circle.

For this reason he should make candles of virgin wax in the day and hour of Mercury; the wicks should have been made by a young girl; and the Candles should be made when the moon is in her increase, of the weight of half a pound each, and on them thou shalt engrave these characters with the Dagger, or the Burin of Art. (See Figure 84.)

After this thou shalt repeat over the Candles, Psalms cli.; ciii.; cvii., and shalt say:--

O Lord God, Who governest all things by Thine Almighty Power, give unto me, a poor sinner, understanding and knowledge to do only that which is agreeable unto Thee; grant unto me to fear, adore, love, praise, and give thanks unto Thee with true and sincere faith and perfect charity. Grant, O Lord, before I die, and descend into the realms beneath, and before the fiery flame shall devour me, that Thy Grace may not leave me, O Lord of my Soul. Amen.

After this thou shalt add:--

I exorcise thee, O Creature of wax, by Him Who alone hath created all things by His Word, and by the virtue of Him Who is pure truth, that thou cast out from thee every Phantasm, Perversion, and Deceit of the Enemy, and may the Virtue and Power of God enter into thee, so that thou mayest give us light, and chase far from us all fear or terror.

After this thou shalt sprinkle them with the Water of the Art, and incense them with the usual perfumes.

And when thou shalt wish to kindle them thou shalt say:--

I exorcise thee, O Creature of Fire, in the Name of the Sovereign and Eternal Lord, by His Ineffable Name, which is YOD, HE, VAU, HE; by the Name IAH; and by the Name of Power EL; that thou mayest enlighten the heart of all the Spirits which we shall call unto this Circle, so that they may appear before us without fraud and deceit through Him Who hath created all things.

Then thou shalt take a square Lantern, with panes of Crystal glass, and thou shalt fit therein the Candle lighted, to read by, to form the Circle, or any other purpose for which thou shalt require it.

BOOK TWO

CHAPTER XIII

Concerning[120] the Precepts of the Art

HE who hath attained the rank or degree of Exorcist, which we are usually accustomed to call Magus or Master according to grade, whensoever he desireth to undertake any operation, for the nine days immediately preceding the commencement of the work, should put aside from him all uncleanness, and prepare himself in secret during these days, and prepare all the things necessary, and in the space of these days all these should be made, consecrated, and exorcised.

The which being duly completed, let him go on the day and hour of the commencement of the work, unto the place set apart for the same, as hath been said, in the place concerning the formation of the Circle. Let him instruct his Disciples on no cause whatsoever to move from their assigned places. And the Magus should exhort them with a bold and confident voice as follows:--

THE EXHORTATION OF THE COMPANIONS

Fear ye not, my beloved Companions, seeing that we draw near unto the desired end; therefore, all things being rightly done and the Conjurations and Exorcisms diligently performed, ye shall behold Kings of Kings, and Emperors of Emperors, and other Kings, Princes, and Majesties with them, and a great crowd of followers, together with all sorts of musical instruments, yet nothing should either the Magus or his Disciples fear.

And then let the Magus say:--

I exhort you by these Holy Names of God, ELOHIM, ADONAI, AGLA, that none of you now presume to move or cross over from your appointed stations.

This being said, let the Magus and his Disciples uncover the Holy Pentacles and show them towards each quarter, and they being shown in each place, there shall be noises and rushings.

Then shall the Emperor of (the Spirits) say unto you:--From the time of the Great Addus until now, there hath not been an Exorciser who could behold my person, and unless those things[121] which ye have showed unto us had been made, ye would not now have seen me. But seeing that ye have powerfully called us, as I believe, by the rites derived from Solomon, and which but few of your comrades, or Exorcisers, possess, also they compel us against our will, and I therefore say unto thee that we wish to be obedient in

---

[120] This Chapter is only given in 10862 Add. MSS.
[121] The Pentacles.

all matters.

Then shall the Magus place the petitions of himself and his companions, which should be written down clearly on virgin card, or paper, beyond the Circle towards the King or Prince of the Spirits, and he will receive it and take counsel with his Chiefs. After this he will return the Card, saying:--That which thou desirest is accomplished, be thy will performed, and all thy demands fulfilled.

BOOK TWO

CHAPTER XIV

Of the Pen, Ink, and Colours

ALL things employed for writing, etc., in this Art, should be prepared in the following manner.

Thou shalt take a male gosling, from which thou shalt pluck the third feather of the right wing, and in plucking it thou shalt say:--

ADRAI, HAHLII, TAMAH, TILONAS, ATHAMAS, ZIANOR, ADONAI, banish from this pen all deceit and error, so that it may be of virtue and efficacy to write all that I desire. Amen.

After this thou shalt sharpen it with the penknife of the Art, perfume it, sprinkle it, and place it aside in a silken cloth.

Thou shalt have an Inkstand made of earth or any convenient matter, and in the day and hour of Mercury thou shalt engrave thereon with the Burin of Art these Names:--Yod, He, Vau, He, Metatron, Iah Iah Iah, Qadosch, Elohim Tzabaoth (see Figure 85); and in putting the ink therein thou shalt say:--

I exorcise thee, O Creature of Ink, by ANAIRETON, by SIMULATOR, and by the Name ADONAI, and by the Name of Him through Whom all things were made, that thou be unto me an aid and succour in all things which I wish to perform by thine aid.

As it sometimes happeneth that it is necessary to write with some noble colour, it is well to have a new and clean box wherein to keep them. The principal colours will be Yellow or Gold, Red, Celestial or Azure Blue, Green, and Brown; and any other colours that may be requisite. Thou shalt exorcise, perfume, and sprinkle them in the usual manner.

Chapter XV

Of the Pen, Of the Swallow, and Of the Crow

TAKE the feather of a Swallow or of a Crow, and before plucking it thou shalt say:--

May Holy MICHAEL the Archangel of God, and MIDAEL and MIRAEL, the Chiefs and Captains of the Celestial Army, be my aid in the operation I am about to perform, so that I may write herewith all things which are necessary, and that all the experiments which I commence herewith may through you and through your Names be perfected by the power of the Most High Creator. Amen.

After this thou shalt point and complete the pen with the Knife of the Art, and with the pen and ink of the Art thou shalt write upon its side the Name, ANAIRETON (see Figure 86), and thou shalt say over it the following Psalms: cxxxiii.; cxvii.

BOOK TWO

CHAPTER XVI

Of the Blood of the Bat, Pidgeon, and Other Animals

TAKE a living Bat and exorcise it thus:--

THE EXORCISM OF THE BAT

CAMIACH, EOMIAHE, EMIAL, MACBAL, EMOII, ZAZEAN, MAIPHIAT, ZACRATH, TENDAC, VULAMAHI; by these Most Holy Names, and the other Names of Angels which are written in the Book ASSAMAIAN,[122] I conjure thee O Bat (or whatever animal it may be) that thou assist me in this operation, by God the True, God the Holy, the God Who hath created thee, and by Adam, Who hath imposed thy true name upon thee and upon all other animated beings.

After this, take the Needle or other convenient Instrument of Art, as will be said later on, and pierce the bat in the vein which is in the right wing; and collect the blood in a small vessel over the which thou shalt say:--

Almighty ADONAI, ARATHRON, ASHAI, ELOHIM, ELOHI, ELION, ASHER EHEIEH, SHADDAI, O God the Lord, immaculate, immutable, EMANUEL, MESSIACH, YOD, HE, VAU, HE, be my aid, so that this blood may have power and efficacy in all wherein I shall wish, and in all that I shall demand.

Perfume it and keep it for use.

The blood of other winged animals may be taken in the same manner, with the proper solemnities.

Note by Editor.--I cannot too strongly impress on the readers of this volume that the use of blood is more or less connected with Black Magic and that it should be avoided as much as possible.

---

[122] The 'Sepher Ha-Shamaiim,' or 'Book of the Heavens.'

Chapter XVII

Of Virgin Parchment, Or Virgin Paper, and How it Should be Prepared

VIRGIN paper, or card, is that which is new, pure, clean, and exorcised, never having served for any other purpose.

Virgin parchment is necessary in many Magical Operations, and should be properly prepared and consecrated. There are two kinds, one called Virgin, the other Unborn. Virgin parchment is that which is taken from an Animal which hath not attained the age of generation, whether it be ram, or kid, or other animal.

Unborn parchment is taken from an animal which hath been taken before its time from the uterus of its mother.

Take whichsoever of these two classes of animals thou pleasest, provided only that it be male, and in the day and hour of Mercury; and take it to a secret place where no man may see thee at work. Thou shalt have a marsh-reed cut at a single stroke with a new knife, and thou shalt strip from it the leaves, repeating this Conjuration:--

The Conjuration of the Reed

I conjure thee by the Creator of all things, and by the King of Angels, Whose Name is EL SHADDAI, that thou receivest strength and virtue to flay this animal and to construct the parchment whereon I may write the Holy Names of God, and that it may acquire so great virtue that all which I shall write or do may obtain its effect, through Him who liveth unto the Eternal Ages. Amen.

Before cutting the Reed recite Psalm lxxii.

After this, with the Knife of the Art, thou shalt fashion the Reed into the shape of a Knife, and upon it thou shalt write these Names: AGLA, ADONAI, ELOHI (see Figure 87), through Whom be the work of this Knife accomplished. Then thou shalt say:--

O God, Who drewest Moses, Thy well beloved and Thine elect, from among the Reeds on the marshy banks of the Nile, and from the Waters, he being yet but a child, grant unto me through Thy great mercy and compassion that this Reed may receive Power and Virtue to effect that which I desire through Thy Holy Name and the Names of Thy Holy Angels. Amen.

This being done, thou shalt commence with this Knife to flay the Animal, whether it be Virgin or Unborn, saying:--

ZOHAR, ZIO, TALMAÏ, ADONAI, SHADDAI, TETRAGRAMMATON, and ye Holy Angels of God; be present, and grant power and virtue unto this parchment, and may it be consecrated by you, so that all things which I shall write thereon shall obtain their effect. Amen.

The Animal being flayed, take Salt, and say thus over it:--

God of Gods, and Lord of Lords, Who hast created all things from Negative Existence, deign to bless and sanctify this Salt, so that in placing it upon this parchment which I wish to make, it may have such virtue that whatsoever I may write on it hereafter may attain its desired end. Amen.

Afterwards rub the said parchment with the exorcised salt, and leave it in the Sun, to imbibe this salt for the space of an entire day. Then take a large earthen vessel glazed within and without, round the outside of which thou shalt write the characters in Figure 88.

After this thou shalt put powdered lime into the vessel, saying

OROII, ZARON, ZAINON, ZEVARON, ZAHIPHIL, ELION, be ye present and bless this work so that it may attain the desired effect, through the King of the Heavens, and the God of the Angels. Amen.

Take then exorcised Water and pour it upon the said lime, and place the skin therein for three days, after which thou shalt take it thence, and scrape therefrom the lime and flesh adhering, with the Knife of Reed.

After this thou shalt cut, with a single stroke, a Wand of Hazel, long enough for thee to form a Circle therewith; take also a cord spun by a young maiden, and small stones or pebbles from a brook, pronouncing these words:--

O God Adonai, Holy and Powerful Father, put virtue into these stones, that they may serve to stretch this parchment, and to chase therefrom all fraud, and may it obtain virtue by Thine Almighty Power.

After this, having stretched the said parchment upon the Circle and bound it with the cord and stones, thou shalt say:--

AGLA, YOD, HE, VAU, HE, IAH, EMANUEL, bless and preserve this parchment, so that no Phantasm may enter therein.

Let it dry thus for three days in a dark and shady place, then cut the cord with the Knife of Art, and detach the Parchment from the Circle, saying:--

ANTOR, ANCOR, TURLOS, BEODONOS, PHAIAR, APHARCAR, be present for a guard unto this Parchment. Then perfume it, and keep it in silk ready for use.

No woman, if her flowers be upon her, should be permitted to see this parchment; otherwise it will lose its virtue. He who maketh it should be pure, clean, and prepared.

But if the preparation of the aforesaid parchment seemeth too tedious, thou mayest make it in the following manner, but it is not so good.

Take any Parchment, and exorcise it; prepare a censer with perfumes write upon the parchment the characters in Figure 89, hold it over the incense, and say:--

Be ye present to aid me, and may my operation be accomplished through you; ZAZAII, ZALMAII, DALMAII, ADONAI, ANAPHAXETON, CEDRION, CRIPON, PRION, ANAIRETON, ELION, OCTINOMON,

ZEVANION, ALAZAION, ZIDEON, AGLA, ON, YODHE VAU HE, ARTOR, DINOTOR, Holy Angels of God; be present and infuse virtue into this Parchment, so that it may obtain such power through you that all Names and Characters thereon written may receive due power, and that all deceit and hindrance may depart therefrom, through God the Lord merciful and gracious, Who liveth and reigneth through all the Ages. Amen.

Then shalt thou recite over the parchment Psalms lxxii.; cxvii.; and cxxxiv.; and the 'Benedicite Omnia Opera.' Then say:--

I conjure thee, O parchment, by all the Holy Names, that thou obtainest efficacy and strength, and becomest exorcised and consecrated, so that none of the things which may be written upon thee shall be effaced from the Book of Truth. Amen.

Then sprinkle it, and keep it as before said.

The Cauls of newly-born children, duly consecrated, may also be used instead of virgin parchment. Also paper, satin, silk, and the like substances, may be employed in operations of less importance if duly exorcised and consecrated.

Chapter XVIII

Of Wax and Virgin Earth

WAX and Virgin Earth are also employed in many Magical Operations, whether to make Images, or Candles, or other things; therefore they should never have been put to any other use. The Earth should be dug up with thine own hands, and reduced to a paste, without touching it with any instrument whatever, so that it be not defiled thereby.

The Wax should be taken from bees which have only made it for the first time, and it should never have been employed for any other purpose; and when thou shalt wish it to avail thyself of the one or the other, thou shalt before commencing the work repeat the following conjuration:--

Conjuration

EXTABOR, HETABOR, SITTACIBOR, ADONAI, ONZO, ZOMEN, MENOR, ASMODAL, ASCOBAT, COMATOS, ERIONAS, PROFAS, ALKOMAS, CONAMAS, PAPUENDOS, OSIANDOS, ESPIACENT, DAMNATH, EHERES, GOLADES, TELANTES, COPHI, ZADES, ye Angels of God be present, for I invoke ye in my work, so that through you it may find virtue and accomplishment. Amen.

After this repeat Psalms cxxxi. xv.; cii.; viii. lxxxiv.; lxviii.; lxxii.; cxxxiii.; cxiii.; cxxvi.; xlvi. xlvii.; xxii.; li.; cxxx.; cxxxix. xlix. cx.; liii.; and say:--

I exorcise thee, O Creature of Wax (or of Earth), that through the Holy Name of God and His Holy Angels thou receive blessing, so that thou mayest be sanctified and blessed, and obtain the virtue which we desire, through the Most Holy Name of ADONAI. Amen.

Sprinkle the wax and put it aside for use; but take note that the Earth which should be dug up with thy hands should be prepared every time thou hast need thereof.

Chapter XIX

Concerning the Needle and Other Iron Instruments

THERE are several steel instruments necessary in various Operations, as a Needle to prick or to sew; a Burin, or instrument wherewith to engrave, etc.

Thou shalt make such instruments in the day and hour of Jupiter, and when it is finished thou shalt say:--

I conjure thee, O Instrument of Steel, by God the Father Almighty, by the Virtue of the Heavens, of the Stars, and of the Angels who preside over them; by the virtue of stones, herbs, and animals; by the virtue of hail, snow, and wind; that thou receivest such virtue that thou mayest obtain without deceit the end which I desire in all things wherein I shall use thee; through God the Creator of the Ages, and Emperor of the Angels. Amen.

Afterwards repeat Psalms iii.; ix.; xxxi.; xlii.; lx.; li.; cxxx.

Perfume it with the perfumes of the Art, and sprinkle it with exorcised water, wrap it in silk and say:--

DANI, ZUMECH, AGALMATUROD, GADIEL, PANI, CANELOAS, MEROD, GAMIDOI, BALDOI, METRATOR, Angels most holy, be present for a guard unto this instrument.

Chapter XX

Concerning the Silken Cloth

WHEN any Instrument of the Art is properly consecrated, it should be wrapped in silk and put away, as we have said.

Take, then, silk of any colour except black or grey, whereon write the words and Characters in Figure 90.

Perfume it with incense of good odour, sprinkle it, and recite Psalms lxxxii.; lxxii.; cxxxiv.; lxiv.

After this thou shalt put it aside for seven days with sweet spices and thou shalt use this silk to wrap all the Instruments of the Art.

Chapter XXI

Concerning Characters, and the Consecration of the Magical Book

WHENSOEVER in any Operation it is necessary to write Characters, and thou fearest that thou wilt fail, do this: Write at the beginning the Name EHEIEH ASHER EHEIEH (Figure 91), and at the end the Name AIN SOPH (Figure 92); between these Names write what thou wishest, and if thou hast anything especial to do bear the said written Names upon the wrapper in silk, and thou shalt say over them:--

Most Wise and Most High Creator of all things, I pray Thee for Thy grace and mercy that Thou mayest grant such virtue and power unto these Holy Names, that Thou mayest keep these characters from all deceit and error, through Thee, O Most Holy ADONAI. Amen.

After having repeated this thou shalt write the requisite Characters, and thou shalt not fail, but shalt attain thy desired end.

The Consecration of the Book[123]

Make a small Book containing the Prayers for all the Operations, the Names of the Angels in the form of Litanies, their Seals and Characters; the which being done thou shalt consecrate the same unto God and unto the pure Spirits in the manner following:--

Thou shalt set in the destined place a small table covered with a white cloth, whereon thou shalt lay the Book opened at the Great Pentacle which should be drawn on the first leaf of the said Book; and having kindled a lamp which should be suspended above the centre of the table, thou shalt surround the said table with a white curtain; clothe thyself in the proper vestments, and holding the Book open, repeat upon thy knees the following prayer with great humility:--

(For the Prayer beginning 'Adonai Elohim,' etc., see Book I., Chapter XIV., where it is given in full.)

After which thou shalt incense it with the incense proper to the Planet and the day, and thou shalt replace the Book on the aforesaid Table, taking heed that the fire of the lamp be kept up continually during the operation, and keeping the curtains closed. Repeat the same ceremony for seven days, beginning with Saturday, and perfuming the Book each day with the Incense proper to the Planet ruling the day and hour, and taking heed that the lamp shall burn both day and night; after the which thou shalt shut up the Book in

---

[123] The rest of this Chapter is from 1203 Lansdowne MSS.

a small drawer under the table, made expressly for it, until thou shalt have occasion to use it; and every time that thou wishest to use it, clothe thyself with thy vestments, kindle the lamp, and repeat upon thy knees the aforesaid prayer, 'Adonai Elohim,' etc.

It is necessary also, in the Consecration of the Book, to summon all the Angels whose Names are written therein in the form of Litanies, the which thou shalt do with devotion; and even if the Angels and Spirits appear not in the Consecration of the Book, be not thou astonished thereat, seeing that they are of a pure nature, and consequently have much difficulty in familiarising themselves with men who are inconstant and impure, but the Ceremonies and Characters being correctly carried out devoutedly and with perseverance, they will be constrained to come, and it will at length happen that at thy first invocation thou wilt be able to see and communicate with them. But I advise thee to undertake nothing unclean or impure, for then thy importunity, far from attracting them, will only serve to chase them from thee; and it will be thereafter exceedingly difficult for thee to attract them for use for pure ends.

Chapter XXII

Concerning Sacrifices to the Spirits, and How They Should be Made

IN many operations it is necessary to make some sort of sacrifice unto the Demons, and in various ways. Sometimes white animals are sacrificed to the good Spirits and black to the evil. Such sacrifices consist of the blood and sometimes of the flesh.

They who sacrifice animals, of whatsoever kind they be, should select those which are virgin, as being more agreeable unto the Spirits, and rendering them more obedient.

When blood is to be sacrificed it should be drawn also from virgin quadrupeds or birds, but before offering the oblation, say:--

May this Sacrifice which we find it proper to offer unto ye, noble and lofty Beings, be agreeable and pleasing unto your desires; be ye ready to obey us, and ye shall receive greater ones.

Then perfume and sprinkle it according to the rules of Art.

When it is necessary, with all the proper Ceremonies, to make Sacrifices of fire, they should be made of wood which hath some quality referring especially unto the Spirits invoked; as juniper, or pine, unto the Spirits of Saturn; box, or oak, unto those of Jupiter; cornel, or cedar, unto those of Mars; laurel unto those of the Sun; myrtle unto those of Venus; hazel unto those of Mercury; and willow unto those of the Moon.

But when we make sacrifices of food and drink, everything necessary should be prepared without the Circle, and the meats should be covered with some fine clean cloth, and have also a clean white cloth spread beneath them; with new bread and good and sparkling wine, but in all things those which refer to the nature of the Planet. Animals, such as fowls or pigeons, should be roasted. Especially shouldest thou have a vessel of clear and pure fountain water, and before thou enterest into the Circle, thou shalt summon the Spirits by their proper Names, or at least those chief among them, saying:--

In whatsoever place ye may be, ye Spirits, who are invited to this feast, come ye and be ready to receive our offerings, presents, and sacrifices, and ye shall have hereafter yet more agreeable oblations.

Perfume the viands with sweet incense, and sprinkle them with exorcised water; then commence to conjure the Spirits until they shall come.

This is the manner of making sacrifices in all arts and operations wherein it is necessary, and acting thus, the Spirits will be prompt to serve thee.

Here endeth our Key, the which if thou thoroughly instillest into thy memory, thou shalt be able, if it pleaseth thee, even to fly with the wings of the wind. But if thou takest little heed hereof, and despiseth this Book, never shalt thou attain unto the desired end in any Magical experiment or operation whatsoever.

For in this Book is comprised all science of Magical Art, and it should be strictly kept by thee. And hereunto is the end of our Key, in the Name of God the righteous, the merciful, and the eternal, Who liveth and reigneth throughout the Ages. Amen.

THE END OF THE KEY OF SOLOMON THE KING

Ancient Fragment of the Key of Solomon

Translated from Hebrew by Eliphaz Levi

I will now give unto thee the Key of the Kingdom of the Spirits.
This Key is the same as that of the Mysterious Numbers of Yetzirah.[124]
The Spirits are governed by the natural and universal Hierarchy of things.
Three command Three through the medium of Three.

There are the Spirits of Above, those of Below, and those of the Centre; then if thou invertest the Sacred Ladder, if thou descendest instead of ascending, thou wilt discover the Counter-Hierarchy of the Shells, or of the Dead Spirits.

Know thou only that the Principalities of Heaven, the Virtues, and the Powers, are not Persons, but dignities.

They are the Degrees of the Sacred Ladder upon which the Spirits ascend and descend.

Michael, Gabriel, Raphael, and the others, are not Names but Titles.

The First of the Numbers is the Unity.

The First of the Divine Conceptions called the Sephiroth is Kether or the Crown.

The First Category of the Spirits is that of Chaioth Ha-Qadesh or the Intelligences of the Divine Tetragram, whose Letters are symbolised by the Mysterious Animals in the Prophecy of Ezekiel.

Their empire is that of unity and synthesis. They correspond to the Intelligence.

They have for adversaries the Thamiel or Double-Headed Ones, the Demons of revolt and of anarchy, whose two Chiefs, ever at War with each other, are Satan and Moloch.

The second Number is two; the second Sephira is Chokmah or Wisdom.

The Spirits of Wisdom are the Auphanim, a Name which signifieth the Wheels, because all acts in Heaven like immense Wheels spangled with Stars. Their Empire is that of Harmony. They correspond to the Reason.

They have for adversaries the Chaigidel, or the Shells which attach themselves to Material and Lying Appearances. Their Chief, or rather their Guide, for Evil Spirits obey no one, is Beelzebub, whose Name signifieth the God of Flies, because Flies haunt putrefying corpses.

The third Number is three. The third Sephira is Binah or Understanding.

The Spirits of Binah are Aralim, or the Strong. Their empire is the creation of ideas; they correspond to activity and energy of thought.

---

[124] The 'Sepher Yetzirah,' or 'Book of Formation,' one of the most ancient Books of the Qabalah.

They have for adversaries the Satariel, or concealers, the Demons of absurdity, of intellectual inertia, and of Mystery. The Chief of the Satariel is Lucifuge, called falsely and by anti-phrase Lucifer (as the Eumenides, who are the Furies, are called in Greek the Gracious Ones).

The fourth Number is four. The fourth Sephira is Gedulah or Chesed, Magnificence or Mercy.

The Spirits of Gedulah are the Chaschmalim, or the Lucid Ones. Their empire is that of beneficence; they correspond to the imagination.

They have for adversaries the Gamchicoth or the Disturbers of Souls. The Chief or Guide of these Demons is Ashtaroth or Astarte, the impure Venus of the Syrians, whom they represent with the head of an ass or of a bull, and the breasts of a woman.

The fifth Number is five. The fifth Sephira is Geburah or justice.

The Spirits of Geburah are the Seraphim, or the Spirits burning with zeal. Their empire is that of the chastisement of crimes. They correspond to the faculty of comparing and of choosing.

They have for adversaries the Golab or incendiaries, Genii of wrath and sedition, whose Chief is Asmodeus, whom they call also Samael the Black.

The sixth Number is six. The sixth Sephira is Tiphereth the Supreme Beauty.

The Spirits of Tiphereth are the Malachim, or the Kings. Their empire is that of the Universal Harmony. They correspond to the judgment.

They have for adversaries the Tagaririm, or Disputers, whose Chief is Belphegor.

The seventh Number is seven. The seventh Sephira is Netzach, or Victory.

The Spirits of Netzach are the Elohim or the Gods, that is to say the representatives of God. Their empire is that of progress and of life; they correspond to the Sensorium or to sensibility.

They have for adversaries the Harab-Serapel, or the Ravens of Death, whose Chief is Baal.

The eighth Number is eight. The eighth Sephira is Hod or eternal order.

The Spirits of Hod are the Beni-Elohim or Sons of the Gods. Their empire is that of order; they correspond to the inner sense.

They have for adversaries the Samael or jugglers, whose Chief is Adramelech.

The ninth Number is nine. The ninth Sephira is Yesod, or the fundamental principle.

The Spirits of Yesod are the Cherubim or Angels, those powers which fecundate the earth, and which are represented in Hebrew symbolism under the form of bulls. Their empire is that of fecundity. They correspond to true ideas.

They have for adversaries the Gamaliel or obscene, whose Queen is Lilith, the Demon of debaucheries.

The tenth Number is ten. The tenth Sephira is Malkuth, or the kingdom of Forms.

The Spirits of Malkuth are the Ischim, or the virile ones; they are the souls of the Saints whose Chief is Moses. (Let us not forget that it is Solomon who speaks.--Eliphaz Lévi.)

They have for adversaries the wicked ones who obey Nahema, the Demon of Impurity.

The wicked are symbolised by the five accursed nations whom Joshua was to destroy.

Joshua, or Jehoshua the Saviour, is a symbol of the Messiach.

His Name is composed of the Letters of the Divine Tetragram changed into the Pentagram by the addition of the Letter Schin (see Figure 94).

Each letter of this Pentagram represents a power of good attacked by the five accursed nations.

For the real history of the people of God is the allegorical legend of Humanity.

The five accursed nations are:--

1. The Amalekites or Aggressors;
2. The Geburim or Violent Ones;
3. The Raphaim or Cowards;
4. The Nephilim or Voluptuous Ones;
5. The Anakim or Anarchists.

The Anarchists are vanquished by the Yod, which is the Sceptre of the Father.

The Violent are vanquished by the Hé, which is the Gentleness of the Mother.

The Cowards are vanquished by the Vau, which is the Sword of Michael, and Generation by travail and pain.

The Voluptuous are vanquished by the second Hé, which is the painful bringing forth of the Mother.

Lastly, the Aggressors are vanquished by the Schin, which is the Fire of the Lord and the equilibrating Law of justice.

The Princes of the Perverse Spirits are the False Gods whom they adore.

Hell has then no other government than that fatal law which punishes perversity and corrects error, for the false Gods only exist in the false opinion of their adorers.

Baal, Belphegor, Moloch, Adramelech, have been the idols of the Syrians; idols without soul, idols now destroyed, and of whom the Name alone remaineth.

The True God hath vanquished all the Demons as Truth triumphs over

Error. That is past in the opinions of men, and the Wars of Michael against Satan are the symbols of movement, and of the progress of Spirits.

The Devil is ever a God of refusal.

Accredited idolatries are religions in their time.

Superannuated idolatries are Superstitions and Sacrileges.

The Pantheon of Phantoms, which are then in vogue, is the Heaven of the Ignorant.

The Receptacle of Phantoms, whom Folly even wisheth for no longer, is the Hell.

But all this existeth only in the Imagination of the Vulgar.

For the Wise, Heaven is the Supreme Reason, and Hell is Folly.

But it must be understood that we here employ the word Heaven in the Mystical sense which we give it in opposing to it the word Hell.

In order to evoke Phantoms it is sufficient to intoxicate oneself or to render oneself mad; for Phantoms are ever the companions of drunkenness and of vertigo.

The Phosphorus of the imagination, abandoned to all the caprices of over-excited and diseased nerves, fills itself with Monsters and absurd visions.

We can also arrive at hallucination by mingling together wakefulness and sleep by the graduated use of narcotics; but such actions are crimes against nature.

Wisdom chaseth away Phantoms, and enables us to communicate with the Superior Spirits by the contemplation of the Laws of Nature and the study of the Holy Numbers.

(Here King Solomon addresseth himself to his son, Roboam):--

Do thou, O my son Roboam, remember, that the Fear of Adonai is only the beginning of Wisdom.

Keep and preserve those who have not Understanding in the Fear of Adonai, which will give and will preserve unto thee my crown.

But learn to triumph thyself over Fear by Wisdom, and the Spirits will descend from Heaven to serve thee.

I, Solomon, thy father, King of Israel and of Palmyra, I have sought out and obtained in my lot the Holy Chokmah, which is the Wisdom of Adonai.

And I have become King of the Spirits as well of Heaven as of Earth, Master of the Dwellers of the Air, and of the Living Souls of the Sea, because I was in possession of the Key of the Hidden Gates of Light.

I have done great things by the virtue of the Schema Hamphorasch, and by the Thirty-two Paths of Yetzirah.

Number, weight, and measure determine the form of things; the substance is one, and God createth it eternally.

Happy is he who comprehendeth the Letters and the Numbers.

The Letters are from the Numbers, and the Numbers from the Ideas, and the Ideas from the Forces, and the Forces from the Elohim. The Synthesis of the Elohim is the Schema.

The Schema is one, its columns are two, its power is three, its form is four, its reflection giveth eight, which multiplied by three giveth unto thee the twenty-four Thrones of Wisdom.

Upon each Throne reposeth a Crown with three Rays, each Ray beareth a Name, each Name is an Absolute Idea. There are Seventytwo Names upon the Twenty-four Crowns of the Schema.

Thou shalt write these Names upon Thirty-six Talismans, two upon each Talisman, one on each side.

Thou shalt divide these Talismans into four series of nine each, according to the number of the Letters of the Schema.

Upon the first Series thou shalt engrave the Letter Yod, symbolised by the Flowering Rod of Aaron.

Upon the second the Letter Hé, symbolised by the Cup of Joseph.

Upon the third the Letter Vau, symbolised by the Sword of David my father.

And upon the fourth the Hé final, symbolised by the Shekel of Gold.

These Thirty-six Talismans will be a Book which will contain all the Secrets of Nature. And by their diverse combinations thou shalt make the Genii and Angels speak.

HERE ENDETH THE FRAGMENT OF THE KEY OF SOLOMON

BOOK TWO

THE QABALISTICAL INVOCATION OF SOLOMON

Given by Eliphaz Levi

POWERS of the Kingdom, be beneath my left foot, and within my right hand.

Glory and Eternity touch my shoulders, and guide me in the Paths of Victory.

Mercy and justice be ye the Equilibrium and splendour of my life.

Understanding and Wisdom give unto me the Crown.

Spirits of Malkuth conduct me between the two columns whereon is supported the whole edifice of the Temple.

Angels of Netzach and of Hod strengthen me upon the Cubical Stone of Yesod.

O GEDULAHEL! O GEBURAHEL! O TIPHERETH!

BINAHEL, be Thou my Love!

RUACH CHOKMAHEL, be Thou my Light!

Be that which Thou art, and that which thou willest to be, O KETHERIEL!

Ishim, assist me in the Name Of SHADDAL

Cherubim, be my strength in the Name of ADONAL

Beni Elohim, be ye my brethren in the Name of the Son, and by the virtues of TZABAOTH.

Elohim, fight for me in the Name of TETRAGRAMMATON.

Malachim, protect me in the Name Of YOD HE VAU HE.

Seraphim, purify my love in the Name of ELOAH.

Chaschmalim, enlighten me with the splendours of ELOHI, and of SCHECHINAH.

Aralim, act ye; Auphanim, revolve and shine.

Chaioth Ha-Qadosch, cry aloud, speak, roar, and groan; Qadosch, Qadosch, Qadosch., SHADDAI, ADONAI, YOD CHAVAH, EHEIEH ASHER EHEIEH!

Halelu-Yah! Halelu-Yah! Halelu-Yah. Amen.

THE END

About the Authors

Samuel Liddell (or Liddel) MacGregor Mathers, born Samuel Liddell Mathers, was a British occultist. He is primarily known as one of the founders of the Hermetic Order of the Golden Dawn, a ceremonial magic order of which offshoots still exist today.

Mathers was born in January 1854 in Hackney, London, England. His father, William M. Mathers, died while he was still a boy. His mother, whose maiden name was Collins, died in 1885. He attended Bedford School, subsequently working in Bournemouth, Dorset, as a clerk, before moving to London following the death of his mother.

The "MacGregor" surname was added by Mathers as a claim to Highland Scottish heritage, although there is little evidence of such in his family background. He was a practicing vegetarian, or (according to some accounts) vegan, an outspoken anti-vivisectionist, and a non-smoker. It is known that his main interests were magic and the theory of war, his first book being a translation of a French military manual. He became more and more of an eccentric towards his later years, as was noted by W. B. Yeats.

Mathers was a polyglot; among the languages he had studied were English, French, Latin, Greek, Hebrew, Gaelic and Coptic, though he had a greater command of some languages than of others. His translations of such books as The Book of Abramelin (14thC.), Christian Knorr von Rosenroth's The Kabbalah Unveiled (1684), Key of Solomon (anonymous 14thC.), The Lesser Key of Solomon (anonymous 17thC.), and the Grimoire of Armadel (17thC.), while probably justly criticized with respect to quality, were responsible for making what had been obscure and inaccessible material widely available to the non-academic English speaking world. They have had considerable influence on the development of occult and esoteric thought since their publication, as has his consolidation of the Enochian magical system of John Dee and Edward Kelley.

Mathers died in November 1918 aged 64.

Aleister Crowley

Aleister Crowley was an English occultist, ceremonial magician, poet, painter, novelist, and mountaineer. He founded the religion of Thelema, identifying himself as the prophet entrusted with guiding humanity into the Æon of Horus in the early 20th century.

Born to a wealthy Plymouth Brethren family in Royal Leamington Spa, Warwickshire, Crowley rejected this fundamentalist Christian faith to pursue an interest in Western esotericism. He was educated at the University of Cambridge, where he focused his attentions on mountaineering and poetry, resulting in several publications. In 1898 he joined the esoteric Hermetic

Order of the Golden Dawn, where he was trained in ceremonial magic by Samuel Liddell MacGregor Mathers and Allan Bennett. Moving to Boleskine House by Loch Ness in Scotland, he went mountaineering in Mexico with Oscar Eckenstein, before studying Hindu and Buddhist practices in India. He married Rose Edith Kelly and in 1904 they honeymooned in Cairo, Egypt, where Crowley claimed to have been contacted by a supernatural entity named Aiwass, who provided him with The Book of the Law, a sacred text that served as the basis for Thelema. Announcing the start of the Æon of Horus, The Book declared that its followers should adhere to the code of "Do what thou wilt" and seek to align themselves with their Will through the practice of magick.

After an unsuccessful attempt to climb Kanchenjunga and a visit to India and China, Crowley returned to Britain, where he attracted attention as a prolific author of poetry, novels, and occult literature. In 1907, he and George Cecil Jones co-founded a Thelemite order, the A∴A∴, through which they propagated the religion. After spending time in Algeria, in 1912 he was initiated into another esoteric order, the German-based Ordo Templi Orientis (O.T.O.), rising to become the leader of its British branch, which he reformulated in accordance with his Thelemite beliefs. In 1920 he established the Abbey of Thelema, a religious commune in Cefalù, Sicily where he lived with various followers. His libertine lifestyle led to denunciations in the British press, and the Italian government evicted him in 1923. He divided the following two decades between France, Germany, and England, and continued to promote Thelema until his death.

CPSIA information can be obtained
at www.ICGtesting.com
Printed in the USA
BVHW040933161221
624197BV00015B/577